Mike, Nice cov... ...t!

D1756007

Ashes of the Mind

Ashes
of the Mind

War and Memory in
Northern Literature,
1865-1900

Martin Griffin

University of Massachusetts Press

AMHERST

Copyright © 2009 by University of Massachusetts Press
ALL RIGHTS RESERVED
Printed in the United States of America

LC 2008043127
ISBN 978-1-55849-689-7 (library cloth); 690-3 (paper)

Designed by Steve Dyer
Set in ITC Bodoni by Binghamton Valley Composition
Printed and bound by The Maple-Vail Book Manufacturing Group

Library of Congress Cataloging-in-Publication Data

Griffin, Martin, 1956–
    Ashes of the mind : war and memory in northern literature, 1865–1900 /
Martin Griffin.
        p. cm.
Includes bibliographical references and index.
ISBN 978-1-55849-689-7 (lib. cloth : alk. paper) –
ISBN 978-1-55849-690-3 (pbk : alk. paper)
    1. United States–History–Civil War, 1861-1865–Literature and the war.
    2. American literature–19th century–History and criticism.
    3. Authors, American–19th century–Political and social views.   4. Memory in literature.
    5. Literature and society–United States–History–19th century.   6. War and Literature.
    7. Memorials in literature.   8. Bierce, Ambrose, 1842-1914?–Criticism and interpretation.
    9. Lowell, James Russell, 1819-1891–Criticism and interpretation.
    10. Melville, Herman, 1819-1891–Criticism and interpretation.
    11. James, Henry, 1843-1916–Criticism and interpretation.
    12. Dunbar, Paul Laurence, 1872-1906–Criticism and interpretation.   I. Title.
    PS217.C58G75 2003
    810.9'358737–dc22
                            2008043127

British Library Cataloguing in Publication data are available.

For my mother, Dorothy Griffin,
and in memory of my father, John R.Griffin

There was an American war. Just as much an American war as when there is, that it is, where they come and they do not come, where they were there where they were, not there where they meant. They did not mean where they will, they cannot will. It would mean that they would write a will which they did not. Of course why they did not.

Gertrude Stein, 1934

CONTENTS

ACKNOWLEDGMENTS

A NUMBER OF PEOPLE made important contributions to *Ashes of the Mind* along the way, most of which remain as unpaid debts on my part. The list must begin with Barbara Packer and Michael North at UCLA, who always had both a sympathetic ear and an exacting eye for the project, and who continued to be generously available for intellectual and scholarly advising long afterward. Special thanks for responses and suggestions on particular themes and chapters are owed to Joan Waugh, Richard Yarborough (who told me once, "You'd have to dig for days to reach irony in Dunbar's poetry"), and Maurice Lee. Cristanne Miller, my former department chair at Pomona College, encouraged me at a crucial moment and pointed me in the right direction. Clark Dougan and others at the University of Massachusetts Press made being a first-time academic author as painless an experience as possible. Finally, Emmy Goldknopf devoted a lot more attention to the development of this book than she should have, for which I'm endlessly grateful.

Chapter 3 first appeared in *Prospects: A Journal of American Cultural Studies* 29 (2004): 251–88, under the title "The Road from Memorial Hall: Future Imperfect in *The Bostonians*"; it is reprinted here in a slightly different form with permission from Cambridge University Press.

Ashes of the Mind

Introduction

It is language, and the whole system of social conventions attached to it, that allows us at every moment to reconstruct our past.

Maurice Halbwachs

THE BROAD THEME of this book is the literature of Civil War memory in the North from 1865 to 1900 in the shape of works by five authors who can be described as Northerners by virtue of birthplace, upbringing, and cultural identity. Four were adults during the Civil War, two older (James Russell Lowell and Herman Melville) and two younger, one of whom fought in the war (Ambrose Bierce) and one of whom did not (Henry James), and the fifth was born a few years after it was over (Paul Laurence Dunbar). In the texts I examine in this study, however, all of these writers are engaging, in their fashion, with the memory of what is still the bloodiest conflict in American history, with memorials, and with the legacy of the Union victory for individual lives and for the spectrum of political and cultural ideas that obtained in the Northern states. The roles that individual memory and commemorative politics play in these narratives and poems are the narrower focus of the book, and, for three of these authors, I also discuss their own legacy, the status of their writings as they persisted, or maybe just survived, in American cultural memory. In particular, the shifting and uncertain canonical status of Lowell, Dunbar, and Bierce over the past century can, I believe, cast some light on larger questions about how American collective memory has dealt with the war and its range of meanings within both a national and a regional historical imaginary.

Language and its interdependent social conventions are, as Maurice

Halbwachs argues, the indispénsable tools for our capacity to reconstruct the past.[1] Reconstructing the American past, however, even in the languages of literature, leads inevitably to a difficult confrontation with established social and historical conventions, the frameworks of expression and interpretation. The aftermath of the Civil War saw the emergence of a number of such ideological frameworks, many of which had the urgent and primary purpose of managing the meanings of the nation's recent conflict. The white South regarded the neutralization or defeat of Radical Reconstruction as their most important goal and set about reaching it in ways that were as much about words, ideas, and sensibility as they were about the mounting of an armed and covert insurgency aimed primarily at nominally emancipated and enfranchised black communities. A narrative of injured racial honor and restored hegemony was enshrined in the late 1860s and dominated Southern thinking for many decades, on into the twentieth century. In the North, the framework of the rescue of the Union continued to thrive after 1865, and that fiction (in the sense of a coherent and explanatory story) was the touchstone of political virtue for decades. Nevertheless, the intensity of the social and economic changes in late nineteenth-century America, from urbanization to highly rationalized business models, and from technology to mass immigration, demanded other meanings, and more flexible and pragmatic metaphors, especially to mediate between citizens and a universe of new corporate entities that operated on a formerly unknown scale of size and value and whose industrial power seemed to intimidate or even invalidate the notion of representative politics as understood until then. Literary naturalism, the uncompromising study of the new social forces created by a scientific and industrial order, would be the most sophisticated of those cultural efforts. In contrast, the fictions of the Civil War in the South did not give way before social change in the postwar decades as readily as they did in the North – leaving the matter of the collective memory of the war in the North, at the turn of the twentieth century, in a curious and vulnerable position.

The War over Cultural Memory

The politics of victory are often more complex and more fraught than the politics of defeat, and something of the same distinction can be applied to literature and other cultural traditions into which such politics are threaded. For the United States and its civil war, the relationship between victory and defeat, and between the cultural expression of these complementary experiences, played itself out within a set of common perceptions of the American world. This world was largely English-speaking, generally republican with a small r, and committed to various notions of individual liberty, some more limited in their range of application than others. The idea of a shared American culture was, paradoxically, both undermined and strengthened by the war: the violence of the conflict itself seemed the ultimate proof that such a culture had evaporated in the face of implacable political differences, yet the postconflict decades revealed that culture – especially when it came to the matter of a racial hierarchy – to be in many ways more robust than the bitterness of the war and its aftermath might have suggested.

The war was also a time of intense human suffering, especially for the South, which lost almost 20 percent of its white male population between the ages of sixteen and forty-five. The devastation of the war was visited ultimately and decisively on the territory of the Confederacy because of the aggressive military leadership of Ulysses S. Grant and William T. Sherman, who declared, sometimes openly, sometimes by implication, all methods of warfare to be legitimate in retribution for secession, the crime against the Union. The concept of total war, in which the civilian population and the economy are targeted along with any other enemy asset, fell outside the parameters of contemporary military thinking, and its introduction provided some disturbing premonitions of the conflicts of the twentieth century.[2] The final collapse of chattel slavery, at least as a legal property regime, was a moment of great historical power and some irony, because it removed exactly that which the South had courted ruin in order to protect.

The defeated Confederacy responded with the emotional weapon of the "Lost Cause," a powerful convergence of several discrete elements: a spiritual isolationism, a deep conviction of moral superiority (in relation to the North), an aggressive assertion of racial superiority (in relation to African Americans), and the language of historical romance. The concept of the Lost Cause, as both cultural metaphor and political fiction, outperformed any other model of how the white South would deal with the defeat of 1865 and the dismantling of the slave-based economy. It continually eclipsed the "New South" and similar attempts to generate a narrative of modernity for the region and survived well into the twentieth century, providing a base line of cultural resonance even for the more subversive texts of Southern modernism by William Faulkner, Robert Penn Warren, and others – indeed, in certain ways even for African American modernists such as Jean Toomer.

The historical arc of ideas and expression in the North after the war was significantly different. Initially, the popular attitude was that a grim but ultimately well-deserved lesson had been administered to the secessionist forces and leadership, bringing them after four savage years to the ultimate recognition that the Union could not be dissolved at will by any state or grouping of states. The Emancipation Proclamation of 1863 that had placed the issue of slavery front and center for the final two years of the war had been grudgingly accepted by a large number of Northern whites, even though the goal of full citizenship for black Americans was supported by only a minority. The collapse of the Confederacy, capped by Lee's surrender at Appomattox, had created for a brief period a Northern political complex marked by an acceptance that the war was also about freeing the slaves, a desire to make Southerners pay – at least for a short time – some kind of retributive price for the failed attempt to destroy the Union, and a recognition that significant changes in the industrial and governmental structure of the United States had come about as a result of wartime requirements and would positively inflect the development of the society in the years ahead.

At the same time, however, the psychic mosaic of victory could be interpreted in a somewhat different light. The future of black Americans in general was not a project around which popular support was gathering. Most Northern states disabled or banned voting by African Americans, and the reputation gained by the black regiments such as the 54th Massachusetts Volunteer Infantry had been regarded with more goodwill and approval in the midst of the fighting than it would be afterward, in peacetime. The belief held by influential black leaders such as Frederick Douglass had been that military service in the cause of the United States would be a major source of credit for blacks' push for equal citizenship. This assumption would prove to be more fragile than many had thought. Also, although the desire to exact retribution from the South for the war was indeed a powerful force, especially after Andrew Johnson succeeded Lincoln in the White House and appeared to want to restore the 1861 constitutional status quo ante without further discussion, the North was also uncertain about how far it wanted to go with the dismantling of the Southern system and Southern political traditions, and even more uncertain about how it would deal with Southern resistance, if such came about. The punitive desire to impose a new order on the South lasted probably about seven or eight years, until 1873, and had dissipated long before Reconstruction was officially terminated in 1877. It was a psychic as much as a political process, in fact, and in Ralph Ellison's intriguing and quite contemporary-sounding phrase, the North was "eager to lose any *memory traces* of those values for which it had gone to war" (my emphasis).[3]

Behind the political maneuvering and the shifts in public attitude is, however, the more complex economic question. All the markers of American modernity – railroads, industrial plant, urbanization, immigration, political genuflection to corporate needs – increased after 1865, but the knowledge that these assets had also contributed definitively to the North's victory in the Civil War was counterbalanced by an increasing sense that commercial and social forces had been unleashed in a way that now made them difficult to supervise and control. The increasingly intense hierarchies of industrial work, the sense of free American labor turning into a "legacy" proletariat, without access to the presumed upward social mobility granted by an earlier economic and cultural model, the political inability to deal with the implications of massive concentrations of financial power in individual hands – for some, these were nothing more than the unfortunate but unavoidable by-products of dynamic capitalist development. For others, however, they were the troubling phantasms of a deeper social alienation, an alienation of American society from its roots and its original strengths.

For those others, the implicit and explicit critique of Northern industrial society on the part of the South, despite its anachronistic style and, often, shallow and sentimental glorification of plantation life, became rather attractive. Writers such as Joel Chandler Harris, Thomas Nelson Page, Constance Fenimore Woolson, and Mary Noailles Murfree (whose chosen setting was the rugged mountain culture of the Appalachians rather than the plantation South) communicated a sense of regional identity and social warmth in a period marked by the gradual flattening of social and regional distinctions in the rest of the United States. They created an alternative world of stability, loyalty, and community in which racial problems and tensions disappeared behind a rose-tinted fiction of plantation slavery in which everyone knew his or her place and a kindly paternalism was the dominant manifestation of white authority. For Southern authors, this form of writing was not necessarily a predetermined campaign of cultural manipulation (and there were talented and less talented exponents), but it did serve the purpose of wrestling into place an attitude to the South and its past completely different from the one that had obtained in the North in 1865. The politics of defeat had opened up a field of imaginative work in which what one might call a realist history of the war and its origins was slowly replaced with a romance of nobility, nostalgia, and lost, "organic" social relations. In the performance of cultural memory, commemorating the Southern past and the sacrifice of the war years, Southern writing played the most plangent if not the most subtle chords.

Northern literature was part of the map too, but it seemed to have no such obvious mission, nor did it have the materials out of which to construct an equivalent myth. The major intellectual achievement of the antebellum United States was New England Transcendentalism, but that movement had dissipated by the early 1850s and, more problematically, its high-minded commitment to philosophical rigor and the most demanding of cultural forms meant that little had come out of Boston in the prewar era that appealed to ordinary tastes. To a great extent, that same philosophical rigor – despite its optimism – doomed Transcendentalism to live on in intellectual history rather than American popular memory. As Vernon L. Parrington expressed it at the end of the 1920s in his influential study of American cultural history: "The transcendental dream . . . was in an even worse plight, for it left no tragic memories to weave a romance about the fallen hopes."[4] A little more accessible than the chilly altars of Emersonian idealism, the popular, so-called Fireside Poets, such as Henry Wadsworth Longfellow and John Greenleaf Whittier, who combined lyric gifts with a sense of where the public taste was moving, would continue to enjoy a large audience over many years. In comparison with the literature of the Lost Cause, however, their social ideas and poetic styles were marked by a cheerful decorum and thematic primness that left them, ultimately, bringing up the rear in any competition to secure a broad national cultural authority. To take one example: even powerful evocations of the New England sensibility and natural environment such as Whittier's famous and much-loved poem "Snow-Bound: A Winter Idyl" (1865) failed to influence the national imagination in a way comparable to the effect of Southern plantation whimsy. Significantly, the type of Southern popular writing that won a large supra-regional audience, such as Joel Chandler Harris's Uncle Remus stories, managed to represent both (overtly) a quasi-mythical past recovered within an exotic present and (covertly) the political and social tensions of the contemporary period. By deploying openly a fantasy of African American deference within a vision of a pastoral order of society, these texts were also playing on the racial fears and related prejudices of the post–Civil War decades. Whittier's poem, despite its status as a popular classic, was in the end only about nostalgia for a rural Massachusetts childhood. Furthermore, the fiery abolitionist verse of the Fireside Poets seemed suddenly but not unexpectedly, at the end of the war, to have become anachronistic; a new ideological formation was beginning to crystallize, which rendered earlier ones moot.[5]

Northern writing about the war, therefore, had a more difficult task and met a more complicated fate, which included, to some degree, ultimately finding itself in an obscure corner of American cultural memory, in a way that the South did not permit to happen to its own history. The growling tones in Robert Lowell's 1961 poem "For the Union Dead" embody one of the most confrontational expressions, at the middle of the twentieth century, of despair at the marginalization of the sacrifice made by the Federal soldier in the Civil War, at the casual forgetting that Lowell saw as the morbidity infecting the nation's grasp of historical meaning.[6] My argument is that the literature of the North (or the literature of the Union) has also been the victim of a kind of forgetting, the amnesia that ensues when a historically contingent identity fails to become a robust subgenre of culture. Some individual authors and texts fared better than others: for example, Herman Melville and his work vanished from memory during the last quarter of the nineteenth century while Henry James never lost public attention, although he, at times, stimulated as much irritation as admiration. But what was forgotten was that there was such a thing as a Northern writer at a time when that distinction meant something. One can see the results of this today. Courses on Southern literature abound in college undergraduate catalogs and job descriptions request specific qualifications in that field, but somehow the assumption is that the rest of the country is covered by other rubrics: "American naturalism"; "nineteenth century"; "women writers in America." Occasionally classes in the writing of another regional concentration are offered (e.g., New England, California, Chicago, or Appalachia), but these have nothing like the stamina and institutional presence of Southern literature as a field.

In the immediate postconflict decades, from 1865 to the end of the century, it was all a little more open, however. The topics of war and commemoration did not yet belong entirely to the South, and many authors had their own memories of military service to draw on (indeed, the dramatic arrival of Stephen Crane's *Red Badge of Courage* on the scene in 1895 marks a critical moment at which the memory of the war devolves from lived experience to literary metaphor). The Northern journey through loss, uncertainty, memory, and self-criticism was undertaken in different ways by the authors I discuss in this book – James Russell Lowell, Herman Melville, Henry James, Ambrose Bierce, and Paul Laurence Dunbar – as well as by John W. DeForest in *Miss Ravenel's Conversion from Secession to Loyalty*, Albion Tourgée in *A Fool's Errand*, Elizabeth Stuart Phelps in *The Gates Ajar*, William Dean Howells in *A Hazard of New Fortunes*, and Walt Whitman in *Specimen Days* and *Democratic Vistas*, to name a few figures who would each warrant more extensive treatment. Not only did all of these authors, as Northerners, take up matters of collective and personal memory and the sacrifices of the war years, but they had to deal also with the politics of victory and with the cultural and rhetorical forms that victory offers, which may be considerably less imbued with emotional clarity and tragic elegance than those associated with defeat. In many ways, therefore, *Ashes of the Mind* is an exercise in the recovery of memory, an effort to move the cultural furniture slightly to give a better view of an obscured pattern of American writing. Indeed, writing as memory, in certain instances even as countermemory that challenges an established consensus, is an explicit theme in this book.[7]

The Memory of American Literature

American literary texts are one of the vehicles of American memory. They take their place in the array of cultural forms that retain and communicate experience across generations. Other forms are well known:

autobiographical accounts, oral or written; professional historical research and writing; theater, television, and movies; and the diffuse field of collective or public memory, passed down through a range of channels from family stories to regional or national folklore, and from commemorative and memorial sites to educational and cultural institutions. Literature, however, even a strongly autobiographical text, is something more than individual memory, and yet enjoys something less than institutional power. If there is a potential for influence there, it is embodied in the literary text as words from the past, a construction of language from an earlier and now lost moment in time.

The literary texts that concern us in *Ashes of the Mind* are fiction and poetry, but in the subjective reality of cultural memory it is always, however, the operative elements of the genre, rather than the abstract genre itself, that are important. Readers recall poetry not as a form of language but as a couple of lines from a particular poem or as the dominating image of a short lyric; in drama, audience members retain a powerful theatrical moment, or a familiar line, in their memory (indeed, even without seeing an actual performance: more people today may be able to quote Stanley bellowing "Stella!" than have ever seen Tennessee Williams's *A Streetcar Named Desire*); rather than a whole novel, often the opening and closing sentences take up residence somewhere in the unconscious, to emerge at odd times when we experience an unexpected reminder or read something that strikes us as similar. Clearly, also, there are areas of generic convergence, where an image in a poetic text, for example, may transmit a sharper or more enigmatic description of an experience or a location than a passage in a narrative text. Equally, the rhythms of prose fiction may, at one moment or another, open out into a more charged, more emotionally modulated, even more prophetic style of writing, bringing that text briefly closer to poetry. All forms of literary expression, in their somewhat different ways, carry memory and transmit it, through language, to the reader or audience.[8]

The work of retaining, reconstructing, and disseminating memory in writing and rhetoric can have several different active dimensions. One might sketch out four such dimensions as follows: (a) the memory of an earlier historical period manifested in the language, narrative structure, or imagery of a text; (b) the degree to which that text is itself constructed around the work of memory or engages in a commemorative act, whether it assumes a positive, neutral, or even negative posture toward that work; (c) the text's own role as a kind of memorial in language; (d) the negative, or ironic, tensions between memory and cultural context set up by the multidimensionality of the literary text itself: a text invoking a collective memory for which the natural audience is no longer at hand, for example.

With category (a), the act of reading means simultaneously identifying and embracing the language, narrative movement, architecture, and imagery of a text in the sense that the reading of literature demands some time, attention, and initial empathy. There is also, in any situation in which the reader and the text occupy different historical locations, a meeting of strangers. Indeed, the rules for such a meeting have been altered throughout the modern history of interpretive philosophies for literature. The text has been at times a self-protecting icon, accessible only to those who ignore the distractions of historical and biographical knowledge, at other times a product of the toxic soup of ideology, discoverable only through an analysis of its chemical components and their imprint on the flow of discourse, and at others again a playful negotiation with uncertainty, as unlikely to transmit meaning as anyone is to want to receive it. Here I sketch out an approach that gets beyond this series of new critical, historicist, and deconstructive models and suggest that the text, the poem or prose narrative, contains in its language the past of the culture in which it currently lives and breathes, and that its function as the bearer of memory evades – but does not negate – the legacy of ideology. The text confronts the reader with a past that is a repository of potentially retrievable experience, in a way that reconnects, through language, elements of that now partly objectified past to the subjective but not entirely individuated consciousness of the present. Or, to put it another way: not quite our own man or woman, we confront the literary text, which is both familiar and strange, and in this confrontation both individual and collective identities may be in play.

The theory behind (b), in its focus on the idea of a text as itself a commemorative act, is that the literary text that is consciously "about" memory has to be about two things: first, the putting of the act of memory into operation as an image, narrative element, or plot device within the contours of the text, and second, structuring the emotional and intellectual dynamic of that text around the presence, absence, or ambivalent status (indeterminate presence/absence) of memory. Thus a text can be a commemorative act in itself as well as representing commemoration, and indeed it might achieve this act even when it is not representing commemoration, or when it cannot decide whether it is or not. Many examples of poetry and fiction from various cultural and historical contexts are self-evidently commemorative projects as texts, quite apart from any ostensible theme or leitmotif they are host to, as works from Milton's "Lycidas" to Paul Celan's "Todesfuge" and James Ellroy's *My Dark Places* confirm. The enactment of such a project leads to (c), the status of the text as a memorial within the flow of individual, regional, or national cultures. Many literary texts can be about the act and significance of memory and commemoration but may lose that profile in time and fade from collective or institutional memory; others can retain that profile and even find it sharpened as the processes of collective and institutional memory retain the text and re-examine it in different historical contexts. Two powerful examples, separated by eighty years, would be the Gettysburg Address and Randall Jarrell's World War II poem "The Death of the Ball Turret Gunner."

Lincoln's words at Gettysburg in November 1863 are an act of commemoration, dedicated (as the address both asserts and withdraws) to the men who had died there four months earlier. The words have also, through tunnels of historical change and political struggle and fluctuations in values and perception, become a memorial to Lincoln himself and to a certain relationship between crisis, language, and purpose that has meaning for American culture today. As Barry Schwartz observes in his study of Lincoln in American memory: "Connecting past events to one another and to the events of the present, collective memory is part of the culture's meaning-making apparatus. How this apparatus works is problematic; that we depend on it as part of the nature of things is certain. How collective memory establishes an image of the world so compelling as to render meaningful its deepest perplexities remains to be investigated."[9] The presence of the past within the lived present is inseparable from any engagement with the language of the past, and that in turn is one element, I would argue, of the connectivity Schwarz describes. With certain familiar texts such as Lincoln's four-minute speech, images, abstract terms, perceived emotional tonalities, and even syntax may play key roles in the rendering of meaning across time.[10]

The survival in public memory of Randall Jarrell's bleak five-line poem is something different, although perhaps not entirely so. Published in 1945, it has become a much-anthologized piece about the air war during World War II, the exposed position of the gunner in the semi-spherical turret slung underneath the B-24 bomber; the unequal interaction of the human body and modern technology and weaponry, the efficient disposal of bloody remains, and the final two lines,

> I woke to black flak and the nightmare fighters.
> When I died they washed me out of the turret with a hose.

are, or used to be, exemplary for a certain kind of mordant, masculine emotion-as-lack-of-emotion.[11] Indeed, to call it "much-anthologized" is to indicate that its spread throughout Anglo-American culture cannot be divorced from a discussion of its poetic value. Thus, any attempt to analyze this brief poem must take into account those matters of American popular memory into which it has inserted itself: the risks involved in military service; the value of the war against Nazi Germany and the Empire of Japan; the possibility that sacrifice in a larger cause can be – must be – both brutally anonymous and blessed with individual significance; and the second possibility that it is, unfortunately, only anonymous and thus a kind of traumatic blow to a nation committed to individual self-realization. The poem is an attempt to remember that is embodied in an image of disembodiment; it has, however, succeeded, despite its motif of utter bodily annihilation, in becoming a poetic memorial to Americans who died in air combat in World War II. It is also a remarkably elastic memorial, because it can be "harmonized," as one critic puts it, as effectively "with a patriotic celebration as it can with a pacifist critique of the American war effort."[12]

The Gettysburg Address and "The Death of the Ball Turret Gunner," Lincoln's words and Jarrell's words, diverge somewhat on the cusp of category (d), however. No matter how plain its intention, any language is always open to the ironic undermining that occurs when the cultural context in which the language is read shifts in such a way as to render that language awkward and unconvincing and deprives it of the audience for which it has had significance. We know that, from some often unidentifiable point, archaic formulations may begin to provoke unease or

laughter as opposed to inviting familiarity or solemnity, and thus no literary text that engages in a commemorative maneuver can avoid the potential irony that lurks beneath the agreed meanings of words, images,
and names. This willingness, or indeed necessity, to embrace, and not try
to evade, the depredations of time and an ever-changing perspective
makes the literature of memory different from the detachment of professional history at one end of the spectrum and the ritual invocations of institutional commemoration at the other.

Remembering the Civil War

Civil War memory went through several stages, regionally determined to
a significant degree, over the century that began in the spring of 1865.
The period immediately following Appomattox was marked by a strong
sense of victory and moral achievement in the North, and by bleak bewil-
derment in the defeated South; within a short time, the latter feeling
shifted and grew into intense resentment, marked by a commitment to
retaining white supremacy in the former Confederate states, if necessary
by violence and intimidation. The fifty years from the end of Reconstruction in 1877 until about 1930 were the great period of national reconciliation, in which the unbending hostility of the Southern white population
to the consequences of the Civil War changed again to offer a model of
national reconciliation on the South's terms, canceling slavery as an
issue in the public memory of the war – a position that white America accepted with growing enthusiasm. The South, by legal and extra-legal
means, declared the matter of race and citizenship to be its own, rather
than a national, affair.

At the end of this period, the vast majority of those who had personally experienced the war had died, taking the element of individual memory out of the equation. In the decades between the 1920s and the 1940s
a resurgence of popular interest in the South and the Civil War took
place across the United States and overseas, and in this regard Margaret
Mitchell's *Gone with the Wind* is the defining cultural artifact of the era.
During those decades the pressures of modernity on the social and political assumptions and practices of the South grew in strength, culminating in the civil rights struggle that broke out in the early 1950s. In the
shadow of the centenary of the Civil War, the 1960s saw the emergence

of a new historical paradigm that reopened the questions of slavery and emancipation without which the war and its aftermath could not be properly understood. The centenary activities themselves provided a stage for many an outburst of the kind of political acrimony that had marked the Reconstruction era, history sometimes repeating itself as farce as the nation prepared to commemorate the war in which more Americans died than in any conflict before or since.[13]

To add to this sketch (which is itself a partisan interpretation of historical events), it is important to note that, while the nurturing of the collective memory of the war was a social and often personal duty for Southerners, it continued to be a significant issue in the Northern states too. During the postwar decades of the later nineteenth century, the move to a reconciliationist posture toward the Southern states and the re-establishment of racial segregation as a largely national consensus (sometimes unspoken, sometimes not) was resisted by a rag-tag-and-bobtail alliance of prominent antiracist whites and black activists. At the end of the 1890s, this group included the writer and attorney Albion W. Tourgée, the philosopher William James (who gave the keynote speech at the unveiling of the monument on Boston Common to the 54th Massachusetts in 1897), the human rights campaigner Ida B. Wells, the principled, antisegregationist branches of the Grand Army of the Republic veterans' organization,[14] and the "respectable" black political leadership, of which Booker T. Washington was by then the most prominent representative. These groups and individuals were trying, in a way that seems more obvious now that it did at the time, to keep some measure of control over the memory of the Civil War, its origins and its consequences.

Although the period of this study – from the end of the war until 1900 – was well populated with hundreds of thousands of veterans from both the Union and Confederate forces, of various ranks and different backgrounds, it is also the era during which the dynamic of experience, recollection, and interpretation was moved from the context of individual experience recounted (personal memory) to the wider and more paradoxical field of collective memory. By that, I do not mean that it was a period in which every individual memory was aggressively denied for the benefit of a state-sponsored myth. It was a time, however, during which personal memory, especially in the North, had lost something of its hold on the record of the Civil War. By the turn of the twentieth century, as David Blight comments, it was "the Confederate soldier [who] provided a model of masculine devotion and courage in an age of gender anxieties and ruthless material striving."[15] In most times and places, most individuals are not prepared to resist a degree of manipulation of public memory, and even personal memory can be unreliable, taking on the contours of what appears to be the approved narrative even when such contours do not fit individual recollection. Memory wants to be on board with the dominant social and historical assumptions at large in the world, and it is often easier – and not necessarily deliberately fraudulent or dishonest – to acquiesce in the legends of the tribe than to hold out for a different account of events that few people want to hear. It is nonetheless one of the astonishing successes of the defeated South that it won the cultural struggle over American memory within twenty-odd years of the war's end. Indeed, one might go as far as Nell Irwin Painter does and argue that the history of the memory of the war is itself a remarkable narrative, relating how one race was read out of history in a clever maneuver that removed the ugly embarrassment of slavery and substituted for it the cultural supremacy of a national epic in which only white Americans had speaking roles.[16]

Nevertheless, there were holdouts, and I address two radically different examples – Bierce's fiction, and the narrative of the Robert Gould Shaw memorial and its unveiling – in the final chapters of this book. But suffice it to say that the memory of the Civil War that Augustus Saint-Gaudens embodied in his figures of Shaw and the black soldiers of the 54th Massachusetts, or that resurfaced during the ceremony on Boston Common, had become by 1897 a minority position in every sense of the word, including the contemporary sense of racial minority. The memory of that memory, the meditation on the social meaning of that memory, is the subject of Paul Laurence Dunbar's sonnet "Robert Gould Shaw." But decades before that, in the weeks and months immediately following the end of the conflict in April 1865, there were people who understood that the commemorative act might be both necessary and problematic, an expression of victory and of loss for which the victory may not compensate. When James Russell Lowell stepped onto the podium at Harvard, at the end of the day's commemorative ceremonies on July 21 of that year, he was conscious of the fragility of memory and of the necessity of investing it with the rhetorical energies that can render both the past that is gone and the present in which one speaks, and the long poem he delivered on that occasion, the Harvard Commemoration Ode, echoes that realization. From the earliest moment, the literature of Civil War memory was entwined with the politics of Civil War commemoration, and the relationship would not be easy.

Memorials, Historical and Ideological

Although the desire to build memorials is certainly not uniquely American, the nineteenth century saw Americans embrace the practice with enthusiasm. The dedication of a culture's artistic and productive energies to funerary construction (often notably out of proportion to the economic level at which the people lived) is a feature of almost all stages of human history. What we can make of that history is open to interpretation, but the significance of the effort has clearly to do with a desire to extend meaning beyond the normal span of life, to counter the human tendency to forget (or even to resist the demanding memories of) the departed, whether distantly respected leaders or beloved kin. Because times of crisis, and war in particular, tend to increase mortality (for example, among young men) and make death in conflict a community affair, a merging of private and public bereavement takes place. It was thus to be expected that the years after the Civil War would see a range of cultural expression aimed at commemorating both individual and community loss.

The latter motive – to express a communal or collective emotion – is present in the realistic commemorative statues built by public subscription to stand guard opposite courthouses on New England town squares, the figures Robert Lowell described in his poem "For the Union Dead" almost a century later as "stone statues of the abstract Union soldier" which "grow slimmer and younger every year."[17] It is also visible in the massive logistical effort and emotional investment that went into the construction of the memorial to Robert E. Lee in Richmond, unveiled in 1890. The Lee memorial, however, in its wrought and almost baroque grandeur, is a very different kind of political and aesthetic statement. In contrast to the rational austerity of the statue of the anonymous Union infantryman at Forest Hills Cemetery in Boston, for example, created by Martin Milmore in 1867, the overpowering equestrian figure of Robert

E. Lee speaks of duty and tragedy, aristocratic heroism, and the moral superiority of memory over reality. Indeed, one might call it a refusal of reality for the benefit of memory. But the Union and Confederate monuments represent, in their different ways, a struggle to bridge the abyss between, on one side, the individual consciousness in the quotidian world and, on the other, a community's need to validate itself by appeal to meanings that are not merely responses to daily existence but rather principles embodied by the dead who sacrificed themselves so that those meanings might prevail. The role of a memorial to the deceased of a past conflict is thus less an appeal for a unique individual response and more a signal to the pertinent community in their public lives that they should now (every day or once a year) turn and redirect their emotional commitment, all their attention, to the presence of the sacrifice being thus commemorated. All public monuments have as their goal "a peculiar reshaping of the self around an abstraction of loss," as the psychiatrist Murray Shane has commented, and furthermore: "It is the function of monuments to be a permanent context for the idea of the self forever doubling back over ideas or examples or exemplifications about the self. In this way a monument, like a cultural idea (like a psychotherapeutic idea of the self), shadows its origins and its definitions and its own destination."[18] For the Southern war memorials, the permanent context was the defeat of the Confederacy, while in the North it was victory and the securing of the Union. The monument of the Union soldier, in its classic austerity and reticence, shadows its origins in the guilt over slavery, its definitions in the Union he managed to save, and its destination in a confusion about nation, race, and value that allowed Northerners to sacrifice their principal moral achievement to the ideology against which they had fought. The monument of Robert E. Lee, in contrast, has its origins in racial hierarchy, its definitions in a defeat that was regarded as only military and not social or moral or political, and a destination that provoked more cultural energy after its subject's death than when he had lived. To that extent, it was a "reshaping of the self" around a celebration of public memory rather than a meditation on loss.

The real "doubling-back" came about later. The writing of the white Southerners in the first half of the twentieth century – Allen Tate, John Crowe Ransom, Robert Penn Warren, Donald Davidson, Erskine Caldwell, Carson McCullers, Flannery O'Connor – tapped into a current that

was the product of a self returning doggedly to its origins and definitions.[19] Whatever their individual feelings about history or about race,
the modern literary artists of the South were anything but tentative in
their investigation of the hidden corners of their country's psyche. In the
earlier period, however, over the decades from the end of the Civil War
to the end of the century, Southern writers rarely wanted to confront the
self with anything other than either a ritual invocation of a lost past or a
declaration of Southern virtue. Two exceptions among white artists were
the New Orleans writer George Washington Cable, author of the novel
The Grandissimes (1880) as well as the remarkable antiracist essay "The
Silent South" (1884), and, for one brief moment in his career, Thomas
Nelson Page, author of the collection of sentimental plantation tales *In
Ole Virginia* (1887). Although Page was perhaps unsure of his own true
aims, he counterbalanced the nostalgic parlor-pieces such as "Marse
Chan" with "No Haid Pawn," the nearest that a white author, committed
to the memory of the Confederacy, had come to creating the definitive
gothic horror story about slavery. In that narrative, the local white population's perception of visiting Abolitionists as being "of the devil" is
shadowed by the history of the murderous cruelty of the slave execution
at the remote plantation house.[20] But for Page, that short piece was a
one-time event and had no effect on his long career as an apologist for
Southern exceptionalism – and he was also a vigorous opponent of what
he saw as Cable's cultural treason.[21] By and large, the reality of the late
nineteenth century was that any literature of commemoration and memory that was not merely a morbid picking at the scab of defeat had a hard
time of it. Although efforts were made in the postwar years to create a vital regional publishing industry to resist the increasing weight of New
York in particular, the publishing business in the South was, aside from a
couple of spirited journals, about as weak and comparatively ineffectual
as it had been in the 1840s and 1850s.[22] Traditional restraints on theme
and perspective continued to dog writers and publishers. Even Sherwood Bonner, a cheerfully enthusiastic defender of Southern culture and
values, brought out *Like unto Like* (1878), her only published novel –
with its eccentric and doomed love affair between a politically active Federal soldier and an impetuous young Southern woman – in Boston. It just
would not have been appropriate, anywhere in Dixie.

Politics and Words

Rather than the more culturally familiar motif of Southern collective memory, in this study I take up the issues of memory, memorial, and commemoration in texts by authors from Northern states. The birthplaces of the writers whose works are examined in *Ashes of the Mind* include Cambridge, Massachusetts (Lowell), New York (Melville and James), and the state of Ohio (Bierce – who grew up in Indiana – and Dunbar), and I hope to show that their treatments of memory are nurtured by a complex of sadness and irony that came to them precisely because they were Northern writers. To put it in terms of funerary art in a way that echoes my earlier comments, I am interested here in the significance of the austere Union memorial – the statue of the anonymous soldier – rather than the baroque melodrama of Confederate figuration. The dynamics of remembrance in Northern culture, where one was in any case given to a stoical underplaying of emotion, went from a celebration of victory, through induced self-doubt, to an odd distancing from its own major achievements: victory over the Confederacy and black Emancipation. This shift reflects an accrual of uncertainty. Even the battlefield at Gettysburg, the site of an undisputed Union victory, has, as Edward T. Linenthal describes, a complicated history over which different parties have struggled and which "functions as a place where contending perceptions of war and martial sacrifice can be ritually expressed."[23]

One of my central arguments about communication and memory is that the primary text, even if it is only a week or a month old, always contains a language of discourse that is older than the culture's and the reader's present, and it is both a pleasure and an effort to recognize that and to open oneself to it. But there begins the difficulty, as each genre of expression deploys a dynamic of its own: commemorative inscription; political address; short story; poem. This is the fork in the road for the memorial text and the literary text as memorial, between collective memory as a body of inherited notions and narratives and the history of readings of texts in our culture. Compared with Abraham Lincoln's words at Gettysburg, Herman Melville's words in his poem "Shiloh," for example, published in 1866 in *Battle-Pieces and Aspects of the War*, are both more concrete and more enigmatic. Unlike the public memory of the Gettysburg Address, which has sought to acquire the words, preserve them, and make them applicable to a wide spectrum of political ideas and social visions – wider than Lincoln could ever have envisaged – the public memory of Melville's "Shiloh," his memorial poem on the battle that took place there in April 1862, is restricted by and large to two groups: poets and academics whose field includes the culture and literature of the American nineteenth century. Oddly, though, to confront either text involves similar experiences. There is the need for some historical context; there is the initial readjustment to a slightly older and perhaps consciously more archaic form of English; and there is the need to try to read the play of idea and emotion from some other point of view than the reader's own limited experience. One has to reach out and connect in a way that may take some effort, some temporary jettisoning of one's current limitations.

The comedian Bob Newhart is known for, among other things, a popular sketch from the late 1950s that involves an imagined telephone conversation between a public relations adviser (Newhart) and a somewhat dimwitted Abraham Lincoln (the imagined voice at the other end of the line) about preparations for the Gettysburg Address. After arguments about writing speeches on the backs of envelopes (difficult to read), and what to do about Grant's reputation as a lush (writing a gag for Lincoln about a case of liquor), the PR consultant is taken aback and somewhat irritated when Lincoln informs him that he has made some changes to the opening remarks. But he responds with much-tried patience: "What else, Abe? You changed . . . you changed four-score-and-seven to . . . to eighty-seven? I understand it means the same thing, Abe . . . Abe, that's meant to be a grabber! Abe, uh, we test-marketed that in Erie and they went out of their minds! . . . Trust me . . . well, it's . . . it's sort of like Mark Anthony saying 'Friends, Romans, countrymen, I got somethin' I wanna tell ya!' "[24] Newhart knew that the "eighty-seven" line would always raise a few laughs, because his audience was perfectly aware that, despite the brevity and modernity of the speech as a whole, the formulation at the beginning of the Gettysburg Address was indeed a conscious move to an older and more formal style.

To know that one is being addressed in a particular mode of rhetoric, and that this mode carries certain meanings, is an acceptable and even laudable level of knowledge in a democratic polity. Most of Lincoln's audience, then and now, were and are fully aware that they must stretch a little to connect with the vocabulary and cadences of the address. They were, and are, also conscious of the artificiality of the rhetoric at moments, and that this artificiality falls identifiably within the boundaries of a different kind of speech, one geared to unusual occasions. Despite regular jeremiads about the decline in civic education, one can make a reasonable case for modern Americans' being well able to distinguish between various kinds of informal and formal speech. People are not necessarily confused or intimidated when they are confronted with the mode of rhetoric that demands effort to take it in and, in a way, see through it. Nevertheless, historical documents in elevated, nonstandard English, or the English of a past era, tend to be located in areas of collective memory similar to museums, to be treated with a certain amount of hushed reverence. Only very few records of public speech, and the Gettysburg Address is primary among them, are both stylistically and syntactically demanding and retained actively within popular culture in America.[25]

Herman Melville's poem "Shiloh," however, which I discuss more extensively in Chapter 3, is both a similar and a very different kind of text. It is short, as is the Gettysburg Address. It contains both poetically archaic and prosaically modern language, as does the president's speech. It is about a known place where, on a known date, an event took place, as is the speech. And like the speech, it expresses a memory of that place and event and posits a significance for that memory. Both the president's speech and the poet's poem are also, in a crucial way, memorials themselves. Both texts place their speaker in the way of being a privileged recorder of a great event, with some inevitable and perhaps oppressive responsibility that comes with that privilege. They are not uneasy or mutually hostile if placed side by side, the speech and the poem. But the Gettysburg Address and "Shiloh" live in different worlds, and the cultural collective memory that keeps the one alive has little place for the other.

The distinction being made here is not about genre itself but rather about the often uneasy cultural status of the act of poetry, as opposed to our readier assimilation into public memory of the rhetorical abstractions of the Gettysburg Address, a supremely inclusive and political text in its appeal to clarity of purpose. In poetics of cultural transmission, one might say, the complexities and ambiguities of the Gettysburg Address have been flattened and partly erased, whereas in Melville's

"Shiloh" they have been sharpened. In commemorative expression generally there is an uncertainty about the fragility of language as a compen-
sation for loss – which is exactly what a memorial text is – and an
uncertainty that such language could be a carrier of potential danger, as
the words might be read in a different spirit than they were originally
meant, or in no spirit at all. The difference between literature and almost
any other record in language is that a certain ironic distance on the part
of authors – even authors loyal to a particular subject or audience – is inescapable, and that the literary text is resistant to a greater or lesser degree to attempts to manipulate its vision to fit the prevailing ideological
circumstances. The memory of American literature is not one to be conveniently adjusted: it remains often an uncomfortable, ambivalent, and
complicating presence in a world where historical nuance is suspect and
difficulty is at the very least dubiously elitist. My purpose in writing
Ashes of the Mind has been to look at the uncomfortable, ambivalent,
and complicating presence of Civil War memory and commemorative
culture in the Northern literature of the period 1865 to 1900. Or, as
Michael Kammen has expressed it in his magisterial study *Mystic Chords
of Memory*, to look at the "inertia and indifference, pride and vindictive-
ness, honor and shame."[26]

The Chapters

In the opening chapter, I concentrate on James Russell Lowell's Harvard
Commemoration Ode, a long poem in twelve stanzas that he originally
read – as a somewhat shorter version – to the gathering at the large memorial ceremony on July 21, 1865, organized by Harvard College to
honor the graduates who had served in the Union forces during the recent conflict. My aim in this first chapter is to explore anew the way in
which memory, national and community identity, and a recognition of
loss interact with each other in this long text, and to grasp the interior
dynamic of the poem that, like many of its companions, often seems
abandoned on a lonely siding, along with the body of nineteenth-century
American poetry not written by Poe, Whitman, or Dickinson.

   I explore some of the complications and evasions of this poem, including the ambiguous status of academic study and social privilege, and the
degree to which verses in a clearly nonironic mode can be seen as being

nevertheless haunted by uncertainty and the fragility of the poetic memorial. I argue that the Harvard Commemoration Ode does in fact register more arguably modern intimations, in particular the doubt that can
dog the heels of a text that is itself set up to be a memorial in language to
the losses of the past. The title of this book is taken from the lines in
which the "ashes of the burnt-out mind" are compared negatively to the
existential danger of battle. Although the life of the (academic) intellect
may be indeed lived at a lukewarm temperature compared to military
service in the Civil War, the "ashes" are a powerful image that speak to
more, perhaps, than Lowell imagines: in particular to the residue of the
trauma of the war and to the memory of a lost idealism. I suggest that in
our reading of texts such as this, in which neither the lyric intensity of
Romanticism nor the mythic ambitions of modernism are present, we
should make a more sustained effort to grasp their emotional and intellectual arguments.

I focus in Chapter 2 on Herman Melville's *Battle-Pieces and Aspects of
the War* from 1866 and discuss its democratically anonymous tones and
settings as a commemorative poetry that appears without the markers of
stable community and privilege that buttressed Lowell. I look at selected
poems, and especially at some of the often overlooked "Verses Inscriptive and Memorial" with their rather more conventional techniques, reviewing Melville's attempt to trace the public memory of the war within
a poetic form that is more private and meditative than declarative (while
recognizing that a private thought for public consumption is a good description of the epitaph). In contrast to the deployment of recognizable
epic tropes by Lowell, who structures the Commemoration Ode around a
traditional language that demanded and received a traditional collective
response, Melville is drawn more to a pared-down, minimalist aesthetic.
And yet, in contrast also to Whitman's experimental *Drum-Taps* collection, Melville refuses to leave the metrical boundaries of English verse at
mid-century, while rendering them sometimes alien in their juxtaposition to the American voices and themes of the poetry.

Melville, like Lowell, is conscious also of the inner pressure in memorial poetry for the poem itself to take on the role of a memorial in words,
and in crucial texts such as "An uninscribed Monument on one of the
Battle-fields of the Wilderness" and "A Requiem for Soldiers lost in
Ocean Transports" he grasps and simultaneously distances himself from

the lapidary nature of poetic memorial. He also raises, as a subject for poetry, an individual who, long after his own lifetime, would be bound up with the emotional spectrum of Southern cultural politics: the defeated commander of the Army of Virginia, General Robert E. Lee. In "Lee in the Capitol," a poem that is eerily prescient about the hagiography of Lee that began even before his death in 1872, Melville constructs a poetic representation of Lee as a silent and inwardly directed man, perhaps enigmatic even to himself, who refuses the opportunity for personal expression, or even for explanation, when offered it. Built around the figure of Lee, the intimation of tragic choice in the history of Secession and civil conflict was something that would take root in the collective memory of the South. In some final comments on *Battle-Pieces* and in particular on the final poem, "A Meditation," I argue that the collection, as a totality, never quite transcends its own political limitations.

In Chapter 3, on Henry James's novel *The Bostonians*, I return to the origins of this novel as a story of post–Civil War America (its first appearance was a series of installments in *The Century* magazine, one of the main outlets for Civil War memoir, history, and reminiscence during the 1880s). The pivotal scene in the novel takes place at an existing commemorative site, Harvard's Memorial Hall, opened in the late 1870s to honor those who had died in the Civil War – essentially an architectural expression of the same sensibility that led to the Harvard veterans' ceremony in the summer of 1865 and that inspired Lowell's poem on that occasion. The presence of the Southerner, Basil Ransom, in the vault of New England collective memory and community sacrifice, is more than an overture to a comedy of sexual ambition and gender politics. It is a statement in fiction by James that memory can take different forms, and that virtue is not guaranteed any authority. James himself had always before him the memory of his two younger brothers, Robertson and Wilkie James, who had fought and been wounded in the war but whose respective lives after it was over were not marked by success. The use of a former Confederate soldier as James's main character in *The Bostonians* suggests a move to a different memory of war from the Lowellian idealism of the Commemoration Ode, as if the politics of Union victory now matter less than the rejuvenating effects of Southern masculine virtue.

To a great extent, one can see that *The Bostonians* is about culture, and the way in which culture can manipulate history, politics, and human desire. Cultural influence can also take and reshape public memory in ways that surprise even its practitioners. As the South moved – partly consciously, partly intuitively – to take control of American memory in the postwar era, it was proving a point that a conflict can be won on the field of culture even after it has been lost militarily. Ransom, like Robert E. Lee, has the weapons of enigmatic character and a narrative of tragic choice at his disposal, a constellation James finds irresistible.

Chapter 4 takes up the question of memory and writing at a later stage in history: the late 1880s and early 1890s, when the fiction writer and journalist Ambrose Bierce published his bleak short stories based on his wartime experience. For Bierce, a veteran of the conflict, the act of remembering is something that takes place beyond the borders of individual recollection and public commemoration because both suggest the positive working of time on human experience: in his case, it is more like a dis-membering. In Bierce's vision, manifested in the most powerful of his short narratives, the enigma of time and the randomness of historical event grow to an ominous size and overshadow the notion that experience is somehow, conveniently, clearly "past" and yet "present" in the language of commemoration. His challenge to these assumptions involves a recovery of experience that is neither safely past – it bothers the psyche like postconflict traumatic memory – nor indeed present in commemorative tropes, because such tropes are mistakenly posited on the "pastness" of the past. I explore a cluster of Bierce's stories, "One Kind of Officer" and others, to try to understand how these narratives handle the memory of random destruction. In the reconciliation-oriented United States of the last decade of the nineteenth century, Bierce represents not so much a political opposition to reconciliation between North and South as a philosophical opposition to the casual assumption that the memory of the war had somehow been rendered safe, a kind of folksy addition to the museum of Americana. The memory of the war was, for Bierce, proof that time heals few wounds.

I conclude this chapter with a brief discussion of Bierce's relationship to Stephen Crane, his younger colleague in the 1890s literary milieu and author of a classic of American prose fiction in *The Red Badge of Courage*. Now unshakeable in its historic status, *Red Badge* is the modern masterpiece, a novel of "stark greatness," as Alfred Kazin once called it, setting the tone for the debate at mid-century.[27] One significant difference between Bierce and Crane as war writers, however, is that Bierce had personal experience of the Civil War but Crane did not. There is an issue of memory at work in Bierce's writing that is not so significant for Crane – somewhat to Crane's benefit, since *Red Badge* is perceived as the more imaginative work, the one that actually transforms the raw material of a war story into the achievement of American fiction.

My argument is that the matter of transformation is still an open question. Despite the much-vaunted irony of its narrative structure, *Red Badge* is clearly both a novel about a young man's journey through experience into knowledge and maturity, and a cultural product that transforms writing about the war (which large numbers of people had engaged in over the previous thirty years) into something more ambitious: the creation of American literature. The ruling trope in Ambrose Bierce's fiction, however, is the opposite: the refusal or impossibility of transformation. In "One of the Missing," "Parker Addison, Philosopher," and similar narratives, contingency subverts potential alteration, time shreds memory rather than nurturing it, and the notion of fiction as embodying a moral or aesthetic "resolution" is discounted by pre-emptive authorial act. The fact that what I call the "memory of American literature" tends to favor the transformational energies of one author's work over the representation of negativity in another's should encourage us to look at least a little beyond the assumptions around which such a memory is constructed.

In the final chapter I consider the complicated relationship between the poet Paul Laurence Dunbar and the memory of the Civil War, and in particular his reading of the fading of the cultural memory of slavery and Emancipation as interpretive grids for understanding the conflict. I analyze his well-known sonnet "Robert Gould Shaw," written in response to the new Boston public memorial to the 54th Massachusetts, designed and sculpted by Augustus Saint-Gaudens. Published in the *Atlantic Monthly* in October 1900, the poem becomes itself a kind of negative memorial, ending the century with an arraignment of the failure of the more idealistic and racially progressive elements in American political history. The background to Dunbar's lament is not only the institutionalized and quasi-institutionalized racism of the 1890s but also the concerted national project to deny the black contribution to the North's victory in the Civil War – as indeed black veterans had been denied their space in the increasingly amnesiac commemorative culture that purported to remember that war.[28] In contrast to a more radical critique that might be rooted in concepts of racial identity and counterhegemonic discourse, however, Dunbar never wavers in his admiration for Shaw, the white man whose sacrifice for black freedom was made without quibble or compromise.

It is important, however, to go beyond this one text and ask about the broader dynamic of culture in Dunbar's poetry. His idea of nation, his concept – as an African American writer – of free access to the language and body of the English poetic tradition as much as to the resources of Southern black folklore, are interventions in a new theory of cultural memory that looks toward the twentieth century and parallels aspects of the poetry of W. B. Yeats and Thomas Hardy. That kind of intervention, however, also provoked the refusal that he sensed, arising not just from a racist social order but from a type of cultural parochialism. The efforts to secure the "color-line" (to use W. E. B. DuBois's term) were not only a gesture of American social paranoia but also a barrier to a transatlantic cultural memory that might point the way to a more open and international profile of the American self.[29] The experience of Dunbar at the end of the nineteenth century is one item of evidence that the evocation of the Civil War had, by 1900, been cleansed of any emancipatory dynamic. The anthropological forgetfulness that Lowell foresaw in 1865 had become the political manipulation of collective memory.

In the Coda that concludes the book, I offer brief readings of three texts (more specifically, of one novel, one biographical history, and one collection of essays) that provide noncanonical perspectives on the Civil War and its collective memory. The shifting loyalties of women in relation to history and to struggles about race and political legitimacy point to complications in the picture of Northern memory even for those, such as Josephine Shaw Lowell, who were closely linked to its cultural nervous system. The other two figures I look at in the Coda, Sherwood Bonner and Jane Addams, although they are in terms of social and psychological identity at opposite ends of more than one spectrum, share an understanding of the organic, indeed the bodily nature of memory, that is another way of reading the effects of the Civil War and war in general on American society. In some respects, even accounts that seek most faithfully to record the marks of loss and injury discover the inadequacy of verbal expression: in particular, Jane Addams in *The Long Road of Woman's Memory* wants to make us understand that there are prelinguistic levels of injury to which women are more vulnerable because they are, as women, encouraged to operate with less resilient emotional defenses than men. The potential to be injured by history and the inadequacy of language to compensate for such injury points to the more complex understanding of war and trauma that the twentieth century produced.

To reiterate briefly the elements of the thesis that underpins my readings and explorations in this selection of post–Civil War writing in America: we can regard the work of retaining and communicating memory in language as a multi-dimensional operation, especially with respect to major cultural and individual experiences such as military conflict and traumatic political upheaval. The active elements of this complex are, first, that the memory of an earlier historical period is interwoven, at a cellular level, with the language, narrative, or imagery of a text. Second, the structuring of the work takes place around memory and the ambiguities of a commemorative act. Third, the text aspires to its own status as a memorial in words. And fourth, the potential for ironic subversion in a literary text will emerge when the enchantment of memory is undercut by the train of events in the actual life-world, or by the sobering distance of history. As a final note, it is worth emphasizing that the texts featured in this study are not obscure works recovered for some social-pedagogical agenda: on the contrary, they have all been there in the standard canon, or just hovering at its borders. Some, like *The Bostonians*, are quite famous, and others, like Melville's *Battle-Pieces*, have slowly gained a substantial critical foothold, but it is generally true that these texts have experienced little immediate juxtaposition in recent times – partly, perhaps, because my selection draws on both fiction and poetry, which is a little uncommon these days. In writing *Ashes of the Mind* my aim has been to turn these works at an unusual angle to give access to some of their revealing moments of rhetoric and historical vision. The perspectives gained thereby point – uniquely for each author and text – backward into the past and forward into the future: back to the war that once had been, and forward to how literary culture would engage, or retreat from, the poetics and the politics of Northern memory.

1

Cambridge Interiors

LOWELL'S COMMEMORATION ODE

Well, this is the task before us, to accept the benefit of the War; it has not created our false relations, they have created it. It simply demonstrates the rottenness it found. We watch its course as we did the cholera, which goes where predisposition already existed, took only the susceptible, set its seal on every putrid spot, and on none other; followed the limestone, and left the granite. So the War.

Ralph Waldo Emerson, Journals

We will meet but we will miss him,
There will be one vacant chair,
We will linger to caress him
When we breathe our evening prayer.

"The Vacant Chair," a popular song from the 1860s

Two poems of moderate length, each remembered in a different way and mirroring the rise and fall and rise of its respective author's literary reputation, appeared in the months immediately following the end of the Civil War. James Russell Lowell read the first version of his "Ode Recited at the Harvard Commemoration, July 21, 1865," on the date memorialized in the poem's title, and in November 1865 Walt Whitman published his brief collection *Sequel to Drum-Taps* (the first poem of which was "When Lilacs Last in the Dooryard Bloom'd") along with the longer *Drum-Taps* collection, the latter having been withdrawn from publication by Whitman a few days after Abraham Lincoln's assassination.

Lowell, a respected Boston literary practitioner who had been a committed antislavery campaigner, had composed his Commemoration Ode in
the shadow of a personal knowledge of the human cost of the Union victory: three of his nephews had been killed on active duty between 1862
and 1865.[1] The invitation from Professor Francis J. Child, coordinator of
the planning subcommittee for musical and literary presentations, to
produce an appropriate elegy for the memorial ceremony reflected a
recognition not only of his extended family's sacrifice but also of Lowell's stature as a poet and professor of Romance languages and literatures
at Harvard College. The social context for the emergence of Lowell's
poem offers a distinct contrast to the unofficial and fragile public reputation of his fellow poet Walt Whitman, and the irregular publication
history of Whitman's now more canonical and established elegy for
Lincoln. Whitman, in contrast to Lowell and his largely placid relationship with his intellectual and social milieu, had already suffered the
displeasure of one Washington politician, who fired him from the Department of the Interior that same summer of 1865 because of the
"moral scandal" embodied in *Leaves of Grass*.[2]

During the 1850s and 1860s, Whitman had only rarely met with an expression of direct personal hostility followed by official sanction (and on
this occasion he quickly found employment elsewhere with the federal
government), but uncomprehending dismissal of his poetry was something with which he was more familiar.[3] Henry James's unsigned review
of *Drum-Taps* in *The Nation* in November 1865, for example, was marked
by a sarcastic impatience with Whitman's poetic experiments. A lecture
on poetry and the war by Oliver Wendell Holmes, delivered before a large
audience in New York during the same month, did not mention a single
poem by Whitman or give any indication that Holmes even knew of his existence.[4] Such anecdotes underline, at the very least, that what today's
critical consensus would regard as a traditional exercise by a popular but
ultimately derivative writer of verse (the Commemoration Ode) and a
unique work by a powerfully original American poetic voice ("Lilacs")
occupied rather different niches in the cultural hierarchy of nineteenth-
century America. As the ebb and flow of canon formation has shown,
those characteristics that confirmed the originality and stature of Whitman's work for readers in the twentieth century were precisely those
that rendered it confusing and offensive for the greater number of his

contemporaries. To put it another way, the presence and relative absence of texts reveal, perhaps involuntarily, which strands of poetic history we as a society have consented to remember and which ones we find now slightly embarrassing to recall. James Russell Lowell's principal poetic output, consisting of the four major public poems (the Harvard Commemoration Ode, "Memoriae Positum," "An Ode for the Fourth of July, 1876," and the Concord Bridge Ode), the two series of *Biglow Papers*, the much underrated *Fable for Critics*, the elegy for the Harvard naturalist Louis Agassiz, and a large collection of, at times, derivative Victorian lyric and narrative verse, has the look of a museum cabinet of now-defunct American establishment letters – the broad tradition that was subject to three severe critical evaluations in the twentieth century. These are, first, the influential and decisive rejection of the social elitism of the Brahmin class expressed by Victor Parrington in his *Main Currents in American Thought* at the end of the 1920s; second, the dismissal of Victorian poetry in general by New Critics such as John Crowe Ransom and Allen Tate a little later, on grounds of a fatal lack of ironic resonance and structural complexity; finally, the marginalization of New England poetic culture by more contemporary Americanist criticism, which at the same time regards Poe, Whitman, and Dickinson as almost clairvoyant, seeing in their different intensities a powerful prefiguring of the values and concerns of modern poetry. (In a satirical mood, one might also raise a fourth accusation: the failure of the New England poets to be recovered as the representatives of a strange but fascinating ethnic minority that was, once upon a time, a major cultural power in the Northeast.)[5]

To provide one example of the status enjoyed by James Russell Lowell in his own time compared with that of Edgar Allan Poe, whose prestige has grown almost continuously over the twentieth century: a brief anthology entitled *Four American Poems*, published in 1864 as a German-English dual-language book aimed at immigrant communities in Pennsylvania and elsewhere, contains three of Poe's most famous poems, "The Raven," "Lenore," and "The Bells," with Lowell's early lyric "The Rose" as the final poem.[6] Lowell is given a quarter of the space devoted to Poe, but his right to be there is unchallenged. Representative of contemporary attitudes, in contrast, is the *Norton Anthology of American Literature*, 4th edition, volume 1 (New York: W. W. Norton, 1994), which devotes barely a comment to Longfellow, Lowell, Bryant, Whittier, or Holmes in its survey chapter on the period 1800 to 1865. Sketching the landscape of American literary practice at the middle of the nineteenth century, therefore, the conventional prospect would have the gentle hillocks of Lowell's body of work almost completely disappearing into the ever-expanding shadow of Whitman's *Leaves of Grass*.

This approach conceals, however, as much as it clarifies. It prevents us from recognizing, for example, that the considerations that would connect the Harvard Commemoration Ode with "When Lilacs Last in the Dooryard Bloom'd" might well be at least as strong as those that confirm that the two poems embody completely different types of literary motivation and artistic status. If we are to understand the poetic reaction to the years of war and the Lincoln assassination – at least as far as the passionately pro-Union constituency of the Northern states is concerned – then we have to leave some canonical assumptions behind and begin to see Lowell as responding to the same pressures of experience as Whitman, but in a different way, and try to recognize that the apparent chasm between their respective poetic missions may disguise similarities of ideological focus and elegiac intention. As they attempt to reconcile the self and the community with the memory of violence and loss, the two projects reveal odd parallels in their confrontations and negotiations with the language of traumatic memory and the demands of poetic genre. That is, "When Lilacs Last in the Dooryard Bloom'd" and the Commemoration Ode both take up the motif of the wounded nation and transform it in the course of an elegiac mediation in such a way as to allow the speaker to invoke (and the audience to comprehend) the performance of both individual and community mourning and to explore the significance for national memory of death in wartime. Although the uncompromising interiority of Whitman's text appears to give it the enigmatic depth that (in a somewhat circular fashion) is the warrant for its poetic credentials, the quite different language and thought of the Commemoration Ode are also worthy of investigation and reveal alongside the play of surfaces their own unexpected interiors and enigmas. To recover the poem for ourselves is, in a way, to also unearth a lost memory of American literature.

The phrase "play of surfaces" is not negatively loaded. It does not mean that the Commemoration Ode or any similar text is merely superficial. The work of the New England Poets, as one critic has remarked, "aimed at a solution of conflicts through good social sense [and] comforted not by asking for tears but by being urbane and witty," and ultimately this posture saw to it that their body of poetry slid rapidly – by the second decade of the twentieth century at the latest – into cultural and pedagogic marginality.[7] This emphasis on the humorous, however, itself emerges in part from our inability as readers to engage with the other emotional registers of traditional mainstream poetry from the premodernist era, poetry in which an appeal to tears and sentiment is commonly made. Such appeals have tended to be interpreted – or, more accurately, held at arm's length – as manipulative lachrymosity. Be that as it may, no poet, any more than anyone else, can ultimately choose the pressures of history that confront him or her, but surrender to them is not the only option.

Lowell's Commemoration Ode goes beyond the local cultural parameters of Cambridge, Massachusetts, and beyond patriotic invocation, to embody a complex struggle to both admit and resist the reality of loss, the passing of time, and the slippages of collective and individual memory. The poem also stakes, in a new political context, the old claim for New England as embodying the definitive history and guiding spirit of the United States and suffers from the same provinciality that always shadowed that claim. In the Commemoration Ode, the losses of war are configured as a greater national loss because they were Harvard losses, but the poetic speaker is aware (though one wonders) that to assert such significance brings the poem closer to the local passion of a tribal lay rather than to the mapping of a national political consensus. As in "When Lilacs Last in the Dooryard Bloom'd," the objective of the poem is to put the sacrifice of those whose loss is being mourned into equilibrium with a quantum of historical or moral significance rescued from the fact of death – to consolidate the memory of the dead within the contours of the living society, as it were. Whitman's intense and hypnotic cadences shepherd the reader into a mysterious psychic underground, but even the otherwise declamatory notes of the Commemoration Ode are speaking to something that lies deeper than the level of articulated public discourse.[8]

What lies deeper is, again, the instinctive belief in the nation and the assumption on the part of the audience – vindicated at least by the surface rhetoric of the poem – that that nation had as a result of war been purified of compromise and corruption. I use *the nation* with some freedom in this chapter, but it was not an uncontested term in the discourse of 1865. It is clear that the word had been (and, as they saw it, legitimately) appropriated by those in the North who regarded the defeat of the Confederacy as the final victory in a historic, costly but utterly justified struggle to save the Union. That the new journal founded in New York City in late summer of 1865 should be called *The Nation* was no accident. Nevertheless, the swirl of emotion around the ceremony at Harvard, evoking both sacrifice and healing, could not obscure the fact that the United States was an intensely divided society and would continue to be so, despite rather than because of the resolution of the slavery and secession issues through war. The party loyalties of Americans – which had been formed out of the more fluid affinities of the early national period and had hardened over the quarter-century between the Jackson and Lincoln administrations – were in many ways not only unaffected by the Civil War but even more difficult to budge afterward as the Republicans used the raw feelings of the war years for political capital, and Democrats became even more resentful toward federal authority.[9] The selfless and unalloyed love of the nation that Lowell demands in the Commemoration Ode, although crucial for the kind of political aesthetic that the poem embodies, was probably largely out of tune with the social realities of the greater Boston area, let alone those farther afield. Furthermore, at the moment of its maximum rhetorical assertiveness, the cultural authority of the Brahmin class and the Boston-Cambridge establishment – of which Lowell was in many ways one of the most outstanding representatives – was giving way to "the age and the dreams of a middle-class sovereignty," as Vernon Parrington once called it.[10] Thus the curious paradox of the provincialism of Cambridge staging the invocation of a redemptive national leadership may be the defining – and largely unnoticed – historical irony shaping the Harvard memorial ceremony. Despite the potentially awkward combination of parochial self-regard and epic hyperbole, however, the invocation is woven in the Commemoration Ode into a statement of high expressive power.

In sum, then, the poem has to be brought back into memory to discover that it is indeed worth remembering. The "Ode Recited at the Harvard Commemoration," as performed by Lowell before an audience at the end of the afternoon of July 21, 1865, is, with the exception of the "Lincoln" stanza, the same text as was published immediately afterward (unsigned) in the September issue of the *Atlantic Monthly*, subsequently in a private printing of fifty copies sent by Lowell to friends and colleagues, and finally published as the introductory verses to the *Harvard Memorial Biographies*, the two volumes of brief life stories of the deceased soldiers compiled by Thomas Wentworth Higginson. The long stanza on Abraham Lincoln that became eventually one of the most often-quoted sections of the poem was not in the recited text but inserted by Lowell shortly after the public reading.[11] In the 1869 collection *Under the Willows and Other Poems*, the Commemoration Ode appeared with a completely new section, the ninth stanza ("But is there hope to save / Even this ethereal essence from the grave?"). Lowell made some minor emendations immediately after the reading and in succeeding years, but the "Lincoln" and stanza IX interpolations are the main alterations made to the text as it crossed from performance to a series of publications. The "Ode Recited at the Harvard Commemoration," in its post-1869 form, has twelve stanzas, with a total length of 426 lines, in the irregular Pindaric ode form as appropriated and transformed by English poets from Abraham Cowley to William Wordsworth. The complex of motifs in the poem is, broadly, that of the classical and English elegy projected against the history of the Civil War as an American experience of singular violence and significance.[12] The following brief overview suggests that the poem can be described as an elegiac meditation progressively organized around the themes of the poetic confrontation with personal and collective loss, the ever-present danger of life slipping continuously, unredeemed, into the past, heroism and readiness to make an irreversible sacrifice, and the nation as the symbolic form of that sacrifice made meaningful.

As the Commemoration Ode begins, it moves from an admission of its own inadequacy when faced with the task of comprehending loss and making it meaningful to the invocation of the scholarly life and its values as represented by Harvard; the search for Truth, called for by the university motto *Veritas*, can take many forms, including going to war (stanzas I–III). The poetic speaker asserts the difficulty of recovering significance from the passage of time that drains all human energies and reduces men's lives (in an echo of *Hamlet*) to "our little hour of strut and rave" and describes a different path that opens up for those destined to prove themselves against a harder fate than normal existence offers. Abraham Lincoln was such a man (IV–VI). The struggle to recognize and honor appropriately both the dead soldiers and the murdered president occupies the speaker, who cannot free himself from the painful realization that those lost will never return: the elegy is not easily won out of the discords of the dirge, which is the more spontaneous response. Those living seem, in contrast to the example of those who made the sacrifice, "the dead that stayed behind" (VII–VIII). The universe is one of randomness, chaos, and unpredictable change; the heroic example of those who gave their lives can be, however, the one island of stability in the flux of time. A nation, if it can claim any legitimacy, has to be built on such examples (IX–X). The poet's identification with his people enables him to celebrate the national destiny, and the values for which the trauma of war was, and continues to be, suffered. The nation is what makes the individual life meaningful (XI–XII).[13]

As Elaine Scarry has argued in her influential study of armed conflict and its consequences, there are three primary areas in which war effects change and injury: embodied persons; the material culture or the self-extension of persons; and immaterial culture, aspects of the national consciousness, political belief, and self-definition.[14] The war dead, among them Lowell's three nephews, suffered the first of these; Lowell himself was as aware of the second as any informed individual could be; and he seeks to enter imaginatively into the third, that of trauma and memory, of cultural sensibility and mourning, to construct a poetic response to its demands. The "Ode Recited at the Harvard Commemoration" involves an attempt to understand the changes imposed by acts of war on the bodies of human beings, on the structures and environments they inhabited, and most of all on the "immaterial culture" of the psyche, the interior landscape of consciousness. The poem, moreover, also takes up the theme of the significance and the efficacy of language as a common American inheritance of expression and understanding, an inheritance that had been damaged and obscured by, on one side, the destructive oratory of slaveholding and Southern bullying and, on the other, the rhetoric of radical Abolitionism that seemed willing to sacrifice the Union for a moral principle:

> the war of tongue and pen
> Learns with what deadly purpose it was fraught,

> And, helpless in the fiery passion caught,
> Shakes all the pillared state with shock of men.   (V)

The war could be seen as a sublime effort to dismantle the rhetorico-political corruption of the 1850s and force a reinterpretation of the nation as both a functioning body politic and a balanced psychic identity – a note echoed by Lowell when, in an essay on Lincoln a year earlier, he had suggestively described the president's memorable capacity as a speaker "to give his *I* the sympathetic and persuasive effect of *We* with the great body of his countrymen"; or, as a contemporary study of language and politics expresses it: "In 1863 in the person of Lincoln the democratic idiom of the straight tongue of Hawkeye . . . fights a war to edit the Constitution of its tortured language that sanctions slavery."[15] Before any purification of political discourse, however, is the invocation of the Union dead as the source of moral strength, who

> glorify our clay
> With light from fountains elder than the Day;
> . . . .
> A light across the sea,
> Which haunts the soul and will not let it be,
> Still beaconing from the heights of undegenerate years.   (IV)

But what haunts the soul can also be the memory of the absence left by the deceased, and the soul can belong, as the poem seeks to affirm, to both the individual and the nation. The nation, for Lowell a social manifestation of the theory of republican citizenship, has undergone a sea-change into an allegory of spiritual destiny and a testimony of remembered injury. Destiny and injury are not easily integrated, however, and the dichotomy between the justification won by heroic sacrifice and the fact of blind chance on the battlefield is not resolved so much as illuminated and accepted within the Commemoration Ode – perhaps to the benefit of the poem, which is energized by unexpected combinations of assertion and concession, victory and resignation.

The conventions of the elegy, as a poetic genre, demand such combinations and shifts. Lowell's poem sets the scene with the declamatory opening line of the first stanza: "Weak-winged is song" is an assertion of poetic limitation at the moment of authorial emergence. This striking but paradoxical demolition of poetic authority and justification in such a clear and decisive tone is followed by the slightly nervous caveat that the rituals of mourning, of which this poem is clearly one, are inappropriate when it comes to honoring the memory of those who died in battle for a sacred cause:

> We seem to do them wrong,
> Bringing our robin's-leaf to deck their hearse
> Who in warm life-blood wrote their nobler verse,
> Our trivial song to honor those who come
> With ears attuned to strenuous trump and drum,
> And shaped in squadron-strophes their desire,
> Live battle-odes whose lines were steel and fire.   (I)

The dead soldiers are reconstituted as subjects insofar as their war experience is an allegorical enactment of the making of poetry. The sudden reversal of metaphoric energy from our "song" to their "squadron-strophes" and their lines of "steel and fire" appears to celebrate as something superior to mere words the ordinary man's contribution to the pursuit of victory under the prospect of injury and death. Nonetheless, the governing metaphor, despite the assertion of the opening line, is the creation of a poetic text. The deployment of an infantry unit is a poetic act at least equivalent, if not superior, to a linguistic construct.

The initial confession of weakness is a rhetorical turn within the generic procedures of the poem. Complicating this maneuver, however, is not only the figurative cross-mapping that links poetry and war but also the interweaving of uneasily coexisting motifs of, on one hand, academic passivity and, on the other, scholarly rigor. The site of the poetic act itself, Harvard, offers an easily embraced model of the soldier-scholar, the figure in stanza III whose search for a capitalized Truth finds its ultimate expression in his role as the uniformed archaeologist of the nation's soul:

> They followed her and found her
> Where all may hope to find,

> Not in the ashes of the burnt-out mind,
> But beautiful, with danger's sweetness round her.   (III)

Despite the slightly odd syntax ("Where" to "beautiful"), this might be a quatrain that secures its own entry in any respectable anthology of American poetry, because it, surprisingly, succeeds in walking a very narrow line between hollow solemnity and laconic elegance.[16] Nevertheless, the assuredness of the statement points back ambiguously at the poetic speaker. The force of the "not" in the third line of the quatrain is eclipsed by the image of the ashes. Beauty belongs with the vital and the dangerous, but the fourth line – although expertly balanced in meter and syntax – is in danger of being poetically eclipsed in its turn by the greater focus and coherence of the image of the ashes and the mind. The historical immediacy of the poem, its close proximity to the fires that transformed Southern farmhouses and towns into smoking embers, makes the implications of ashes and burnt-out places, and their hold on the poem, as much reportage as metaphor. For the South, it was a simple equation: "Defeat follows war as ashes follow fire."[17] For the victorious Union, however, it was a more complicated experience. The speaker of the Commemoration Ode, who seems to be closer to the seekers of Truth in books than he is to the soldiers who met her in the field, appears uncertain about whether the act of poetry might not need the ashes, perhaps as in Longinus's motif of the poetic sublime in the form of the glow of burnt-out coals the moment before extinction, more than the sweetness of vindication. The creative and compositional abilities may need a different kind of truth from the moment of moral testing in combat. The ashes of the mind survive also in the ironic moments of doubt, contingent destiny, and recognition of the cost of sacrifice that make up Northern memory.

The search for truth, however it may be qualified, is nevertheless reflected clearly in the willingness to sacrifice one's life for the Union cause, in effect the pursuit of scholarly achievement transformed into a commitment to defend the meaning of the nation. In stanza VII the "ideal Good" is the defining principle behind the superficial differences between "Freedom, Law, [and] Country." The apposition of those three concepts merges the abstract with the concrete, and they all possess, to a greater or lesser degree, an ideal coherence within a broader moral

truth. The most concrete of these elements, "Country," would seem to
be the balancing element to the most abstract, "Freedom." In the subsequent stanza VIII, the country is "the Promised Land" in which those
alive enjoy the political fruits that have been won for them by the fallen.
These lines are followed by the well-known passage declaring that the
elegiac act must, perhaps inevitably, fail to integrate any vision of the
positive consequences of the sacrifice:

> I strive to mix some gladness with my strain,
>> But the sad strings complain,
>> And will not please the ear:
> I sweep for them a paean, but they wane
>> Again and yet again
> Into a dirge, and die away, in pain.   (VIII)

As Henry James writes in *Notes of a Son and Brother*, quoting these
lines, Lowell's Commemoration Ode had to take up the challenge of giving expression to the meaning of a sacrifice "particularly radiant to
memory," in respect of the significance of the loss and the character of
the dead men themselves.[18] The radiance of the dead is, I would argue,
one of the defining pressures in this poem with which the speaker has to
come to terms. Lowell is writing within the traditions of later New England Puritanism (in particular Unitarianism, with its transformation
into a spiritual identity governed by political idealism rather than theological rigor), and the redemptive moment is a complex but indispensable rhetorical element in his attempt to understand the meaning of his
nephews' and others' deaths in combat. Indeed, the audience expectations in the context of the commemoration ceremony would have seen
no other configuration as appropriate. Nonetheless, Lowell's poem begins to show here the peculiar tensions between the need for a national
memorialization that has the potential to legitimize, by virtue of a quasi-
sacred authority, the loss of life on the battlefield, and the individual demand for recognition of the darkness of personal bereavement.

But Lowell has to try to resolve this potential difficulty. The poem
shifts onto a higher level of intensity in stanza IX (inserted for the 1869
version), where the threat of a capitalized Change leers out of the image
of the flow of history that seems to owe something to Shelley, some-

thing to Emerson, and something to nineteenth-century archaeological research:

> Shadows of empire wholly gone to dust,
> And many races, nameless long ago,
> To darkness driven by that imperious gust
> Of ever-rushing Time that here doth blow:
> O visionary world, condition strange,
> Where naught abiding is but only Change,
> Where the deep-bolted stars themselves still shift and range!
> Shall we to more continuance make pretence?   (IX)

The evocation of the disinterested ravages of time and their capacity to render contingent all value, all criteria for commemoration and significance, raises the stakes for the notion of Christian redemption and the meditation on individual loss. The nation (originally entering the poem as "a rescued Nation" in stanza X but now arriving – as the result of the subsequent interpolation by Lowell – in stanza VI, the "Lincoln" stanza) becomes the guarantee of some fixed point of reference in the flux of history, human value, and the "thoughtless drift of the deciduous years." It becomes the bridge between individual mourning and collective memory.

The determination of this poem to transform the justifying referent of the illuminated soul of New England's social and religious traditions (the kingdom of God) into the secular nation (the United States) is visible in its assertion of the religious character of that soul's willingness to be a tool of the collective national ideal: "The single deed, the private sacrifice, / So radiant now through proudly-hidden tears" is eclipsed, despite its power, by the community act "whereby a people rise / Up to a noble anger's height . . . set on flame / By the pure fire that flies all contact base" (IX). The motif of the "pure fire" is intriguing because of its biblical implications and the note of prophetic intensity. There is within the Judeo-Christian tradition a type of border skirmish, as Harold Bloom has suggested, between the psyche and the soma, particularly in the sense of the manifestation of the divine will. The intervention of God into human affairs may fail to observe our ideas about the appropriate line of separation between consciousness and what it walks around in. Bloom quotes chapter 20 of the Book of Jeremiah: "Then there is in my

heart as it were a burning fire / Shut up in my bones, / And I weary myself
to hold it in, / But cannot" to suggest that, in the prophetic tradition, it
is not only the soul but also the body that cannot seal itself off from the
divine command, and that the dividing line between conscience and vis-
cera, so to speak, is not as sharply drawn as we might believe.[19]

The "endless wars" between the mind and the body, so goes Bloom's
argument about both Freud's conception of the drive and the cultural
origins of prophetic speculation itself, might be understood as follows:
these conflicts arise from a mutual fear of the implications of time and
death that each part of us, psyche and soma, flinches from when it comes
into contact with the other. Appearing at a moment of commemoration
and aftermath, when both the individual and the collectivity had en-
dured wars of political hatred and of armed conflict, Lowell's poem discovers, I would argue, an analogous area of psychic injury and explores a
speculative map of healing. The Commemoration Ode asks whether, at
an intersection of history and consciousness marked by the unavoidable
recognition that those lost are indeed lost to all but memory, an authority such as the nation – or the national virtue embodied in a particular
class of young men and their families – could stabilize psychic identity,
counteracting fear and resignation in the face of the passage of time.
Time, in Lowell's words, is that which washes all lives and all history into
"the silent hollow of the past." At certain moments within the text, Lowell is concerned with what appears to be a physical disintegration that,
fatally, mirrors the disintegration of man's ability to act in some way
other than with a set of routine exercises designed to ensure his safety
and psychological comfort. The duration of human life needs rescuing
from the chronological succession of moments, as the society needs values that provide for more complex responsibilities than the purely economic or functional ("Man on the farm" instead of merely "the farmer,"
as Emerson declared in "The American Scholar").

Such an intellectual and moral focus had been, as it emerged almost
thirty years earlier, the principle that linked together the colorful regiment of Unitarian rebels, social reformers, abolitionists, and poetic
thinkers that dominated New England culture and politics from Emerson's "Divinity School Address" in 1838 to John Brown's guerilla war in
the Kansas territory some twenty years later. With implications for the
manifold traces of a once-powerful complex of Transcendentalist ideal-

ism in the perception of the Civil War and its physical effects, Bloom argues in his essay that for the "Romantic Ego, whether in Hegel or Emerson, the body is part of the Not-me," the external phenomenal world.[20] This is the point where Lowell diverges from the more idealist streams of Transcendentalist culture. Although the values of truth and testing in Lowell's poem are those of the broad cultural and intellectual community that included Emerson, the Commemoration Ode begins to point in a direction that Emerson might have been tempted to disagree with, in respect of the philosophical distinction between the self and the world: the "Ode Recited at the Harvard Commemoration" has to do with resonances in the body as much as conceptual illumination in the head. When the "dreadful" fire of the martial purpose in the nation's eyes dies down in the penultimate stanza of the poem, the state reverts to a quiet mental repose, a physical release, and an attentive relaxation. The vision that has driven the struggle, the "live coal behind the thought" in stanza V, is not isolated in a uniquely individual dimension removed from the social fabric within which real lives take place but rather shares in its existence. If the conflict is over, then that vision must be willing to recognize that the consequences of conflict are registered not merely on abstract forms but also on physical entities. Bloom's theory of a speculative dualism, a dynamic of the borderlands of psychic and physical experience, applied to the traditional movement of Lowell's text, suggests that the Commemoration Ode could be read as trying to map an emotional response to violent disruption onto the hypothesis that the nation is the one collective entity that can meet, on both the physical and psychic levels, the totality of injury to the series of individual bodies and individual psyches that constitutes its citizens, and that the poetic or authorial objective is a fiction that could form a protective narration, so to speak, around the scar of memory (a scar that is both psychic and somatic).[21]

Ultimately for the poetic speaker, however, the matter remains ominously open, as the movement of stanza VIII seeks to confront the presence of absence:

> In these brave ranks I only see the gaps,
> Thinking of dear ones whom the dumb turf wraps,
> Dark to the triumph which they died to gain:

Fitlier may others greet the living,
For me the past is unforgiving.   (VIII)

Little protection here, and little speculative healing. The dead remain
the "gaps" in the ranks of the returning Union armies, subject to the silence imposed by burial in the earth. The darkness that surrounds them
seems to be impenetrable, and the possibility that the dead men have departed to some Christian afterlife, and are looking down upon the victory ceremonies at their alma mater, is not entertained by the poem in
any way. To suggest a rough parallel to the model sketched by Scarry in
The Body in Pain, the dead embody the injury to persons, the commemoration ceremony seeks to repair the injury to the community that suffers the loss, and the poem attempts to get to grips with the injury to
the individual psyche, manifested for Lowell by the memory of three
nephews whom he had known since they were children. The ironic tension working its way through "Ode Recited at the Harvard Commemoration" is to a large degree activated by the half-suppressed admission that
even the impressive weight of an elegiac poem, performed within a complex of social, political, and spiritual traditions conscious of their influential history, cannot satisfy the past that is "unforgiving," the memory
that comprises only the emptiness of the places where the dead had
stood. That the poem can "speak" is perhaps an act of repair, but against
the blank "dumb turf" that hides the dead soldiers it must struggle with
the inadequacies of its existence as a metaphoric signal in language des-
ignating, like an epitaph on a gravestone, an absence in reality.

The argument I am making, that there is a significant dimension of
complexity and a substratum of irony in the poem, is in essence an attempt to understand the text as a communicative act produced within a
certain matrix of cultural and social relations, rather than as a document
defined by American literary histories of various interpretive stripes. For
much of the modernist era in criticism, Victorian poetry and nineteenth-
century American poetry have suffered from two complementary but
radically dissimilar attitudes. The one derives from the New Critical
avoidance of poetry that appears to exclude division and internal dissonance from the text, or relocates it downstream from the immediate
poetic project. This critical practice was unwilling to devote attention to
such work as Lowell's because of the fear that its own critical standards

might have been debased on contact with any poetry that seemed too organizationally and emotionally one-dimensional – as John Crowe Ransom once asserted, the nineteenth century was "the century of the simplest poetry in English literary history."[22] The other attitude is the largely overlooked popular partisanship for lyric directness and traditional sentiment that, although reflective of the wider public taste, was sidelined by modernist poetic practice and academic pedagogy during the first half of the twentieth century. The former declared ironic complexity or the play of paradox to be absent, the latter had no desire to register them even if they were there. Caught between these two opposing attitudes – the popular, antimodernist desire to cling to the expression of mainstream experience embodied in a conservative literary aesthetic, and the critical marginalization of poetry that would not allow the procedures of close reading to shine in the way its practitioners wanted – much of nineteenth-century American poetry has, until recently, found itself demoted, adrift, and without influential supporters.[23]

Ironically, the scholar who identified this problem was one of the most influential voices of the New Criticism in poetry, Cleanth Brooks. In his discussion of Tennyson in *The Well Wrought Urn*, Brooks makes the following observation:

> Tennyson is perhaps the last English poet one would think of associating with the subtleties of paradox and ambiguity. He is not the thoughtless poet, to be sure: he grapples . . . with the big questions which were up for his day – and he struggles manfully with them. But the struggle, as Tennyson conducted it, was usually kept out of the grammar and symbolism of the poetry itself. . . . Yet substantially true as this generalization is, Tennyson was not always successful in avoiding the ambiguous and the paradoxical; and indeed, in some of his poems, the failure to avoid them becomes a saving grace.[24]

Despite many crucial differences between the two poets, one could replace "Tennyson" with the name of James Russell Lowell in the passage and have a reasonably judicious assessment of the latter's achievement in "Ode Recited at the Harvard Commemoration." Indeed, Brooks' description of Tennyson's failure to avoid the intrusion of paradox into his poetry is particularly interesting in respect of Lowell's Commemoration

Ode, because Lowell is without doubt sensitive to the pressure, emerging from inside the compositional history of the poem itself, to do justice to the institutional requirements of the occasion for its formal delivery at the ceremony at Harvard. Lowell did not necessarily set out with the intention of introducing disruptions and aporia into the text. Rather, the public aspect of the ambitious poetic task he has undertaken, allied with the inescapable facts of personal bereavement that he is unable to keep out of the weave of implicit narratives shaping the poem, generates odd energies, momentary gaps, in the course of his efforts to integrate the disparate emotions into one aesthetic formulation. Indeed, to concede the presence of any dramatic power in the poem, one has to also concede the presence of some degree of "ironic contrast and paradox," as Brooks argues in his discussion of Tennyson's "Tears, Idle Tears."[25]

Another, and in some ways more obvious, source of drama is the history of the reading of the Commemoration Ode as a public elegy at an occasion of collective and personal confrontation with memory, loss, and the peculiar status of the victor. An important element in the composition of a public elegy is the performative nature of the genre. Peter Sacks has observed that the public elegy "develops the effect not only of an event but of a performance. The performance is . . . foregrounded by the genre's staging devices, a convention that draws attention to the mourner or cast of mourners."[26] This is a point worth remembering when reviewing the scholarly consensus that has crystallized around Lowell's poem in the past century and more, a consensus expressed even in Marjorie Kaufmann's otherwise sympathetic introduction to the 1978 republication of *The Poetical Works of James Russell Lowell*, in which the reader finds the comment that, compared to "the magnificence we find in 'When Lilacs Last in the Dooryard Bloom'd' . . . Lowell's ode has importance as an historical document, but its pulse has faded."[27] Kaufmann's remark does at least concede that the poem had possessed some kind of emotional or ideological energy at some time in the past. As suggested earlier, however, to assume too much from the apparent excision of internal contradiction and dissonance from the poetic text may well be a critical misreading not only of the poem itself but, more crucially, of the kind of literary text the poem is supposed to be.

The "Ode Recited at the Harvard Commemoration," in its version of July 1865, was composed to be delivered to a large gathering in a relatively open space within the parameters of a formal, commemorative event. As a matter of historical research, reconstructing this environment would be possible. One could review, painstakingly, details of the actual proceedings at Harvard on July 21, 1865, about which we have considerable documentary testimony. There were over twelve hundred guests gathered there, probably the largest number thus far for any one event in the history of the college; Harvard Hall, University Hall, and the Yard were festooned with flags and banners; the sun shone brilliantly on that July day, three months after the surrender of the Confederacy and Lincoln's death; there was a cash bar dispensing "whiskey, brandy, hock, claret, champagne, and sherry."[28] No doubt, a contemporary American academic audience would reveal less of a positive consensus on the ideology of military sacrifice that Lowell's poem seeks to valorize. Nevertheless, if one fails to keep in focus the sense of the high regard in which James Russell Lowell was held and the popular resonance he had achieved earlier with satirical verse such as *The Biglow Papers* in particular, one must fail also to understand the social and psychological dynamic that was operating behind and around the Harvard commemoration event itself. Even if not every member of the audience on that day lived in the Boston area or even in Massachusetts, the community of affinity they belonged to was nonetheless as definitive in its own way as a geographical location. As all communities in some way have to, this social and cultural milieu depended on certain traditional orientations such as the loyalties and expectations mentioned earlier that, as Jörn Rüsen expresses it, "present the temporal whole which makes the past significant and relevant to present actuality and its future extension as a continuity of obligatory cultural life-patterns over time." Rüsen, in the course of an original and amusing essay in which he examines the ways in which traditional obligations might be received and acted on by the current generation, goes on to say: "Traditional orientations guide human life externally by means of an affirmation of obligations requiring consent. . . . They shape identity-formation as a process in which roles are assumed and played out."[29] The reading of the Commemoration Ode at Harvard can be regarded, therefore, as being shaped by particular desired objectives: the structuring, by way of a performed text, of a temporal whole to make a particular past significant and relevant to the contemporary audience; the affirmation of a complex of obligation and consent; the managing of a process of identity-formation for and within the postwar nation.

Lowell's sense of the unstoppably approaching deadline of the July 21 ceremony at Harvard became a part of his memoir of the composition of the Commemoration Ode. After more than twenty years he confessed to R. W. Gilder that the poem was "an improvisation." Two days before the commemoration, Lowell writes, "I had told my friend [F. J.] Child that it was impossible [but] . . . the next day something gave me a jog and the whole thing came out of me with a rush."[30] Lowell's account, irrespective of any factual truth it may contain, is an unmistakable trope of what one might term "creation under pressure." As in the seminal narrative of the Anglo-Saxon peasant Caedmon who is asked to sing at a festive gathering and confesses that he cannot, escapes from the gathering into the night, has a vision, and returns to the hall to recite a religious poem, Lowell's remembrance of the creation of the Commemoration Ode appears to be a metaphor of inspirational origins and the impossibility of poetic production suddenly, against all odds, made possible.[31] The story of Caedmon and his hymn as recounted in Bede's *Ecclesiastical History* is just one example of the psychologically realistic, but historically unreliable, narratives standing in a patrilineal sequence of authorial testimony behind Lowell's account of the origin of his Commemoration Ode. Unreliable or not, however, Lowell continued to assert this mystical account of the poem's compositional history, including in an interesting exchange of letters published over twenty years later by William James and the American Society for Psychical Research.[32]

As it turned out, Lowell's actual performance of the poem on that July evening in 1865 was, according to contemporary accounts, something less than spellbinding. Or perhaps, even had his delivery been everything it might have been, the audience was distracted and failed to bring the focus and span of attention required to absorb Lowell's lengthy text. Oddly, despite extensive newspaper coverage, in particular detailed reports in the *New York Daily Tribune*, the *New York Times* and the *Boston Daily Advertiser*, with briefer bulletins in other publications, there is no press record of Lowell's reading of his poem. The press coverage of the event in general, however, is clear evidence of its local as well as its regional (and perhaps even national) significance – although the style of local as opposed to national reporting of the ceremony was somewhat different. As Hamilton Vaughan Bail comments in his detailed recreation of the event, one of the main differences between the Boston papers and the others was that the former did not feel that their readers would require a translation of the Latin mottoes inscribed on the ceremonial banners that fluttered over Harvard Yard.[33]

In his biography of Lowell, Martin Duberman comments that Lowell had "hoped that the Ode might prove the feature of the day's exercises" although he knew that the presence of major literary figures, Emerson and Holmes to name but two, would mean a difficult and, in a sense, theatrically unbalanced context in which to try to make an impact.[34] "Theatrically," because the Commemoration Ode is not the kind of text that can, in either its language or its structure, offer a foothold to wandering audience receptivity, and because both Emerson and Holmes had the reputation and the rhetorical resources to make any contribution of theirs memorable, particularly before such a gathering. The audience expectations and circumstances require consideration also. Although many of the speakers would have aimed at getting their contributions as much in tune with the atmosphere of the event and its local significance as possible, there is no reason to assume that the audience would have been able to devote the same level of attention at the end of a very long day that they would have given to those presenting their speeches, prayers, songs, and poems earlier in the proceedings.[35] Lowell's position in the sequence of events (toward the end) and his own modest public-speaking skills would have combined to obscure the originality and ambition of his poem. Indeed, the irony of the poem's first unveiling may be that the assigned slot for the performance of the Commemoration Ode emphasized its more ambivalent elements. The "Ode Recited at the Harvard Commemoration" may have embodied, performatively, a signal of the recognition – manifested in turn through the poetic text – that even the most achieved elegiac act brings inevitably its own sense of inadequacy with it.

Despite its deployment of confessional emotion and its embodiment of a vital and uncompromising historical dynamic, the "Ode Recited at the Harvard Commemoration" ultimately lacks an obvious mechanism of rhetorical domination, the kind of assertion of power that acts as a paradigm of authority and the commanding synthesis of experience. Indeed, the Commemoration Ode is remarkable for its willingness to embody weakness and the circumstantial, to approach the questions of death, mourning, and memory – and justification – from behind admissions of poetic and possibly even moral inadequacy. In stanza VIII, for example:

> We sit here in the Promised Land
> That flows with Freedom's honey and milk;
> But 't was they won it, sword in hand,
> Making the nettle danger soft for us as silk.   (VIII)

The speaker, at more than one juncture in the poem, whittles down the status of the commemoration participants and by implication puts the credentials of his poem in question. Indeed, that might in fact be Lowell's peculiar trope of rhetorical authority: to take the risk, in a poem first unveiled at a public occasion of some importance, of challenging the audience at the point of its most obvious identification with the dead – that of shared background and common values. The poem's maneuvering is not subtle: the casually introduced, gendered disapproval of "honey," "milk," and "silk" undermines the assumption of common identity with the soldiers. Their act has made them different, and the poem, in an unexpected way that combines a somewhat tentative New England masculinity with the old Puritan assumption of universal feminine status in relation to God, has doubts that its language or the language of the memorial ceremony can claim for itself any of the absolute, unapproachable reality that the dead created for themselves with their sacrifice.[36] The speaker goes on, however, to state baldly:

> Little right has he to sing
> Through whose heart in such an hour
> Beats no march of conscious power,
> Sweeps no tumult of elation!   (XI)

Reasserting that "little right" is also and always a right, the poem's gesture of deference becomes, simultaneously, the assertion of its cultural authority.

Shortly after the reading at the commemoration ceremony, Lowell was asked to make the poem available as a verse introduction to the two-volume *Harvard Memorial Biographies*, edited by Thomas Wentworth Higginson, that appeared in 1866. These were the ninety-nine biographical sketches of the Harvard graduates killed on active duty during the war, who were, at a later date, to be commemorated on the marble tablets in the newly built Memorial Hall, completed in 1877. The biographies are essentially short stories, narratives of an achieved ideal of New England character and integrity. As a tribute to the dead young men, it cannot be expected otherwise.[37] Although Lowell's "Ode Recited at the Harvard Commemoration" is, in one way, the ideal preface to the sequence of controlled encomiums that make up the *Biographies*, my argument is that the poem does not, in fact, represent a verse cognate of Higginson's biographical sketches. The Commemoration Ode was, like the biographies, composed on behalf of a community seeking justification (and the trace attaching to the term from early Puritanism – where one was or was not justified by faith – seems appropriate) for its actions and its ideas as embodied, as a physical and not just a social or cultural reality, in its people. Nevertheless, the imaginative unfolding of Lowell's text involves an unsettling recognition that the trauma of the Civil War was double-edged, and the injury was deeper than the consolidated casualty totals of the five preceding years. While the *Harvard Memorial Biographies* express in the assumptions behind their narratives a traditional Christian message of redemption, Lowell's poem, beyond the simple act of mourning, invokes a different symbolic valency of war and sacrifice as gestures that confront the depredations of time. Time will be redeemed only by something brought about by heroic intervention ("Is earth too poor to give us / Something to live for here that shall outlive us?" [IV]), and for that there must be some source of motivation, but it need not be strictly religious. In making this move to open up a kind of Cambridge regional existentialism, the poem activates one of the more intriguing, but sometimes obscured, elements of the history of New England at mid-century: the welcoming of war as a tool of moral cleansing and – a significant bonus – as an arena in which to prove one's manhood. In fact, the phrase used by Higginson in his preface to the *Harvard Memorial Biographies*, that the outbreak of hostilities in 1861 was an exhilarating moment in which "the past was annihilated [and] the future was all," concedes that aspect in so many words.[38] Here is an embracing of violence and disruption, rather than an avoidance of them.

The beginnings of the conflict touched off an intuition that it would become, as indeed it did become, the zone of the uncontrollable. The reality of the war, as Ralph Waldo Emerson recognized, sought out the weaknesses in human beings and social structures and eradicated them without mercy, after the analogy of the cholera epidemic in the quotation from the *Journals* at the head of this chapter.[39] Welcomed originally or not, however, the years of anxiety and death brought a generation face-to-face with a process of attrition that was as much subjectively random as it was, in a broader calculation of the various conditions for, and probability of, injury and fatality, objectively predictable. Such traumatic contingency causes Lowell to become concerned with a "form" in his text that has as much to do with observing "good form" in public ceremonies of mourning as with aesthetics. Rather than invoking the interior nation that Walt Whitman finds in the undergrowth of his psyche, and assimilating to his elegy the plaintive birdsong from the lonely swampland that is the geographic objective correlative of his meditation on death and sacrifice in "When Lilacs Last in the Dooryard Bloom'd," Lowell's poem is a negotiation seeking a different and in some ways more difficult path. The Harvard Commemoration Ode is designed to manifest, at least provisionally, an emotional configuration that can give a form to both private mourning and the public commemorative voice. Its problem is that it must try to discharge the impossible duty of encompassing the national and the individual losses in the kind of language that matches audience expectations, and with meeting the pressure for reconciliation between the knowledge of the war's casualties and the value that may or may not be justifiably ascribed by the community to such a sacrifice.

The difficulty of giving expression to this complex of tasks is the background against which Lowell achieves, in his poem, a kind of provisional assertion of stability. The ironic dimension of this lengthy and at times diffuse poem emerges from the major difference between it and Whitman's "Lilacs": where Whitman has challenged and neutralized the parameters of nineteenth-century poetic art and is attempting in his poem to construct the emotions of an elegy anew and from the ground up, James Russell Lowell has accepted what is, in some ways, a more sensitive mission. Lowell chooses to embrace, but also to struggle with, the same parameters that Whitman rejects – but the very different poetic result does not mean in any way that his poem is merely an exercise that illuminates the limits beyond which the text cannot go. Rather, the reader of the "Ode Recited at the Harvard Commemoration" discovers, below its expected and declamatory public tones, the deeper notes of an exercise that confronts and deploys the irony of contingency, thereby making the poem one of the more memorable texts in nineteenth-century American writing for its embracing of the tradition of literary and critical thought that says that while the work is impossible it also must be completed. As Anne Mellor has remarked in her study of the presence of irony in the works of English Romanticism:

> Romantic irony, then, is a mode of consciousness or a way of think-ing about the world that finds a corresponding literary mode. The artist who perceives the universe as an infinitely abundant chaos; who sees his own consciousness as simultaneously limited and in-volved in a process of growth or becoming; who therefore enthusi-astically engages in the difficult but exhilarating balancing between self-creation and self-destruction; and who then articulates . . . a literary structure that reflects both this chaos or process of becom-ing and the systems that men impose upon it; and a language that draws attention to its own limitations.[40]

Chaos and destruction can take place on many different levels, however, and they may be read in a typological structure that sees the present as implicated in the transgressions of the past. Although the trauma of the war means that invoking a sense of recovered integrity is more impor-tant to Lowell than the pleasurable exercise of intellectual display, the attempt is also being made in this poem to mediate between process, sys-tem, and the limits of language in a way that draws on elements of Ro-mantic irony.

Indeed, that attempt might well be the echo of the Transcendentalist mode of consciousness in the Commemoration Ode. The shifting config-uration of skepticism and faith that marks so much Transcendentalist writing from Emerson on is that mixture of elements that make the Com-memoration Ode able to evade clear theological or ideological defini-tion. Lowell's poem is an attempt to sketch a commemorative statement that does not deny the problem of chaos or the contingency of experi-ence and human projects or the way in which the achieved poetic work is overshadowed by knowledge of the limited extent of its authority. As Lowell writes in an earlier poem, "Memoriae Positum," composed in memory of Robert Gould Shaw, commander of the African American troops of the 54th Massachusetts Volunteer Infantry regiment:

> we, who make pretence
> At living on, and wake and eat and sleep,
> And life's stale trick by repetition keep,
> Our fickle permanence
> (A poor leaf-shadow on a brook, whose play
> Of busy idlesse ceases with our day)
> Is the mere cheat of sense.[41]

These lines suggest (and there are analogous passages in the Commemoration Ode) that the poetic speaker of "Memoriae Positum" clearly recognizes the corrosive effect of the passage of time on any moment – for example, the regiment's courageous but disastrous attack on the Confederate lines at Fort Wagner, led by Shaw – that disrupts, or cuts across, the contingent flow of random event and the "cheat of sense," as well as the inadequacy of the poetic act as it seeks to represent the moral sublime of unselfish sacrifice. With respect to the objectives of commemorative posture and elegiac coherence in particular, "Ode Recited at the Harvard Commemoration" is an elaboration and a further exploration – and to some degree a riskier exploration – of the uncertainties of community identity and art on the borders of poetry and religious conviction. Indeed, the role of the Emersonian prophet-poet as a new, antidoctrinal ambassador between community need and individual creative inspiration (and up one notch, between the nation and creativity as well) is one that should not be overlooked in any attempt to interpret a text such as Lowell's poem.[42] As Walt Whitman once expressed in different terms, national crisis may be the social petri dish for generating a poetry of prophecy.

Writing some years after the Civil War, at the beginning of *A Backward Glance o'er Travel'd Roads* in the 1888 edition of *Leaves of Grass*, Whitman suggests that literary texts are not iconic works of art existing in a kind of autonomous glow of inner power, and that any "luminosity" ascribed to the poetical work should not be taken at face value but is rather "lunar and relative at the best." Poems "grow of circumstances, and are evolutionary," he writes, arguing for a gradual process of literary production rather than an idealizing of authorial utterance in and for itself. Commenting on the unique historical circumstances offered by the United States during the nineteenth century, he goes so far as to suggest that *Leaves of Grass* cannot be read and understood without the reader's sensibility being educated by a consideration of the "preparatory background" of this national experience. Whitman then proceeds to the center of gravity of his discussion, declaring that "in estimating first-class song, a sufficient Nationality, or, on the other hand, what may be call'd the negative and lack of it, (as in Goethe's case, it sometimes seems to me) is often, if not always, the first element."[43] Despite the sequence of rather tentative qualifying notes in this statement, its central thesis remains clear: first, that literary excellence and poetic achievement cannot be divorced from the surrounding social, cultural, economic, and political context in which the work is generated and nurtured, and second, that "Nationality," whether present or absent, is a formative energy that can be evaluated as part of a critical understanding of literary production. The evolutionary growth of circumstance is, I would suggest, a necessary context for reading Lowell's Commemoration Ode as it is for "When Lilacs Last in the Dooryard Bloom'd."

Whitman asserts more than once during *A Backward Glance* that the Civil War, the "war of Secession," gave his poetry its most powerful motivation and justification. Shadowing Whitman's claim is the implication that if *Leaves of Grass* is indeed the poem that not only represents in language but in some way even embodies its subject, America, then the threat to that national formation was in some way a threat to the poetry itself, and poetry had to defend itself, to offer resistance and protection, as did the Union. This sentiment connects the stanza with the runaway slave and the "firelock leaned in the corner" in "Song of Myself" in the 1855 *Leaves of Grass* across a gap of ten years to less well-known *Drum-Taps* poems such as "The Veteran's Vision" (retitled "The Artilleryman's Vision" in later editions of *Leaves of Grass*) with its mechanic-like gunner haunted by recurring dreams of battle, and "Spirit Whose Work Is Done," in which a Union soldier is addressed: "Leave me your pulses of rage! bequeath them to me! fill me with currents convulsive! / Let them scorch and blister out of my chants, when you are gone."[44] From the motif of the lone farmer with his slightly archaic weapon to the invocation of the massed firepower of a modern battlefield, the willingness to take up arms defines the moral posture. In contrast to the unperturbed note struck by the earlier poem, however, that suggests that the "firelock" is merely a precautionary symbol of republican principle (the slave recovers and moves on, the speaker is not put to the test), the language of the post-war image permits no such de-escalation and sketches a much grimmer picture of men and weaponry. The lines from "Spirit Whose Work Is Done" evoke the irrational feelings of fury that can exert a powerful grip on soldiers in combat, enabling them to overcome inner surges of fear and panic, and also the effect of individual rifles, side arms, and larger artillery pieces on the bodies of their users, quite apart from their targets. The speaker invites that concentrated violence to remain on duty, as it were, alert and ready to respond to the poetic call.

As noted in the context of Lowell's merging of poetic composition and battlefield maneuvers, however, violence and poetry can, together, create a complex metaphor, and the scorched and blistered hands (in Whitman's poem) may not only evoke images of a workmanlike application of military training to the national cause but offer themselves as outward manifestations of an injured interior; also, such visible signs of invisible states of affairs can likewise – and this is an implication of Whitman's poem – remain long after the conflict that caused them has been laid to rest. Or not laid to rest: either way, the motif of scarred flesh and the rhythm of the nervous convulsions of soldiers in combat is extended into the future and by implication across the nation, which exists both in and across time.[45] Looking at the ambitious profiles of both Lowell's and Whitman's poems, it could be asked how much potential does the "sufficient Nationality," identified in *A Backward Glance* as a source of power for poetic achievement, possess when it comes to integrating the experience of large-scale civil war and intense cultural acrimony into a poetic text – as Whitman suggests its role is – and how much has it retreated before the corrosive presences of scorched earth and blistered skin? The nation may now be simply the memory of injury. "All serious poetry of war," John Carlos Rowe has argued, "is obsessed with the problem of memory, for it appears to be the hopeless task assigned to the poet either to memorialize gloriously war or simply remind us of its pain."[46]

As Whitman did, Lowell too enters a confrontation with violent and disruptive national experience in a way that tries to work out an emotional equation between the implacable process of history and the subjective truth of irrecoverable loss both for the reader and, in a sense, for the literary work itself, but the matter of community political memory is also subject to new and strange attentions in "Ode Recited at the Harvard Commemoration." The historical pressures, the consequences of the violence and disruption that cannot be ameliorated by the elegiac act, are manifest in the poem as, among others, an unresolved tension between ideology and emotion. The memory of injury in Lowell's text is not identical to its evocation in "When Lilacs Last in the Dooryard Bloom'd," but it is close enough in nature and origin to make the motives for these elegies, as suggested above, manifestly alike: the victory for which the sacrifice was made must be more than the inevitable and mechanical result of the superior logistical organization of the Northern war effort. It must in some way be co-extensive with the emotional struggle driving the elegy, and not merely involve a detached or distanced political principle or a statement of historical fact. Furthermore, these poems embody, besides ritual sorrow, praise, attraction to death, and ultimate recovery, a declaration of the right to mourn. As Peter Sacks has pointed out in his study of the genre as a structure of public discourse and private meditation, the right of inheritance and the right to mourn are significantly connected to each other in the genesis of the classical elegy.[47] I would extend Sacks's implication and suggest that, in Lowell and Whitman, the privilege of mourning the injury to the nation, an injury on the various levels that Elaine Scarry describes, becomes an assertion of the nation as real subject – not merely a philosophical entity and not only the ethnic underpinning of a constitutional order – and of the poet's status as its mediator in language.

In Lowell's text the poetic center of gravity lies close to the fault line where national history and private memory meet. The stages of the elegy as a genre involve the attempted expression of a perhaps ultimately inexpressible private loss and give concrete form to a subtle act of reconciliation and assertion in which the sexual powers of regeneration manifest in nature are called on to compensate for the deceased hero, and the legacy of that hero is claimed – in a public forum, as it were – by the poet-director of the elegiac ritual. The elegy does not merely meditate on a struggle with death and suffering but rather makes present that struggle in both its linguistic and emotional configuration. In other words, the elegy can, as a poem, be described as a construct of language, but the reason for the existence of this verbal construct is, in this old and powerful genre, also an act of mourning in the sense that the poem objectifies memory and captures it – memorializes it – within the alternative existence of the literary text. This alternative existence, for Lowell, tends toward an Augustan statement of victory over the disorder that the original trauma caused and might appear to be almost bland in its rationality and sense of decorum. But even Lowell's seemingly unapologetically traditional poetic exercise points in a direction similar to Whitman's "When Lilacs Last in the Dooryard Bloom'd": it is embedded in a cultural and historical situation that demands a closer reading of the poem itself and of its context than is usually offered and embodies a realization of physical experience that suggests, as does Whitman, a close relationship between injury and memory, sacrifice and gain. The public context for the Commemoration Ode does indeed put it at a remove or two from "Lilacs" as well as from more private experiments with the elegy such as, for example, Shelley's "Adonais" or Tennyson's "In Memoriam"; indeed, the context itself might contribute to the assumption that the Commemoration Ode is no longer readable and, in a sense, no longer accessible to criticism. Despite the large-scale public energies of the poem, however, it offers moments when simplicity of expression merges with a controlled turn of thought in an aphoristic but unforced poetic moment:

> The little that we see
> From doubt is never free;
> The little that we do
> Is but half-nobly true.   (IV)

Luckily, the sound of the public occasion does not always drown out the notes of lyric brevity that hide among the declamatory gestures of Lowell's poem.

The relative distribution of lyric and epic moments does not, however, determine a poem's complexity and depth. Again, reifying formal characteristics into evaluative criteria is often a disingenuous maneuver used to apply a critical paradigm in a negative manner, in effect declaring the poetic object to be unworthy of the examining procedure before any examination can take place.[48] Again, Cleanth Brooks, in a discussion of Wordsworth's "A Slumber Did My Spirit Seal," makes the following simple but often overlooked point:

> Yet to intimate that there are potential ironies in Wordsworth's lyric may seem to distort it. After all, is it not simple and spontaneous? With these terms we encounter two of the critical catchwords of the nineteenth century, even as *ironical* is in danger of becoming a catchword of our own period. Are the terms *simple* and *ironical* mutually exclusive? What after all do we mean by *simple* or *spontaneous*? . . . What is likely to cause trouble here is the intrusion of a special theory of composition, . . . *a theory as to how a poem is written is being allowed to dictate to us how the poem is to be read* [my emphasis]. There is no harm in thinking of Wordsworth's poem as simple and spontaneous unless these terms deny complexities that actually exist in the poem.[49]

Brooks's point is not really that simple, but my own point is that neither the political context (official commemorative ceremony) nor the literary environment (Victorian establishment poetics) buttressing the composition of the Commemoration Ode should become a reason for the a priori denial of complexity and depth to Lowell's text.

The epigraphs at the beginning of this chapter open up two very different ways in which a nation might find itself inscribed in a cultural response to trauma. "The Vacant Chair," described by Irwin Silber as "this maudlin piece . . . of unabashed emotional pleading," was an extremely popular song in both the North and the South. With lyrics by Henry S. Washburn and a musical score pirated from an earlier composition entitled "Life Is Like a Mountain Railway," the song first appeared in 1861.[50] Any threat of sentimentality is embraced without reservation by Washburn's lyric. The popularity of the song suggests that honest sentiment, as far as the greater part of American society was concerned, was not in any way seen as breaching the constraints of "form." There is a surprising physicality, despite the aura of disembodied mourning that haunts the lyric, in "The Vacant Chair." Especially the line "We will linger to caress him" suggests that the actual desire to touch the lost father's body is as important a motif for this text as the invocation of Christian redemption involved in his sacrifice or the preservation of his memory as a pious act of family duty.[51] Lowell might well have been wary of this kind of memorialization, because the enthusiastic emotionality of Washburn's song would threaten the "formal" discipline that is so important for the cultural posture of the Commemoration Ode. Lowell wants to legitimize the nation as the configuration of memory and duty anointed by the sacrifice of the war dead, but the ethic of form, of social discipline and observation of the proprieties, pressures him continually, causing the poem to shrink from the emotional violence that the full import of the Harvard casualties might otherwise release.

The other epigraph, from Ralph Waldo Emerson's journals, opens a prospect onto the victory of tough-minded control over emotional sensitivity, a transformation memorably portrayed by George Frederickson in his history of New England intellectuals and the Civil War. Many influential figures such as Charles Eliot Norton, John W. De Forest, the organizers of the Sanitary Commission who transformed field medical services, and Emerson himself found the war a justification for rejecting the middle-class empathy with suffering that had stamped the two decades before Fort Sumter: "Emerson . . . also came to accept and almost welcome a tremendous loss of life," writes Frederickson. "Emerson wrote to the parents of a colonel that had been killed that 'there are crises which demand nations, as well as those which claim the sacrifice of single lives.' "[52] The particular mental posture Emerson assumed in that quotation (echoed in other passages from his writings from the war years, including the one at the head of this chapter) presumably would have led him to find "The Vacant Chair" morbid and effeminate, a public indulgence in self-pity and lamentation that possessed the qualities of form in neither the literary nor the social sense of the term. It would not be the first time that members of a cultural or intellectual elite have abandoned civilized moderation, diplomacy, and a humane distaste for warlike rhetoric and bloodshed to suddenly demand hard, uncompromising, military action to solve a crisis – often harder and more uncompromising than the mainstream of society feels comfortable with. "The Vacant Chair" is in many ways a popular rejection of that position, an assertion of the human cost of war that refuses the kind of blinkered "principled stand" that ignores the real consequences of conflict. Nevertheless, the lyric retains its ideology of patriotic duty: the war fatality whose sacrifice creates the empty place at the dinner table was not a helpless victim or draftee but a volunteer who was aware of the issues at stake and the possibility of his own injury or death. The song was originally written to commemorate the death of Lieutenant John William Grout, 15th Massachusetts Volunteer Infantry, and possibly it was of more comfort to his family than Emerson's reassurance about the crises that demand the lives of nations would have been.

In this sense, "The Vacant Chair" speaks not only to the loss of a loved one in battle but also to the domestic peace and order the war had attacked. The song is working to a different cultural agenda than the "Ode Recited at the Harvard Commemoration," but – in a certain basic way – the two texts are concerned with administering to those who must live with injury and loss. The lyricist Washburn had a good feel for the kind of image that tends to stick:

> We shall meet but we shall miss him,
> There will be one vacant chair.[53]

And what is most interesting here is the poetic imaging of emptiness and absence that also echoes through both Lowell's Commemoration Ode and Whitman's "Lilacs" (the vacant chair in the Oval Office, perhaps?). The song is a useful reminder of the unpredictable cultural mobility and tenacity of popular expression. "The Vacant Chair" survives to become the title of a work of historical scholarship a century and more after the song was first published, for example, and so refuses to be dislodged from history and memory.[54] It also reminds us that beyond the gates of Lowell's Harvard (and beyond the uncompromising individuality of Whitman's "Lilacs") lay another nation that identified and carried out its responsibilities, and commemorated its war casualties, within the framework of a modest and, in many ways, gentle domesticity.

James Russell Lowell seeks, in the Harvard Commemoration Ode, a language that will do justice to both victory and loss and discharge the tasks of both memory and memorial, of the private and the public dimension. Memorial is a responsibility to the nation as conceived by the educated classes of the northeastern United States while memory is the private reality arising from the multitude of sacrifices demanded by the war. In this poem, Lowell wants to bring the dynamic of memory into

harmony with the act of commemoration, to sharpen the individual conscience enough to have it always register the legacy of heroic sacrifice no
matter how faintly it may speak to living generations: "Dream-footed as
the shadow of a cloud, / They flit across the ear" (IX). There is also, however, a consistent expression of doubt regarding the efficacy and legitimacy of the poetic act. That this has a formulaic quality – again, a
question of form in several senses – should not detract from the recognition of its more than rhetorical significance: Lowell is trying to avoid the
irony embedded in the existence of the poem as a verbal inscription that
might, some day, supersede the inscription in history, in American reality, that the Harvard men made in the very act of military service itself.
Indeed, the historical reality of the marginalized cultural authority of
the New England political and social establishment (a process acceler-
ated by the Civil War) lends, as I point out at the beginning of the chapter, an even more perceptible note of uncertainty to this ambitious
commemorative project. For Lowell, the trauma the nation has undergone can easily be rendered worthless, and the deaths of the Union soldiers reduced to a kind of fertilizing process:

> Shall they lie forceless in the dark below,
> Save to make green their little length of sods,
> Or deepen pansies for a year or two,
> Who now to us are shining-sweet as gods?
> Was dying all they had the skill to do?   (IX)

These moments are the darker interiors of the poem that interrupt its
public, declamatory energies. As those interruptions, the ironic undercurrents of the Commemoration Ode, roll like a wave through the text,
the whole poem becomes a struggle to assert the strength of community
and individual values (nation, courage) over the tendencies to resignation, entropy, and collapse in the face of contingency.

The other dimension lurking in the unvisited interiors of Lowell's
poem involves a problem of poetics raised by certain rhetorical moves
within the text. The posing of a rhetorical question in a poem, particularly if the language is highly figural, is usually carried out within the
protective covering provided by the metaphor. The audience under-

stands and accepts the parameters of the figural language within which a question is asked. Should the figurality be deconstructed, reduced to its grammatical, or literal, structures, the rhetorical intention may collapse. One example of this (which is itself a critical polemic of a high degree of intensity) would be Paul de Man's exposing of the poetic assumptions of Yeats's "Among School Children" in *Allegories of Reading*.[55] That poem's concluding question,

> O body swayed to music, O brightening glance
> How can we tell the dancer from the dance?

is supposed to generate an appropriate response such as, Well, of course one can't! This is clearly the meaning of the metaphor, its figural intention, so to speak. The problem is that, at the moment such figurality is misunderstood, refused, challenged, or undermined some way, the query in the last two lines of the poem could be answered by innocent or malicious responses from outside the rhetorical assumptions of lyric poetry of the type: Well, here's two ways to start with! There are some intriguing parallels to be drawn here with the "Ode Recited at the Harvard Commemoration." Clearly the question "Was dying all they had the skill to do?" must be answered by an emphatic no. The entire poem, in fact, could be read as a passionate negation of that query and its implications. Nonetheless, the rhetorical move is somewhat risky. It would be possible to conceive of a moment or situation marked by resignation, grief, or hostility in which the intention of the question (and the language is somewhat less figural here than in the Yeats poem) is understood not as the poetic declaration that opens up the remainder of the stanza to a celebration of the undying significance of the soldiers' deaths but as a literal speech act to which any number of different responses could be made. The fragility of the Commemoration Ode can be sensed at points in the poem such as "Was dying all they had the skill to do?" or at the lines

> Shall we to more continuance make pretence?
> Renown builds tombs; a life-estate is Wit;
>> And, bit by bit,
> The cunning years steal all from us but woe (IX)

where the speaker for a brief moment is aware that he is walking over a psychic and political abyss on a shaky rhetorical bridge. The specter of the "wrong" answers to the question about the value of the Harvard men's deaths in the Civil War haunts the "right" answer the poem quickly moves on to supply. The ironic register that slips in and out of the otherwise magisterial procession of the Commemoration Ode is, I suggest, Lowell's admonition to his audience and himself that nations, communities, and individuals, no matter what their educational and cultural ideals and resources, and even at their moment of victory, have to accept the unpredictable and significance-devouring universe that renders all commemorative poems evanescent configurations of language and emotion.

James Russell Lowell's Harvard Commemoration Ode stands in a tradition of works that take up the challenge of memory and memorial in the aftermath of violent conflict. Radically different from and yet with a generic relationship to Whitman's "Lilacs," it is not free from private obscurity, public grandstanding, or the irony of its own poetic ambitions. It is a cultural statement also, defined if not dominated by its author's prejudices, its period in history, its audience, and the circumstances of its composition. Though to read the Commemoration Ode ourselves must involve seeing it from a critical perspective, we should also not be too discomfited to grasp its profound sadness and the authentic poetic struggle it enacts.

2

A Strange Remorse

MELVILLE AND THE MEASURE OF VICTORY

When Hölderlin envisages poetry as a measuring, and above all himself achieves poetry as taking measure, then we, in order to think of poetry, must ever and again first give thought to the measure that is taken in poetry; we must pay heed to the kind of taking here, which does not consist in a clutching or any other kind of grasping, but rather in a letting come of what has been dealt out.

Martin Heidegger

Cast a cold eye
On life, on death.
Horseman, pass by!

W. B. Yeats

THE PUBLICATION of Herman Melville's collection of poetry *Battle-Pieces and Aspects of the War* in August 1866, almost ten years after his last work of fiction, *The Confidence-Man*, had appeared, was not the same kind of ceremonial unveiling that James Russell Lowell's commissioned piece had enjoyed. There was certainly no equivalent commemorative and communal occasion on which the book was first presented to the public, and Melville had little or no access to the kind of cultural network of recommendation and dissemination to which the Commemoration Ode, as a poem stamped with something of the institutional imprimatur of Harvard, could be entrusted; furthermore, the reviews of *Battle-Pieces* were at best

neutral and the sales extremely disappointing.[1] The facts of Melville's life
and attenuated writing career during the 1860s have been rehearsed in
many places, most comprehensively in *The Civil War World of Herman
Melville*, Stanton Garner's biographical and critical reading of the poetry
against the background of the war years, and in the second volume of Herschel Parker's epic study *Herman Melville: A Biography*, and I mention a
couple of those facts here very briefly.[2] The two closest family members
through whose experiences Herman Melville could register and understand the war were his cousins Henry and Guert Gansevoort, the former
serving in the Union army, and the latter in the navy. Although both men
survived the war, their close proximity to danger was, for Melville, a source
of family apprehensiveness, masculine envy, and ultimately access to an
experience he was conscious of missing.[3] Guert Gansevoort's unpredictable
career, haunted by controversy and accident, does not appear as a direct inspiration for any specific poems in *Battle-Pieces*.[4] Henry Gansevoort's position as commander of the 13th New York Cavalry, however, became the
opportunity for Melville's one real war experience: his participation in the
tense military patrol through the woods of northern Virginia that forms
the narrative thread of the long poem "The Scout toward Aldie."[5] Although Melville saw very little of the war at first-hand, there is, nevertheless, a concern for fact and place in the poems of *Battle-Pieces*, and
Melville did not hide his distance in time and space from the events that
give many of the poems their precise and documentary titles. Indeed, his
reliance on the already documented suggests that Melville in *Battle-Pieces*
does not "bare his soul to the event" but rather "transcribes only prior
transcriptions," as one critic has succinctly expressed it.[6] Whether transcription or invention, however, a sense of dogged engagement with detail
is maintained by intense and exploratory pieces such as "Shiloh: A Requiem" and "A Utilitarian View of the Monitor's Fight," as well as by the
more traditional commemorative poems in the sequence entitled *Verses
Inscriptive and Memorial*. These undramatic poems, which tend to be dis-
regarded even by critics who place a high value on the collection generally,
have the kind of factuality that surrounds a graven inscription on a head-
stone: an act of writing – an act of wording, one could say – that intends to
draw readers' attention to the commemorative act itself rather than to the
particular language used. The horseman in William Butler Yeats's famous
tercet, for example, is meant to cast his cold eye and move on but not nec-

essarily to forget the epitaph he has just read or to dismiss it as inconsequential. Memorial gestures, Yeats suggests, deserve a brief, appraising glance, no more, but were the gravestone and its inscription not in place, there could not even be a passing-by. In some of the individual poems in *Battle-Pieces*, however, Melville's attitude to commemorative inscription seems often haunted by the possibility that inscription in stone, perhaps even the inscription that is poetry itself, has little of the stability and permanence once asserted by the crafted memorial. This sense of ambivalence in *Battle-Pieces and Aspects of the War* generates poems that are often as politically cautious as they are technically complex, and as emotionally distant as they are often unflinching in their observation of the war and how it is perceived by the Northern public. Indeed, *Battle-Pieces and Aspects of the War* is at times an exercise in "linguistic self-retraction," as Shira Wolosky describes it, in which statement and counterstatement, image and counterimage, cancel each other out.[7] With that context in mind, I discuss a selection of poems in terms of memory, nation, and memorial, as a parallel reading to my discussion of Lowell's Commemoration Ode in the previous chapter. The goal is to explore the strange mirror-image of the more unitary Commemoration Ode that *Battle-Pieces* represents, thrown back in the form of a set of ambivalent lyrical meditations that often, also, carry the documentary flavor of bulletins, snapshots, or journal entries.

The undeniable differences between Melville's *Battle-Pieces* and James Russell Lowell's memorial poetry (and indeed also between *Battle-Pieces* and Whitman's war poems in *Drum-Taps*), apart from their aesthetic qualities, involve assumptions of cultural status and genre. Were we to recreate, for a moment, the cultural environment of middle-class America at the end of the Civil War, and place his work against the imposing architecture of Lowell's Commemoration Ode, Melville would be adjudged a curious and unsatisfactory phenomenon. In literary and social status, he would be – indeed, was – the lurker at the threshold, and his low-key and often oblique poems are the notations of an experimentalist at an uncertain stage of development between and older and newer types of language. In terms of poetic composition Melville worked, as one critic has expressed it, "within the confines of rhymed verse while bending those forms to the limit."[8] Where Lowell's commemorative notes ring slowly as if in stately procession, many of Melville's verses have, despite the reassurance provided by traditional forms, a flattened and

intellectually dry tone that refuses easy involvement. Thus the response
they provoked was a mixture of dislike and bemusement: the poems in
Battle-Pieces struck contemporary readers as, in many ways, falling outside the cultural parameters that poetry was meant to occupy. Times and
tastes change, however, and the comparison that worked to Melville's
disadvantage in 1866 had, by the early twentieth century, switched polar-
ity and become a negative judgment on Lowell and, indeed, on much of
nineteenth-century American poetry. In many ways, however, Melville's
disadvantage – if that is what it was – provides us with a crucial lane of
access to his poetry, poised as it is between a memory of the lost past and
a premonition of the inevitable future. The Civil War poems form a kind
of meditative bridge between Melville's pessimistic sense of life as a
stage for potentially traumatic political and moral choices and his recognition of the poet's role as composer of epitaph and performer of elegy
for the nation. And, despite their relative brevity, these poems are often
ambitious and complex in their philosophical intention and cultural reference.

In the poem "Shiloh. A Requiem," for example, the world is a more
dynamic place than the one evoked by the abstract grandeur of the Harvard Commemoration Ode. The nineteen lines of this short poem weave
and plunge, like the swallows in its key motif, darting in and around the
echoes called out by the name of the Tennessee battlefield of April 6
and 7, 1862. The poem, by its own declared title a requiem of sorts, is
nonetheless configured around an unexpectedly energetic interweaving
of natural mobility, agile observation, and brevity of tone, as it wheels
and skims over the ground that saw so much agony and mortality:

> Over the field in clouded days,
>   The forest-field of Shiloh –
> Over the field where April rain
> Solaced the parched ones stretched in pain
> Through the pause of night
> That followed the Sunday fight
>   Around the church at Shiloh – [9]

The poem does unusual things with syntax, since it can be read as one
complete sentence; and with sound, as it risks in its final lines the bathos of

a terminal rhyming of "lie low" with "Shiloh." As with much of Melville's collection *Battle-Pieces and Aspects of the War*, it is a surprising and unexpectedly assured experiment in using the images of pastoral verse to remind the reader that the deserted battlefields of the war are memorial locations and yet remain natural sites, reverting quickly to grass and bird, and burying the traces of men's suffering. Melville, as a recent study of the Civil War and its representations expresses it, "imagines the power of nature turned against the instruments of war."[10] With its structure and cadences evoking the wild countryside rather than invoking the dead soldiers or the reasons for which they sacrificed their futures, the poem "Shiloh" is also a reminder that nature, despite its vitality, lacks the appropriate social forms and commemorative demeanor.

The appearance of the term "Requiem" in the title of the poem strikes a different, more Latinate and Roman Catholic note, especially in contrast to the materially austere, "log-built" church around which the Union and Confederate troops fought so bitterly. The church at Shiloh was a small Methodist meeting-house built from wood, in every way a manifestation of a religious tradition for which the complex harmonies of the requiem mass would have had little resonance. As it stood at the center of the battle on April 6, so does the simple church stand at the center of the poem "Shiloh" as the words and lines swirl and fall around it. The capacity of the poem to be a requiem, however, is measured by the success with which it achieves a kind of memorial sublime. Three contending forces square off within the poem: natural dynamism, religious transcendence, and human suffering, each autonomous although in permanent and porous juxtaposition. In turn, within the arena shaped by these cosmic interactions, the actual battle was fought between men who had, for the most part, grown up in the culture of American Protestantism. "Shiloh. A Requiem" embodies a response to their deaths that activates a cultural framework beyond the rough conventions of frontier mourning or the roughly hewn logs of the little church. Only the measure of this poem can transverse the world of historical memory and the world of "natural prayer," the world of war's fatalities and the world of self-regenerating landscapes, the world of Protestant austerity and that of a Catholic sacred aesthetic. In a final gesture in the last line of the poem ("all is hushed") Melville invokes silence as the most appropriate commemorative expression of loss and suggests thereby that there is also a poetry of the enigmatic and the unexplained, obscured by the distracting explanations of conventional verse and its scaffolding of assumptions. As somewhat of an exception in the library of Civil War poetry from the nineteenth century, this poem, like others in *Battle-Pieces*, plays with silence and absence. In its rich amalgamation of religious, Romantic, and pantheistic sensibilities, "Shiloh: A Requiem" is a hymn sung in memoriam by Nature to wounded humankind.

As styles of mourning and cultural assumptions about the status of the dead in social memory change, so the capacity to read specific commemorative texts and grasp their emotional background fades also, often rendering the older form of expression anachronistic, even indecipherable. This change can lead in turn to false judgments about emotional authenticity. Joshua Scodel argues in his study of the poetic epitaph in British literary history that the community structures that had guaranteed its significance underwent radical change during the eighteenth century, as the so-called Age of Sensibility gave way to the Romantic era. Poets began to abandon inscriptive or commemorative verse in favor of the interior, psychological exploration of one's role as a living connection to the departed. Mirroring the rise of the elegy as the more powerful and responsive form, the epitaph gradually "ceased to be a vital literary genre in the early nineteenth century."[11] As a kind of delayed crisis in American poetic history, *Battle-Pieces* captures this cultural transformation in a uniquely intense way. Neither protected by the certainties manifest in the work of the New England Poets, for example, nor able to exult in its own iconoclastic voice as in Whitman's *Drum-Taps*, Melville's poetry embodies a moment of imaginative writing as it stretches to encompass both retreating and emergent forms. Throughout *Battle-Pieces and Aspects of the War*, the experience of the conflict in the broadest sense forces the emergence of an elegiac psychology as it subjects the traditional epitaph to the ironic cruelties of modern history.

Across a modulation of poetic signals between the epitaph and the elegy, then, *Battle-Pieces* invites the reader to cast a skeptical eye on the writing of memorial verse but also to extend a moment of empathy to men whose names may be unknown or forgotten but whose death demanded that such a poetic inscription be composed. The poems in the sequence *Verses Inscriptive and Memorial*, comprising the last sixteen poems in

Battle-Pieces preceding the longer "The Scout toward Aldie," "Lee in the Capitol," and "A Meditation," express the enigma of commemoration while making a conscious gesture toward traditional memorial language. They raise the question of who deserves to be remembered, and how, as in the poem entitled "An uninscribed Monument on one of the Battle-fields of the Wilderness." The first part describes a place where the silence is as appropriate a memorial as the stone tablet:

> Silence and Solitude may hint
>> (Whose home is in yon piny wood)
> What I, though tableted, could never tell –
> The din which here befell,
>> And striving of the multitude.
> The iron cones and spheres of death
>> Set round me in their rust.   (*B-P*, 173)

The delicate task that Melville sets himself here is to construct, without bathos, the blank stone of the monument as the speaking voice of the poem, proffering its own lack of inscription as a valid bearing of witness. The poem is testimony to the fact that the absence of an epitaph may not be itself a crucial loss, and indeed that a mute act of witness can be as important as any memorial inscription. In memory of the "multitude," the nameless, rather than of those commemorated by resonant and powerful social networks, might well be the leitmotif of this, as of many of Melville's poems. "An uninscribed Monument" concludes with the lines

> Take in the import of the quiet here –
>> The after-quiet – the calm full fraught;
> Thou too will silent stand –
> Silent as I, and lonesome as the land.

The memorial voice now believes that the absence of an inscription may in fact say all that needs to be said about the loss of life and future and recognizes that the human world of bereavement and the surrounding landscape have been brought into a kind of alignment of mourning. Although the formal requirement of an inscription on the memorial has not been met, the poem argues that the very anonymity of the dead requires a more appropriate act of commemoration and offers one: it consists of accepting the monument as it stands, not disturbing the silence of the place, and meditating on the nightmare of pain and sound that once took place there.

Although the poem on the "uninscribed Monument" is somewhat unusual because it has to make what it can out of the absence of a message and indeed offers a virtual inscription in the form of the body of the poem itself, only a few of the poems in *Verses Inscriptive and Memorial* could be described as engaged in experimentation with commemorative verse. Whether such a perception of these poems is accurate or not, however, it has made that section of *Battle-Pieces* the one least interesting to critics – which is one good reason, among others, to look at it again. An important aspect to consider is that these poems are designed not to draw attention to themselves, but they draw precisely such attention because of the apparent modest obedience to conventional forms of poetic mourning embedded in a larger context that often challenges, implicitly at least, the authority of such conventions. Melville does not reject cliché, one could say, in his exploration of loss and the human capacity to deal with such loss and to find the proper form in which to do so. Neither is he unaware of the deeper, unresolved social tensions that can be expressed through the language of mourning. Although the kind of appeal to an audience that was common in the sentimental culture of the nineteenth century now appears artificial and even trite, we need to understand it in part as a popular expression of emotional need and collective memory that sought to challenge, by way of universal religious invocation, the social distinctions that divided casualties into those commemorated and those forgotten. The traditional Christian position on departed souls that "the last shall be first" could be, as Ann Douglas comments in her essay on nineteenth-century attitudes to death, easily adjusted to reflect a greater or lesser note of social resentment.[12] The mass mortality of the Civil War created a more intense context for that feeling. Indeed, that Herman Melville would make his initial foray into American poetic culture with several poems on the theme of national memorial politics, and on the particular question of who does and who does not receive the grace of remembrance, has its own irony. Memory and forgetting were unavoidable motifs in the narrative of the final decades of Melville's life. They also provide a way of reading the history of his absence and of his recovery by the American literary academy through the middle of the twentieth century until today, including that particular subordinate history of how his poetry rather than his fiction has been revisited and interpreted.[13]

The short, enigmatic poems in *Verses Inscriptive and Memorial* make their own contribution, therefore, to the total effect of *Battle-Pieces*. Or, perhaps not so much an enigmatic style as a brief, oblique but plainspoken gesture that both disburses expected sentiment and, simultaneously, allows a poetic troping on that sentiment. In many of the poems in this sequence, the cliché balances out the chasm, in the sense that the idea of so many monuments to so many dead, a plethora of mortalities, is lightened to some degree by formal elegance in the commemorative language: no experiment, no poetic drama, but rather the craft, the exercise of memorial carving, decent and restrained. The poem of eleven lines entitled "On the Men of Maine, killed in the Victory of Baton Rouge, Louisiana," is a perfect example:

> Afar they fell. It was the zone
>   Of fig and orange, cane and lime
> (A land how all unlike their own
> With the cold pine-grove overgrown),
>   But still their Country's clime.
> And there in youth they died for her –
>   The Volunteers,
> For her went up their dying prayers:
>   So vast the Nation, yet so strong the tie.
> What doubt shall come, then, to deter
>   The Republic's earnest faith and courage high.
>   (*B-P*, 168).

One might say, if this were to be judged as a poem, it would be an odd combination of originality and routine: a well-crafted verse encompassing a movement from a pair of suggestive concrete images to pious political invocation and abstraction. If it were to be judged as a memorial inscription, it might be seen as more original, or at least eccentric, in its opening lines, while retreating to a traditional rhetorical formulation at the conclusion.

No matter which criteria are applied to the text of the poem, therefore, the opening is expertly managed. The oddly technical use of "zone" provokes a momentary double take that slows the reader down going into the second line. The names of the fruit and the sugar cane suggest a life of tropical plenty, a kind of effusive gift from nature that is placed, perhaps a little accusingly, next to the image of the far northeast, the gloomy forests and sharp, uncompromising climate. The opening of the poem is an opening onto an American geographical sublime, a country marked by large-scale, spectacular differences in natural environment. Something of the curiosity and even admiration of the soldiers from Maine for their new environment is captured obliquely in the fifth line in particular. In the background is a murmur of regional essentialism, as the ubiquity of exotic fruits is linked to the indolence and corrupted social order of the South: an approximate cause of the war, as often believed by Northerners.

There in any event, argues the poem, they sacrificed their lives for a national ideal, for their comrades-in-arms, for the officers that led them, even perhaps for the cause of human rights, as we might call it today. Capitalized in the isolation of a two-word line, "Volunteers," not draftees or proxies, they went south and failed to return. The memorial speaker assumes their "dying prayers" were for the nation, as opposed to some more vulgar object, such as their own physical survival. And then he departs from the concrete span of Maine and Louisiana, of pine-grove and sugar cane, and declares their abstract existences to be bound together: "yet so strong the tie." The final rhetorical flourish is a bromide, a casual gesture in standard invocatory terms, phrased as a question that does not warrant a question mark and is therefore not really a question.

The poem "On the Men of Maine" memorializes their deaths, invokes the territorial spread of the United States as the exotic context for their war service and the imperative of national unity and transforms, by virtue of this inscription, their sacrifice into a model of republican virtue. To do this is utterly acceptable, as a commemorative act. In fact, even if one takes a more rigorously critical position, even if the images are seen as conventional and uninspired, the poem as a routine exercise in civic mourning, the text does not dissolve into imaginative failure. Whether poetic meditation or public epitaph, "On the Men of Maine" contains a kernel of collective memory that can live with cliché and perhaps even welcome it as a legitimate co-resident of the world of commemorative expression. The presence of traditional, even conventional memorial images in a poem may be part of the strategy for survival enacted by that poem. As one scholar has remarked: "This continuity of meaningful action and custom, which anthropologists designate as human culture, is the social ecology in which both poems and monuments are embedded and on which they depend for their life support."[14] Melville's *Battle-Pieces* is a monument, as the monuments described in *Battle-Pieces* are also vehicles for poetic inscription. The poetry of the monument needs the security of commemorative inscription, as verses inscribed on the monument need the attention of alert poetic judgment. Words and judgment are inextricably linked in so many ways, and there is a kind of negotiation between author and reader of an epitaph that is, in its own way, as distinctive as the more complex and literary dynamic between author and reader of an elegy. The social ecology, to appropriate that useful term, that supports "On the Men of Maine" is clearly one that must accept a kind of doubling between words and judgment; the poem will be judged as a poem, and the lines as an epitaph. Or, to put it another way, Melville does not want to accomplish the job too easily with a stereotypical memorial verse, but neither does he want the subjectivity of the text, its status as a manifestation of aesthetic value, to overwhelm the custom of public commemoration or the poem's accessibility for average readers.

Any discussion of this group of poems must consider the powerful twenty-six-line meditation "A Requiem for Soldiers lost in Ocean Transports." This text represents one ultimately unavoidable limitation of inscription and commemorative culture: the need for physical presence and stability. The poetic speaker is haunted by the impossibility of a monument, in any real sense connected to the place of loss, that could commemorate the soldiers who drowned as their troop-carrying ships went down. On the basis of that recognized impossibility the poem struggles to be the memorial. Indeed its elegiac architecture is, it would seem, all the more accomplished because it is, once again, taking on the responsibility of attempting to commemorate a loss in concrete terms, and not just offering a verbal representation as a metaphorical act of mourning. Complete disappearance has its own implications, and the uneasy realization that the soldiers on the troopship have disappeared into the ocean is emphasized by the manner in which they have no presence – they do not register, as it were – on the surface of the poem.

The self-healing capacity of the natural world is, in "A Requiem for Soldiers," an extreme form of that phenomenon in the requiem "Shiloh." At sea, a permanent and uncompromising confrontation between the human and the natural forces is always in play, and the sudden turn of fate is absolute.

> All creatures joying in the morn,
> Save them forever from joyance torn,
>   Whose bark was lost where now the dolphins play;
> Save them that by the fabled shore,
>   Down the pale stream are washed away. (*B-P*, 176–77)

Where "Shiloh," for example, operates as a frame for images of human conflict and of the recuperative potential of the natural world, asserting as it does so the legitimacy of names and places as signs of a relationship between language and memory, "A Requiem for Soldiers Lost in Ocean Transports" is a poem about no-place, and the difficulty of commemoration in an environment in which human culture is offered no purchase. In terms of American collective memory of the Civil War, the poem is also the vehicle of a marginalized experience. While the naval battles between the *C.S.S. Virginia* and the *Cumberland*, for example, and subsequently between the *Monitor* and the *Virginia*, went into story and song (including Melville's poem "A Utilitarian View of the Monitor's Fight"), the humdrum world of troop transports found no place among the favored settings of popular memorialization. Like "An uninscribed Monument" in this one crucial respect, this poem is Melville's attempt in *Battle-Pieces* to extend the parameters of what can be considered worthy of commemoration; but it is no easy task. Because these soldiers went down with their ships, the link between inscription and memory is denied in absolute terms. Thus, the poem offers a reflexive and ironic comment on the title *Verses Inscriptive and Memorial*. There is nothing there that could carry an inscription; there are only the mindlessly self-renewing processes of ocean chemistry and sea creatures. Indeed, the mammalian status of the dolphins, alongside an echo of their pagan and Christian symbolism as carriers of souls, delivers an extra charge of irony in this poem, as dolphins too hide in "vaults profound," deep below any remotely human location. Even the inscriptionless monument in the Wilderness offered a sense of physical permanence, though it lacked a message, while the "lone spar" of the concluding lines of "A Requiem for Soldiers Lost in Ocean Transports" is nothing except a random piece of flotsam bobbing on the waves:

> Nor heed they now the lone bird's flight
> Round the lone spar where mid-sea surges pour.   (*B-P*, 177)

The short poem "An Epitaph" is different yet again, providing a brief domestic cameo of the minister and his congregation, demoralized by news of the war but taking inspiration from the stoicism and faith of the visiting war widow, "summering sweetly here," who feels "deep at heart her faith content" (*B-P*, 169). The title is minimalist, almost uninformative, because the object of the epitaph is unclear: it might be for some deceased soldier, or for the "Soldier's widow" herself. It might be even a coded criticism of the "priest and people," who lack the placid insight of the bereaved woman. In a wider sense, the epitaph is embodied in the poem itself, negatively, in memory of the lack of courage and sturdiness shown by the citizens of the town. With its oblique gesture toward the many sentimental poems written by or about war widows during and after the Civil War, "An Epitaph" has the flavor of a piece of popular doggerel designed to remind people of the appropriate behavior for the home front. The widow is seen outside the church, however, outside the community almost, and as such is the font of a spirit that seems not to be available from the established institutions of the society, including organized religion. In "An Epitaph," Melville directs the reader's attention to the meaning of the word as the title of a poem in which the precise location and referent of the epitaph are not entirely clear. If, as suggested earlier, the poem itself is the epitaph, then it is a commemorative inscription that opens up the intriguing paradox that no epitaph is really possible for the random moments of individual history. The widow's refusal of hopelessness and resignation, multiplied throughout the North at moments when it looked as though the war was lost, will never receive the public recognition it deserves. The poem is like a marker or a placeholder for the memory of one individual moment among the myriad of such moments that make up the history of the war. Indeed, Melville's choice of the idealized widow as the central figure in "An Epitaph" is itself a register of the degree to which, over the course of the war, the attitudes and responses of women North and South became increasingly significant for the maintenance of individual and community morale.[15]

The final poem in this section of *Battle-Pieces*, "The Returned Volunteer to his Rifle," sketches the brief, largely implicit narrative of an anonymous Union infantryman returning to his home in New York State. The rifle, itself also a veteran of the Battle of Gettysburg, is placed above the hearth, a symbol of "patriot-memory dear" (*B-P*, 183). The poem evokes the Catskills and the Hudson River valley, the "Highlands blue" to which the soldier often returned in his mind while away at war (and, by implication, the area's history during the Revolutionary War and the role the surrounding countryside played as the inspiration for the first distinctly American school of landscape painting). In an almost totemic image, we are told that the man has often spoken to his rifle about his native region. Conversing with an inanimate object is not presented as anything odder than war itself, however, and the returning soldier hangs the rifle alongside other accoutrements: the "belt, and bayonet, and canteen," the deadly and the harmless clustered together in the veteran's memory of war. This is a poem unusually sensitive to material culture, as are several other poems in *Battle-Pieces*. Here, the physical things of the war are carried into the household to be installed within the surroundings of domestic order to survive as souvenirs or mementos of a resolved past rather than an ominous threat of violence and national strife to come.

Thus in both "An Epitaph" and "The Returned Volunteer" the domestic order, as much as the political order, is part of the social ecology that surrounds works of memory, literary or plastic, static or performative. That ecology is a fragile mesh of individual and group emotion, social expectation, material surroundings, cultural adeptness, and the presence or absence of religious belief. The social ecology demands the production of works of memorial and commemoration, reads them appropriately, and responds to their presence. The intersection of the literary work, the text that carries the memory into commemoration, and the community that receives it is the place where the cultural act of remembering an experience succeeds the involuntary remembering of the human being who experienced it. What constituted the web of society and belief for James Russell Lowell was not available to Herman Melville, but neither would Lowell have had access to Melville's world. For Melville and *Battle-Pieces*, that surrounding human community was not the well-defined field of Harvard alumni and their families and circles that makes Lowell's Commemoration Ode, in so many ways, read like a bard's song for his clan. In contrast, the potential audience for Melville's book was a patchwork, diverse and disparate, made up of his own family members and friends, fellow authors and literati, admirers of Melville's early novels, admirers of his more recent fiction (a much smaller group), and perhaps a few interested parties who were curious about what poets were going to do with the war now that it was over.

Melville's poems of memory and memorial inscription, therefore, occupy a peculiar position: they draw attention to the fact that they need to call into existence a surrounding social matrix for remembrance and mourning, rather than having one already in place (to put it another way, they move in more democratically anonymous surroundings than does the Commemoration Ode). Any such matrix will be, as noted, formed out of a physical community, a geographical location or set of locations, a fabric of commonly held values and beliefs, and available cultural forms of expression. Together they become an echo chamber for commemorative acts, communicated by an appropriately qualified individual and received by the appropriate audience. Whether a brief service after a battle, an invitation-only event like the ceremony at Harvard, the unveiling of a public memorial, or the publication of a literary work, the formal structures serve a community purpose, or at least are supposed to. Melville touches the sensitive intersection of commemoration and poetry as discourses that share a language and yet diverge on ultimate value. The question of ultimate value is about whether the literature of memory and mourning can be, successfully, both an invocation of community experience and the elaboration of a highly individual poetic vision. *Battle-Pieces* is a remarkable literary experiment from that point of view alone: it puts a thematic study of the origins, development, and conclusion of the Civil War into poetry and also reveals the increasing disjuncture between the verse styles of traditional public mourning and remembrance on one hand, and the interiority of a Romantic poetry of trauma and loss on the other. In other words, Melville must negotiate between epitaph and elegy, and the *Verses Inscriptive and Memorial* are to that extent generic echoes of a network of shared grief, collective remembrance, and common vocabulary that once would have given that genre meaning. Now these verses stand as reminders that such a complex, such a social ecology, can perhaps only be inferred rather than directly experienced. Melville's short poems in this collection are, together, a measure of this change in commemorative culture. Turning now to the longer poems, we find in them, often, the more ambitious gestures of intervention that Melville makes in the direction of postconflict American culture.

The epigraph from Martin Heidegger at the head of this chapter reflects the mystical theorizing about poetry that marked his later career, but I want to draw attention to the question of "measure," as he borrows the term from Friedrich Hölderlin.[16] The measure is the poetic division of the line, the parceling out of time during the saying of the verse, the active prosodic choices made by the poet. Ideally, the measure is neither clutched at nor distorted but rather paid out, grasped, and applied. I think it is useful, therefore, to consider Melville's *Battle-Pieces* as that kind of taking of measure. But it is a tense act of measuring. The measures of politics, of war, of injury, and of memory and commemoration have each a different pace and rhythm. They place difficult if not impossible demands on poetry, on poetic voice and style, and Melville is wrestling with the measure of these large and dangerous presences as indeed he wrestles with the structures and parameters of English and American verse. But whether the responsible poet is Hölderlin, Lowell, or Melville, the obscure intersection of history, memory, and poetic act is where the different measures meet, jostle, and try to assert their authority. At certain points in Melville's poetry, the traditional measures of poetic form, from which he does not ultimately depart, are placed in such a relationship to historical experience as to suggest that they struggle to match appropriately the traumatic scale of this American conflict. As Helen Vendler has argued, Melville's jaundiced view of American optimism and his religious nihilism are so uncompromising in *Battle-Pieces* that these lyrics still pose a significant critical problem for our map of nineteenth-century literature.[17] In that context, therefore, taking the measure of national recovery, the dominant theme of the concluding poems of the volume, has to be done, but without any guarantees of reassurance. Melville is too well aware of the centrifugal forces in American culture that have already failed to prevent war, and that could prove be weak in the face of other temptations. Indeed, the fear of the potentially immeasurable consequences of the war may well be, as Robert Milder has suggested, the deeper motive for the very structure of the *Battle-Pieces* collection itself.[18] Melville's long, penultimate poem "Lee in the Capitol" is an extended exploration of this premonition.

Appropriately, perhaps, the prosody of "Lee in the Capitol" is relatively conservative, in the context of the sometimes adventurous stylistic range of *Battle-Pieces*: a 213-line dramatic poem in rhymed couplets and quatrains and, for the most part, governed by a fluid combination of iambic pentameter and tetrameter. The implications of age, sacrifice, and the choice between speech and silence are Shakespearean, gesturing perhaps to the figure of an aging hero who has lost his once-admired powers but not his bearing. In historical reality, Robert E. Lee was summoned to testify before the Reconstruction Committee of the Thirty-ninth Congress in late winter 1866. In Melville's poem, he makes his way to Washington, DC, past scenes that recall the recent conflict and the subsequent loss of the Lee family home:

> Demurring not, promptly he comes
> By ways which show the blackened homes,
> And – last – the seat no more his own,
> But Honor's; patriot grave-yards fill
> The forfeit slopes of that patrician hill,
> And fling a shroud on Arlington.   (*B-P*, 230)

The poetic speaker compares Lee's somber arrival with the Union's victory celebrations a year earlier, at which Grant and Sherman "shone in blue," and suggests that Lee is divided, part of him defeated and part still unwilling to concede. An issue of pride is at root, the poem seems to say, as it attempts to empathize with Lee while, almost simultaneously, expressing approval of the confiscation of his family's Virginia estate. At the actual hearing before the Congress, Lee did not take the opportunity offered to add a personal statement to the answers he had given regarding the current state of opinion in the South and the future of the defeated Confederacy.[19] Melville takes up that offer in the fictional dimension of the "Lee in the Capitol" and has his character respond in a long passage

that is, however, prefaced by a note of encouragement, even pleading, by
the poetic speaker:

> Speak out? Ay, speak, and for the brave,
> Who else no voice or proxy have;
> Frankly their spokesman here become,
> And the flushed North from her own victory save. (*B-P*, 233)

The use of the term proxy has a certain edge to it, emphasizing the widespread opportunity in the North for a draftee to pay a sum of money to
have another man recruited in his place. The absence of that method of
avoiding service in the Confederate forces provides Lee with a certain
moral confidence (although slaveholders, in the early period of the war,
could obtain deferments from the Confederate government on the basis
of the number of slaves, much to the disgust of the nonslaveholding population of the South). The more interesting point is that the speaker appeals to Lee to "save" the North from the corroding effects of victory.
Already, in this poem from one year after the war's end, the recognition
that the consequences of victory can be ultimately more complex than
the consequences of defeat is placed on the agenda. In what is in many
ways a startling note of prescience, Melville appears to grasp intuitively
that the South will have the cultural magnetism of loss and defeat at its
disposal, while the North will have the uneasy residue of victory. Lee
stands also, in Melville's vision, before Congress as he stood at home in
April 1861 after receiving Lincoln's offer to take command of Union
forces, debating with himself whether his loyalty to Virginia or to the
United States should take precedence. The line-and-a-half that runs
"The inner feud / He, self-contained, a while withstood" repeats in the
universe of the poem that moment five years earlier, making Lee into a
figure whose meditation and decision are, together, the story of the war,
its opening and closing, and perhaps even the tragedy of an American
political paradox.

There is also some measure of identification, on Melville's part, with
Lee. The question of the why of Lee's decision at the outbreak of war offers a parallel to the story of a man and a society ennobled by defeat at
the end of that war. Despite the concentration on the mechanics of war
throughout the *Battle-Pieces* collection, "Lee in the Capitol" studiously

avoids the detail of the years of fraternal killing and destruction. Rather, the poem is a study of a man who made a decision, lived and survived its consequences, and is called on to speak in his defense. Lee's refusal of that opportunity in real history (or, at least, the failure of the committee members to draw him into making a more substantial contribution to the debate) becomes, in Melville's text, an explanatory speech that instructs the victors in the ambiguous nature of their victory. Lee's capacity to build defeat and resignation into something like an interior protection for the soul is an admirable thing, or at least one worthy of notice. Melville's own buried career as a fiction writer, as it must have looked to him almost ten years after his last published work, could be read as a defeat. The lack of compromise in Melville's journey through the vicissitudes of the late 1840s and early 1850s – the "American Renaissance" of our twentieth-century critical fictions – was, in ways that might have offered a seductive parallel at the time, a story of commitment and misunderstanding matching Lee's.[20] This is not to suggest any substantial identification on Melville's part with the ideology of Southern secession. Nevertheless, Melville understood the burden of making the clearly intelligible choice in all circumstances. Sometimes the only choice is the bad one, the one that requires an impossible compromise between competing sets of principles and beliefs. But the act of transforming Robert E. Lee from a historical individual who made a bad choice into a poetic construct who is now illuminated from within by the defeat that that choice brought about is also a political act. With the Lee of *Battle-Pieces*, one could say, Melville invented a prototype of one of the key motifs of the Southern "Lost Cause." In the pursuit of the culture war that the South would eventually launch to throw off Radical Reconstruction and extend the narrative of racial supremacy into the wider politics of the United States in the latter decades of the century, Lee's own chilly integrity became the fire of Southern refusal. The least populist of all Confederate leaders became, ironically, the popular symbol of a South that would not accept the moral legitimacy of Northern victory – a victory that indeed would be undermined by its own doubts and contradictions. Lee is both Southern general and silent prophet, defeated and yet articulating, by not speaking, the ambiguity of the relationship between success and failure. Melville seems to sense, in Lee, the sadness of a mind that is destined to become a simplified version of itself, as its quiet self-awareness turns into the truculent sloganeering of others.

The intense, interior, focalization of Lee's statement to the Congress through the narrative perspective of the poem might well suggest to us that Herman Melville, author, would have appreciated such a high-level opportunity to explain himself, his choices, and his creative past and future to a responsible body of men (although Lee's silence is a recognition that explanation itself is hardly ever neutral). When the poetic speaker says of Lee,

> His earnestness unforeseen
> Moved, but not swayed their former mien;
> And they dismissed him. Forth he went
> Through vaulted walks in lengthened line
> Like porches erst upon the Palatine.   (*B-P*, 237)

it is not difficult to discern the contours of Melville's own experience with reviewers of his later fiction, from *Moby Dick* to *The Confidence Man*, who were unpleasantly surprised by the turn in style and approach, initially willing to give him a pass on the basis of his earlier popular books, only to conclude that there was nothing more to be gained by reading this author. To explain oneself, whether one is Robert E. Lee or Herman Melville, is to enter into a dialogue about defeat and its meanings, but in a context in which one does not necessarily control the interpretive field. There is often a price to be paid for explaining oneself, and equally often the price is connected to the limits of whatever language of explanation is available. In painting a verbal portrait of Lee in the Capitol, Melville imagines an interlocking performance, one of speech and one of silence, or of silence within speech. The poem holds out the possibility of an alternative history, one of speech and justification, but even this fictional history does no more than project the silence of Lee in real history onto a larger screen. His explanation is well thought out, tense with controlled emotion, and offers rational grounds for the North's proceeding carefully with the defeated South. But even in the universe of the poem, the act of saying does not have any clear effect or consequence. As Melville might have thought, he (Melville) could have explained himself; he could have offered a reading of his own choices as an artist and presented a petition for understanding and re-spect. But in the act of creating the speaking Lee, he also sketches the truth of how it would have been for the speaking Melville: polite atten-tion for a brief few minutes, and then dismissal.

In an intriguing meditation on the relationship between the language of politics and the language of poetry, the poet and critic Allen Grossman once wrote: "Insofar as the actuality of both policy and poetry require sentences a man can speak, the material upon which poetry works and the material upon which policy works are identical because of the ubiq-uity of language, and present the same resistances. The reasons that one cannot make just any poem, or just any policy, good are the same. An en-tailment of any style a person speaks is the structure of a social world that can receive it – a political formation and its kind of conscious life."[21] The referents of Grossman's comment are Abraham Lincoln and Walt Whit-man. He argues that in the context of the breaking up of the Union, Lin-coln's struggle to make present in language the reasons why secession was unconstitutional and needed to be fought and defeated can be re-garded as an intellectual and emotional companion piece to Whitman's struggle to find a seam of democratic utterance among the legacy of es-tablishment poetic forms. As Grossman implies, no more can just any group of words be a poem than can just any set of actions be policy. There are good and worthwhile poems, competent and imaginative policy, but there are also poems and policy that do not withstand the pressures they are placed under. The preferences that shape Grossman's risky but in some ways elegant comparison are clear: Abraham Lincoln and Walt Whitman were outsiders who made it, by luck and intuition as well as by good judgment, to the center of American government and American literature, respectively. Their willingness to sacrifice the easy choice for the hard one, and pay the cost, make them co-sponsors of the rescue and renewal of the national soul: their language and their policy are suf-fused with the passages of isolation, self-doubt, and courageous inven-tion through which they had to walk. In Grossman's analysis, Lincoln knew the poetry of American governance as Whitman knew the policy of American poetry, and – on separate tracks – they each pursued the resolution that would make anew what had been unjustifiably injured or distorted.

On the map formed by the overlay of the poetry of policy and the policy of poetry, however, Herman Melville has a more difficult task finding a place. Whereas Whitman had a small number of supporters who valued his poetry, had chosen a much lonelier path than Melville's ten or fifteen years earlier, and had raised a certain bohemian insouciance as his defense against the sharp-edged norms of literary and social decorum, Melville had in the mid-1860s nothing similar to fall back on. The upshot was that Melville and *Battle-Pieces and Aspects of the War* were, in a way not even suffered by Whitman and *Drum-Taps*, fated to be selected (or self-selected, perhaps) for a distinctly marginal position in postwar culture. The ambiguity of his poetic argument seems to fit only too comfortably with the unsuccessful search for a national audience for *Battle-Pieces*. There were no equivalents in Melville's poetry of 1866 for the dreamlike meditation of "When Lilacs Last in the Dooryard Bloom'd" or, indeed, for the popular success of "O Captain, My Captain!" two examples that show Whitman's ability to embrace all poetic registers from the dimly prophetic to the cheerfully declamatory.

As Grossman notes, however, Whitman and Lincoln are also captives of a system of representation, which they are commissioned to justify and put in place as an order – poetic or political – of the human world.[22] Their achievement was to take those systems and bend them to a new, freer, objective. Lincoln's commission came from his office and, at a farther remove, from his wider political career; Whitman's commission emerged from his poetic curriculum vitae, the increasing body of *Leaves of Grass* that had given him the creative energy and courage to emancipate ordinary language from vulgarity and poetic language from establishment prosody. But who or what commissioned Melville? Neither political office nor a poetic career had prepared – or justified – Melville for writing *Battle-Pieces*. As a work of commemoration and of literature, it lies athwart the chronology of postwar Northern opinion and the poetic norms of that era. Having neither the social privileges of the Boston and Cambridge set, nor the populist swagger of Whitman in the New York of the 1850s (nor, indeed, Whitman's experience in the military hospitals during the war years) to draw on, Melville introduces *Battle-Pieces* into the post-Civil War scene almost as if he were a social scientist and the poetry an experimental entity, a tool for testing responses. The poems might be modulations on a new technology of verse making, conjoining author, text, and audience in a novel relationship whose implications are not yet fixed. As with, for example, the new battlefield photography by Mathew Brady, Thomas Roche, and Alexander Gardner, the critical issue may be the public reception of the new technology rather than the products of the technology itself. As the pictures presented the conflict and its fatalities in a way that was both familiar and yet distancing and distracting, so do the poems in *Battle-Pieces* "demonstrate how war destroys ways of managing, understanding, and honoring the dead."[23]

The poems of *Battle-Pieces and Aspects of the War* are, as Stanton Garner argues, "studied, symbolic, and encyclopedically allusive . . . in which the war was a product of the American past and an anticipation of the nation's future."[24] They are, to put it another way, about poetry and the politics of memory. *Battle-Pieces* can be regarded as a statement about the potential and the limitations of verse, as the millions of words spent by North and South, over many years, embodied the potential and the limitations of political rhetoric. *Battle-Pieces* is also a set of responses to the reports, narratives, and anecdotes about the war that were the bread and butter of all those who were not directly involved in the military or related operations. Melville distrusts people's fragmentary and unreliable recollections of the war, but at the same time he has only memory and the rhetoric of poetic form at his disposal. For readers and scholars today, I would argue, this is the great central convergence of *Battle-Pieces*: the constraints of Victorian aesthetics mapped onto the politics of American memory, mapped in turn onto a desire to test and mold the shape of poetry as Melville had once tested and molded the shape of fictional prose in his earlier career. And yet, despite the complexity of intentions and forms, a lack of visceral involvement is the impression that many readers could take away from *Battle-Pieces*. That impression would be only partially justified, however, since Melville is not averse to risk-taking, or to rendering uncomfortable or unexplored emotions in verse form and pushing at the limits of concept, style, and register. Two poems in particular exemplify this effort: one looks forward to the literature of modern political trauma and the effects of violence and maltreatment; the other looks back to an ideology of vital nationhood that might, in Melville's vision, survive even modern internecine warfare.

One text that seems to reach for a deeper resonance than it ultimately achieves is "In the Prison Pen (1864)," a six-stanza poem describing the slow death of a prisoner of war, presumably (but not certainly) a Union soldier held by the Confederacy. The poem reflects the situation that obtained in the Confederate prison camp at Andersonville in Georgia, a site of starvation and disease that cost the lives of over twelve thousand Union soldiers. Henry Wirz, the commandant of Andersonville, was the only Confederate officer to be executed on the order of a military court after the war ended. The possibility of a kind of death-in-life, of life as a death-in-waiting, becomes the dominating motif of "In the Prison Pen (1864)."

> Listless he eyes the palisades
>   And sentries in the glare;
> 'Tis barren as a pelican-beach –
>   But his world is ended there.
>
> Nothing to do; and vacant hands
>   Bring on the idiot-pain;
> He tries to think – to recollect,
>   But the blur is on his brain.   (*B-P*, 118)

Although mistreatment of prisoners has not been unknown in history, these images, to a twenty-first-century reader, speak to a recognizable and disturbing modernity. The iconography of the poem contains all the markers of a later experience, as we have come to know it. The emaciated and mentally devastated prisoner in the hands of a regime that does not care about the condition or fate of those under its control is projected easily onto the map of modern ideological conflicts and large-scale, militarized political systems.

Unusually for *Battle-Pieces*, "In the Prison-Pen (1864)" permits no middle ground to emerge between the memory of suffering and the fact of the poetry. Nation, military organization, home, thought, feeling: all have shrunk down to a dull mechanism of animal survival. The prisoners have become "ghosts enduring their exile from the world of the living."[25] In a foreshadowing of a genre that one might call "concentration camp minimalism," my term for a kind of literature struggling with images of the political pathologies of the twentieth century – thinking of, for example, Paul Celan or Alexander Solzhenitsyn – Melville sketches out what a future poetry of human degradation and destruction might look like. That he does this within the tradition of plainsong, in a poem of simple quatrains echoing the so-called common measure of English devotional hymns, carries its own implications. They include the problem of both individual and collective memory in a situation in which the social and spiritual contexts for remembrance waste away with the body, and the remains are buried in mass graves. In this text, the experiment of *Battle-Pieces and Aspects of the War* may well have reached its outermost perimeter, a place where the poetic tradition, as it was available to Hermann Melville in 1865 and 1866, could offer as yet no techniques for formulating a response to the organized violence of modernity. Neither "In the Prison Pen (1864)" nor *Battle-Pieces* could go any further.[26]

The questions raised by the longer poem "A Meditation" are somewhat different. The position that particular text occupies as the final poem in the collection generates its own assumptions regarding significance and structural symmetry. Inevitably, attention is drawn to concluding passages, poems, and dramatic scenes because they may offer a clue about an author's own attitudes to the larger text for which a particular passage or poem is the capstone. I use the term symmetry deliberately, because Melville makes the argument in the prose essay entitled "Supplement" at the end of *Battle-Pieces* that, had he been "fastidiously anxious for the symmetry of this book, it would close with the notes" (*B-P*, 259). That concluding essay, the piece that actually closes *Battle-Pieces and Aspects of the War*, asserts the desirability of both sides in the late conflict putting the hatreds of the war years behind them, and Melville's cautious and, at moments, almost tentative tone stands in curious juxtaposition to the historical scale of the themes of nation, violence, race, and reconciliation that the "Supplement" addresses. A sense of unease is a shadowy presence in this text, and the author appears to be less than convinced that the "terrible historic tragedy" that America has suffered, with its accompanying Aristotelian lessons of "terror and pity," has really penetrated the national conscience deeply enough (*B-P*, 272). Indeed, one might as easily say Northern conscience, since the South is, to some degree, relieved of the responsibility for moral and political wisdom by virtue of its status as the defeated party. If that is indeed true, then Melville's fastidious anxiety appears to be just as concerned not to have the policy implications of his poetry misunderstood as it might have been to secure the appropriate "symmetry" for the book. But a writer coming back onstage, Prospero-like, to warn the reader about how his own words might be read out of context is, although an odd one, not necessarily a dishonorable measure to take, after all: that the poetry of war should not be translated into the policy of a postwar settlement might be one reasonable interpretation of the message delivered by the last pages of *Battle-Pieces*.

To strike the final poetic note in *Battle-Pieces*, however, is the responsibility of "A Meditation." The beginning of this poem invokes a legendary moment of civil war in which each side suddenly, at one moment or another, recognizes the fraternal face of the other, and soldiers are overcome by "something of a strange remorse / Rebelled against the sanctioned sin of blood" (*B-P*, 241). The poem circles around the spiritual and intellectual reasons for war, including the slavery question that ultimately broke the Union. In one memorably bitter couplet, the unavoidable recognition that slavery had been the driver of secession is twisted inside-out to look as if it had been entirely the doing of blacks themselves: "Can Africa pay back this blood / Spilt on Potomac's shore?" (*B-P*, 242). Lincoln's remark during the Second Inaugural Address about the blood drawn by the lash being compensated by that drawn by the sword is subverted here to emphasize the trauma of an apparently unstoppable flow of white men's blood in a deadly exchange of wounding and killing. Unlike Lincoln, Melville suggests that the price paid for removing race-slavery may have been too high. In his choice of motifs, Melville seems to want the hostilities of the Civil War in their totality to be reversed in order to reveal the common origins and loyalties of the Union and Confederate forces. The senior commanders were once classmates at West Point, for example, and older veterans on both sides had occasionally come together to talk about the Mexican War, fifteen or sixteen years earlier.

The final two stanzas deserve some attention:

> A darker side there is; but doubt
>   In Nature's charity hovers there:
> If men for new agreement yearn,
>   Then old upbraiding best forbear:
> *"The South's the sinner!"* Well, so let it be;
> But shall the North sin worse, and stand the Pharisee?

> O, now that brave men yield the sword,
>   Mine be the manful soldier-view;
> By how much more they boldly warred,
>   By so much more is mercy due:
> When Vicksburg fell, and the moody files marched out,
> Silent the victors stood, scorning to raise a shout. (*B-P*, 243)

The movement of the poem's conclusion foreshadows, with remarkable closeness, the argument of the prose "Supplement" that follows it. The tendency to ascribe a global moral flaw to the South in its entirety is criticized on both ethical and practical grounds. The courage of the Confederate soldier and an implied racial brotherhood transcending even years of fraternal killing are advanced as the primary justification for treating the South with much circumspection and generosity. Indeed, both poem and "Supplement" represent on Melville's part, as Carolyn Karcher has noted, "a lapse into a racial consciousness that he had exposed as dangerously delusive in *Moby-Dick* and *The Confidence-Man*."[27] The generosity that, fifteen years earlier, gave *Moby-Dick* its vision of a potential interracial democracy is no longer an option, it would seem. To the extent that it is an openly political text, therefore, a poem about the shape and rhetoric of national policy with regard to the defeated Confederacy, "A Meditation" ends on a note of willed self-doubt and reticence, a posture that is approved precisely to the degree that it could, or should, become the official policy of the United States. "A Meditation" might, with some justification, be called Melville's poetry of policy.[28]

The action of the Federal troops at Vicksburg on July 4, 1863, is transformed by Melville into an iconic model for reconstructing the fraternal affections that previously underpinned the American Union. As the ranks of defeated and disarmed Confederate forces were marching away from the town, no exultation or cheering was heard. The silence of the Union soldiers was a gesture of empathy and courtesy toward the despondent and bitter emotions of the Southerners. The use of the word "moody" to describe the Confederate soldiers is a curious choice, however. It carries notes of immaturity and fickleness, and perhaps a tendency toward resentment. The historical irony is that the North, and later the reconstituted United States, came to be rather wary of Southern moodiness. Characterized by often disturbing surges of feeling, the South would face down all threats to its racial and social order for the succeeding century. And the Union soldiers' "scorn" to display any of the usual signs of victory, within the ironic perspective of later history, was ultimately repaid by the contempt directed at the entire Northern war effort by the cultural campaign of the Lost Cause, emphasizing as it did the accidental and contingent, rather than absolute, character of the war's ending.[29] So Melville's vision in "A Meditation," although aimed at avoiding a poisonous continuation of hostilities, and concerned to evoke the proper symmetry of policy, would be in many respects eclipsed by the somewhat asymmetric relationships – of cultural memory, representational power, and sectional reconciliation – that emerged over the decades between 1865 and the early twentieth century.

In its move from war to loss to speculative aftermath, Melville's *Battle-Pieces and Aspects of the War* reveals an understanding that the memory of the war will likely be as distorted and misdirected as the proximate politics of the conflict themselves. The "strange remorse" that the soldiers in "A Meditation" feel at their accidental, anonymous meeting is not only, as might be expected, the natural reaction of two fellow-citizens on opposite sides in an armed civil conflict, something on the lines of, "How did we let it come to this?" It is also a remorse that, counterintuitively, afflicts the victorious side in that very conflict. If this volume is, in its totality, Melville's project of finding an appropriate measure to commemorate the tragic dimensions of the nation's recent experience, then that measure, although embodied in some remarkable poems, may fall short of the most complex task it faces: that is, understanding the contingent position its own politics put it in.[30] Because it cannot, as it were, think outside its own structure, *Battle-Pieces* is unable to fully articulate the peculiar dynamic that, throughout the conflict and afterward, stirred the deep ambivalence of the Northern public mind toward the war, the enemy, and the justification for such an expenditure of blood. The poetry is both relentless in its dour objectivity and, paradoxically, uncertain if not irrationally nervous at moments when it needs to confront the significance of slavery as the one central and irredeemable cause of the Civil War, and of Emancipation as the war's most demanding legacy. One might read Melville's gesture of racial loyalty with respect to the defeated Confederacy in *Battle-Pieces* as foreshadowing that weakness that led to the Northern memory of the war becoming increasingly foreign to itself, and its commemorative politics becoming more tentative over time.

In contrast, the South's readiness to doggedly use the memorial imperative – that which says you will remember and you will remain loyal – would underpin a broadly successful cultural struggle to take control of the psychic territory of post–Civil War America. And Herman Melville saw clearly, however divided he himself was in his responses to the conflict, that the relationship between the past and future of the United States would inevitably be defined by the deeper movements of culture and identity rather than by moral self-examination. In the course of time, the language of memory and memorial would reveal itself to have a significant capacity to shepherd a nation's cultural narrative in one particular direction: that of North–South reconciliation at the cost of inclusive or progressive racial politics. And over that direction, little remorse would be shown.

3

The Road from Memorial Hall

MEMORY AND CULTURE
IN *The Bostonians*

> Irony is no laughing matter. It can have incredibly long-lasting effects.
> *Friedrich Schlegel, 1800*

> Den I wish I was in Dixie,
> Hooray! Hooray!
> In Dixie Land I'll took my stand
> To lib and die in Dixie
> *Daniel Decatur Emmett, 1859*

HENRY JAMES's first substantial artistic engagement with matters of nation, division, and memory – and his last until the "Richmond" chapter of *The American Scene* in 1907 – appeared almost twenty years after the end of the Civil War.[1] Later still is his reference to James Russell Lowell's Harvard Commemoration Ode – a text that James returned to read many times during his life – in the moving and elegiac passage in *Notes of a Son and Brother*, composed almost fifty years after the war ended.[2] James never reviewed Lowell's poem at the time of its public unveiling, with the unfortunate loss that we have nothing to compare with, or contrast to, James's 1865 review of Whitman's *Drum-Taps*, with its caustic dismissal of the collection as "monstrous because it pretends to persuade the soul while it slights the intellect," and its final comment that the nation did not suffer through years of war "to put up with spurious poetry afterwards."[3] Perhaps with an echo of his dismissal of Whitman in his mind, James's 1886 novel *The Bostonians* does not seek to persuade the soul and goes to work on the trope of national reconciliation with tools of irony and distance rather than pathos. The novel could be read as an extended comment on a largely successful rewriting of national memory, over the intervening twenty years, that took on the victory of the Union and the achievement of Emancipation and slowly overpowered them with a seductive tale of Southern resistance and tragic destiny – and as a sketch of the more ominous implications of the convergence of inspirational rhetoric with the resources of modernity. James Russell Lowell's struggle to construct a functional poetic of American national memory and sacrifice that recognizes and negotiates the insecurity of language is also, however, mirrored in James's novel: at a defining moment in *The Bostonians*, James makes Harvard University's Memorial Hall, near the site of Lowell's 1865 performance, the setting for a dialogue on war, commemoration, and history, with the complicating factor that the characters' exchange is also about sexual attraction and the limits of trust.

This dialogue and others are performed in *The Bostonians* in different subjective contexts and languages – those of polite social intercourse, divergent Union and Confederate historical rhetoric, memorial inscriptions, feminist political reform, and sexual diplomacy – all held within the unpredictable perspective of the narrator. But context and language are not only subjective, in the sense of expressing an individual or community locus of perception and identity. They are also vehicles of an ironic recognition of that subjectivity. Whereas Lowell in the Harvard Commemoration Ode is dueling with the problem of Romantic irony within a poetry of the redeemed American nation and Melville is exploring the outer limits of the Union sensibility in verse, Henry James is investigating whether ostensibly unique interpersonal relationships must inevitably fall back into the collective national memory they seek to escape, or whether they can negotiate that challenge. The protagonists of such relationships will have to accept the relativization of their own subjectivity, as Gary Handwerk has suggested in his study of the ethical dimension of irony: "Irony is above all a certain way of dealing with the problem of the subject in language and its apparent communicative isolation. The confrontation of private and public perspectives was already evident in the opposition of Socrates . . . to the Sophists and recurs whenever irony comes to be treated in a philosophical and not merely rhetorical fashion. For irony is necessarily an intersubjective act of confrontation with and mediation through another subject."[4] The question of intersubjectivity is, as critics have observed, important for the form and substance of James's novel, whether it involves, for example, the mutual escalation of intellectual and personal animosity between Basil Ransom and Olive Chancellor or the flow of rhetorical moves on the part of the nameless narrator as he mediates ceaselessly between fiction and reader. The concept of intersubjectivity is not restricted to a dialogue between two people, or even the interactions of a small group of people. It can also be the intersubjectivity of a community of interest or even a national polity, if its members are engaging in some kind of communicative activity. In Handwerk's approach, irony becomes something like a recognition that (a) the position of the subject is open to (b) radical relativization through (c) the presence of the interlocutor's perception of (d) the subject's expression. *The Bostonians* is a fiction in which that complex of perception and relativization occurs in both private and public, or sexual and civic, contexts and often where the meshing of private and public domains generates its own ironic penumbra, as during the exchange in Memorial Hall.

Some thirty years before William Faulkner's doomed Quentin Compson, in a more dramatic moment, screams, "I don't hate the South. I don't!" out the window of his student quarters at the hostile New England winter, Basil Ransom, the exiled and unmarried Mississippian protagonist of *The Bostonians*, has called on the young, histrionically gifted Verena Tarrant at her parents' house, with a somewhat covert personal agenda. Verena, intrigued by Basil and his unannounced arrival on her doorstep, suggests taking a stroll in the neighborhood; the couple wander through the streets of Cambridge, eventually ending up at Harvard's new Memorial Hall. That building, under construction during the late 1860s and most of the 1870s, was intended to provide a permanent commemorative structure for the Harvard men who had been killed serving with the Union forces during the Civil War. The exact period during which *The Bostonians* is set is never established precisely, but the evidence suggests a two-year period, approximately, very close to 1877, when Memorial Hall was completed.

Verena Tarrant is the only child of self-absorbed parents who, together, represent a heady combination of elements of the mid-century

Boston political fringe – Abolitionism on her mother's side, mesmerism and an early flirtation with a communitarian sexual economy on her father's. She is beginning to make a name for herself with eloquent and moving public orations on women's rights and the state of relations between the sexes. Ransom first observes her at a suffrage campaign soirée to which he has been brought, with a certain malicious intent, by his cousin Olive Chancellor, a women's rights activist,. Olive comes to develop an emotional, political, and – probably – sexual interest in Verena and suspects Ransom of "intentions" regarding the younger woman. (Realizing the situation, Basil wants Verena to keep their meeting in Cambridge confidential.) Verena herself, somewhat to Olive's distaste, is generally at ease among men and is able at least to engage in cheerful banter with them, and regards Ransom's knotty mix of Southern conservative rhetoric and anachronistic behavior as both peculiar and amusing. He represents a more interesting social challenge that that offered, for example, by the Harvard students who pretend solemnly to a serious interest in the female suffrage question.

Their afternoon excursion becomes a narrative component of some importance in *The Bostonians*. The significance of this scene is later echoed and intensified at the moment of Olive Chancellor's tragic recognition, toward the end of the novel, of the central role played by that visit in the collapse of her relationship with Verena. The confrontation with Harvard, the "great University of Massachusetts" as the narrator's hyperbole has it, is an interaction with a place that provokes a sudden moment of self-doubt or at least personal regret in Basil Ransom, and his response is thrown into sharper light by the subsequent confrontation with the Civil War memorial itself. Throughout these passages the dialogue between Ransom and Verena Tarrant is tense with a certain kind of political, although not personally acrimonious, thrust and parry:

> The rectangular structures of old red brick especially gratified his eye; the afternoon sun was yellow on their homely faces; their windows showed a peep of flower-pots and bright-coloured curtains; they wore an expression of scholastic quietude, and exhaled for the young Mississippian a tradition, an antiquity. "This is the place where I ought to have been," he said to his charming guide. "I should have had a good time if I had been able to study here."

"Yes; I presume you feel yourself drawn to any place where ancient prejudices are garnered up," she answered, not without arch-
ness. "I know by the stand you take about our cause that you share
the superstitions of the old bookmen. You ought to have been at
one of those really mediaeval universities that we saw on the other
side, at Oxford, or Göttingen, or Padua. You would have been in
perfect sympathy with their spirit."[5]

Basil Ransom's seemingly guileless remark may be nothing more than an
oblique admission that the great majority of Southern colleges had less
than impressive educational qualifications and that their degrees were
not to be taken seriously as certificates from institutions of higher learning, at least when compared with Harvard.[6] It is not clear what kind of
education Ransom has enjoyed but he does have ideas ("ill-starred
views," as the narrator characterizes them), of which the reader gets occasional glimpses over the course of the novel. These appear to be less
conservative than provocatively reactionary. The name of Thomas Car-
lyle is mentioned, by the narrator rather than by Ransom himself, as a
model to be admired, but there are various other notes to be heard in *The
Bostonians*, including Edmund Burke and perhaps also a certain ethnic
stoicism popular among postwar Southern intellectuals and constructed
around tropes drawn from Old English heroic literature.[7] Whether
Ransom suspects that his intellectual and authorial ambitions might
have taken on a different shape – and perhaps even a better chance of
realization – as a result of a Harvard education is not clear, but the tone
of his remarks suggests a moment of recognition that a valuable experience has been lost to him, perhaps even some alternative life-path closed
off. This psychological movement, however, no matter how substantial a
rupture it might represent in the fabric of Ransom's own ideas and personality, is immediately identified and exposed by Verena as still fitting
in perfectly with the objectionable ideological assumptions he always
carries with him.

Her response is to bring Harvard down to size, rather at Ransom's ex-
pense, suggesting that neither he nor the university would be anything
other than comfortable with each other's narrow and obscurantist view
of the potential of the female sex. In the gendered diplomacy of Verena
Tarrant's negotiations with Basil Ransom, his meditation on the college

experience he never had as a result of secession and war becomes a gesture trapped at the level of individual idiosyncrasy with an exotic regional flavor. Ransom's Harvard represents the desire for the recovery of
a lost, presecession America rather than, say, for the intellectual and
moral legacy invoked by James Russell Lowell's sacralization of the
Union dead. Verena's reaction is not aimed only at Basil, however:
against the background of male sexual and political intransigence, as the
intuitively feminist Verena sees it, the Civil War recedes into proper perspective as one more example of the malaise of human society dominated
by the "ancient prejudices." Neither Ransom's nostalgia nor, one imagines, Lowell's nationalist aesthetic would have much to say to her.

Verena's side-thrust at "the superstitions of the old bookmen" summons up the medieval scholasticism of the European universities she
mentions in her next sentence – presumably stations on her recent trav-
els in Europe with Olive – and puts Harvard into a direct line of descent
from these institutions.[8] Her judgment, reproducing at a distance the
unmistakable tones of Olive Chancellor's mentorship, translates several
hundred years of volatile European intellectual and social history into an
unchanging ritual of masculine phobia and politico-religious mystification. Confronted with a Basil Ransom, however, Verena's feeling that
there is something like a conspiratorial tradition of paternalism and arrogant dismissal of women's desires for equal social recognition and professional opportunity is more than understandable.

As the scene progresses the pair eventually arrive at Memorial Hall at
the end of their walk. Verena comments that it is a place to which it
would be "indelicate" to take a Mississippian, but Ransom is aware of
the meaning of the building and prepared to deal with "the worst that he
should have to suffer there." Verena is unsure of Ransom's, and perhaps
her own, response to the site. She remarks in a warning tone that Ransom may not like what he finds inside.

> "It says they were brave, I suppose."
> "Yes, it says so in Latin."
> "Well, so they were – I know something about that," Basil Ran-
> som said. "I must be brave enough to face them – it isn't the first
> time." And they went up the low steps and passed into the tall
> doors . . . [to] a chamber high, dim, and severe, consecrated to the

sons of the university who fell in the long Civil War . . . they lin-
gered longest in the presence of the white, ranged tablets, each of
which, in its proud, sad clearness, is inscribed with the name of a
student-soldier. The effect of the place is singularly noble and
solemn, and it is impossible to feel it without a lifting of the heart.
It stands there for duty and honour, it speaks of sacrifice and example, seems a kind of temple to youth, manhood, generosity. Most of
them were young, all were in their prime, and all of them had
fallen; this simple idea hovers before the visitor and makes him
read with tenderness each name and place – names often without
other history, and forgotten Southern battles. For Ransom these
things were not a challenge or a taunt; they touched him with respect, with the sentiment of beauty . . . [and] he forgot, now, the
whole question of sides and parties; the simple emotion of the old
fighting-time came back to him, and the monument around him
seemed an embodiment of that memory. (245-46)

There are a number of intriguing strands of expression in this passage,
including several phrases that echo, at a distance, notes heard in the
broader narrative of *The Bostonians*.

The first is the exchange about bravery. As is always possible with gen-
tler forms of sarcasm, it is not certain that Verena is making a barbed
comment about ideological implications of Latin inscriptions or about
her ability to understand Latin and her assumption that Ransom would
suspect her of not being so qualified or that she regards memorials to
male heroism as being, in general, as obscure with regard to their use to
humanity as any classical language. But however her tonal inflection
might be read, Ransom responds with a colloquial phrase ("so they
were") designed to deflect or defuse any potential awkwardness or tension on Verena's part. His subsequent remark, "It isn't the first time"
suggests both a reminder to her of the reality of his war experience and
an equanimity, a lack of embarrassment, in the face of the commemorative dynamic that Memorial Hall and its secular shrine represents. Ransom realizes that what he has to expect is an engagement with an
architecture of mourning. A commemorative architecture is one designed to provoke and, if possible, control its audience's emotional response in order to legitimize or strengthen the ideology for which the

object to be memorialized, either as an individual or collective entity, stands. Memorial Hall is the later embodiment, as an act of institutional and physical memorialization, of the ideological energies present at the commemoration ceremony at which James Russell Lowell first read his Commemoration Ode, thirteen years earlier.[9]

Somewhat in the role of a cultured travel writer concerned to underline the significance of a particular building, and communicate the value of a pilgrimage to the place, the narrator describes the feeling of solemnity in Memorial Hall, the odd "lifting of the heart" inspired by thoughts of "youth, manhood, generosity." He sketches in a map of social origin. The names without "other history," presumably those soldiers whose families had failed to achieve any particular recognition, suggest a broad and, within the constraints of that period in American history, diverse social landscape from which the student-soldiers were drawn. The visitor – and by implication the reader – should understand, the narrator insists, that this is not a commemorative edifice for a small group belonging to an elite military class who inherited their status (as, for example, the officer class of European monarchies did) but a memorial to democratic citizen-soldiers who volunteered to exchange modest social privilege for danger and sacrifice in a legitimate cause.[10]

A peculiar note, however, is struck by the phrase "forgotten Southern battles." It is not clear from the passage why, or in what way, these battles are "forgotten." The locations were inscribed on the tablet to commemorate the place at which the individual soldier died and thus are remembered within the narrative of each memorial element along with the biographical details. They are also, the reader might assume, remembered by Basil Ransom, at the very least in the sense that he would have a geographic knowledge of the South that would enable him to grasp the information on the tablets. They cannot be forgotten by Verena Tarrant, because she is in no position to remember them. The narrator's tendency to lyrical hyperbole might be getting the better of him here, but this segment of the passage is suggestive: the place names have already, a little more than a dozen years after the end of the conflict, taken on the character of a forlorn appeal to memory as if the memorial tablets have not only to secure the meaning of the individual death they record but also to prevent – and that only with immense difficulty – the location of that death from becoming victim to collective amnesia. Indeed, the correct designation might be "grimly remembered Southern battles," because the commemorative vehicle – Memorial Hall and its tablets – represent an attempt to hold the place names in a configuration of permanent relationship to the Union fatalities that occurred there, to occupy the place, in a sense, with the memory of the dead soldier.

Transported back to his own youth as a Confederate, however, Ransom is able to respond generously to the "embodiment of that memory," as the passage has it. But Verena Tarrant is not in that position, and the reader is brought to respect her feelings also: she recognizes the peaceful ambience of Memorial Hall but refuses the logic of a commemorative architecture that justifies war and death by means of the solemnity and elegiac closure of the commemorative act. Verena Tarrant represents the resistance against the ideological process of stabilizing what was in the form of what ultimately had to be. As a feminist, she regards that particular teleological fallacy as a fraudulent mystification trying desperately to cover up the irrationality of the public, historical sphere as defined by men. Her assertion that women would "reason so well" that "they would usher in the reign of peace" (246) as she puts it, is designed to subvert the commemorative ideology behind the construction of Memorial Hall: Verena Tarrant is the voice that challenges, quietly but without apology, the trope of national redemption through individual sacrifice that James Russell Lowell forms within the expressive movement of his Harvard Commemoration Ode. She remains seated as Ransom moves through the room to examine more closely the inscriptions on the various tablets. Seated, but not hostile. She permits Ransom, in a civil fashion, to leave her and spend some time exploring whatever subjective feelings, memories, and sense of value the memorials arouse in him.[11]

As Elizabeth Young has remarked in her study of women's writing from the Civil War period, the meaning of the term *civil* takes interesting implications when the sphere of domestic life and the norms of civilized feminine behavior are included in a sociology of the war. We become aware of the changes that the war wrought in individuals, social milieus, and psychological sensitivities.[12] The pretense that the incivility of the belligerents remained sealed in some guarded area far from home and did not threaten the basic fabric of social life and the relations between the sexes is, as Young argues, clearly exposed by the history of a significant embracing, on the part of many women, of the potential to subvert concepts of *civil* and *uncivil* in various ways:

> In a nation turned upside down, uncivil behavior, such as laughter or anger, might find full expression, whether illicit or authorized. For white Southern women, for example, the aggressive adoption of a new nation, the Confederate States of America, could legitimate the assertive refusal of civility's norms. Conversely, for women writers denied access to the terms of civility, a civil war might be as much a battle for civility as a flight from it . . . [and] "civil wars" might center on the liberatory movement from coerced servility to chosen civility.[13]

Verena Tarrant's handling of Basil Ransom during their walk is civil in every way, but her challenge to his intellectual assumptions is distinctly not servile. Her ability to subject his conservative attitudes to an interrogative irony while remaining positively engaged with him on the level of personal conviviality would suggest that she has, at least, little time for pointless displays of hostility on the basis of gender alone. Civility is the mortar of her relationship with Ransom, at least up until the point in the narrative when they part in Central Park at the end of their afternoon together in New York City. There is one region, however, where Verena cannot accompany Basil, and that is memory. She cannot guarantee him any stability of the self in relation to the shifting landscape of that phenomenon. Indeed, the stability of the self in relation to memory is not only an individual problem but also a site of a struggle over national culture, the interpretation of recent history, and the possible but nonguaranteed futures open to individual lives. The emotional tense in which this novel is written might be called the future imperfect, a modality in which a confrontation with memory is required to establish the coherence of the present and the potential of what may yet come.

The Memorial Hall passage in *The Bostonians*, I am arguing, is central in two respects. First, it appears at the temporal and spatial axis of the narrative – the moment, approximately halfway through the novel's timeline, when the Boston–New York–Boston movement gives way to the New York–Cape Cod–Boston arc. Second, it links a crucial remark by the narrator about Olive Chancellor's family history – the loss of her brothers, killed in the war – at the beginning of the novel with a paranoid

thought by Olive herself much later in the narrative, as she reflects bitterly on the consequences of Basil and Verena together at Memorial Hall.
The walk to Memorial Hall is, in many senses, a journey to the intersection of memory and injury, of self and community. It is also a journey that
Olive Chancellor could have made with Basil Ransom, in the way of a recuperative exploration.

On the face of things, Ransom would appear to be the principal character in *The Bostonians* on whom the burden of memory has come to rest.
He has seen action in the Civil War, and he is a Southerner who speaks in
honest terms of his homeland and "its social peculiarities, the ruin
wrought by the war, the dilapidated gentry, the queer types of superan-
nuated fire-eaters, ragged and unreconciled, all the pathos and all the
comedy of it" (214) but also one who feels a "passionate tenderness" for
the South and despises the cheap and entertaining anecdote, preferring
to "leave her alone with her wounds and memories" (75). The feminization of the region reflects both the tradition of nationalist iconography
that seeks, from Columbia to Cathleen ní Houlihan, to represent the
nation with an image of female quasi-divinity and Ransom's own desire
to recover and stabilize this construction of gender relations on empiri-
cal and symbolic levels. Olive Chancellor, in contrast, is the very embodiment of the aggressive demystification of such ideological fluff, and on
that basis the conflict between her and Basil is preprogrammed, so to
speak, merely awaiting an appropriate – and early – moment to emerge.
Many readings of the novel focus on the raw emotional undercurrents of
Basil Ransom's and Olive Chancellor's dysfunctional interactions, however, while underestimating the importance of the dysfunctional relationship between Olive Chancellor and her own dark areas of memory.[14]
The origins of Olive's invitation to her cousin Basil to visit her in Boston,
as the narrator reveals them, are obscured by a certain semi-conscious or
unconscious ambivalence. As the narrative would have it, Olive's motives arise from her feeling that her mother, now deceased, would have
wished some attempt to be made to reconnect the Northern Chancellor
and Southern Ransom branches of the family after the war. This intuition is complicated by her own drive to "look out for duties, to appeal to
her conscience for tasks" (42). Her conscience is, in turn, directed by the
memory of her two dead brothers, both killed in action serving with the

Union army. It is a memory of loss that is also a sense of another kind of loss, of frustration, that she herself has not been given the opportunity to make an ultimate sacrifice in a worthy cause, "that she might be a martyr and die for something" (43). Oddly enough, her need for self-sacrifice appears to be oriented toward her imagining of the Ransom family's experience of the defeat of the Confederacy, rather than the memory of her brothers who died in the national conflict "within her own vivid remembrance" (43). Furthermore, Olive Chancellor's personality wants to invite danger, to provoke disagreement and contention, and the narrator suggests that Olive realizes that her cousin will be a productive source of ideological friction: "That he should agree she did not in the least expect of him; how could a Mississippian agree?" (44).

The mention of her two deceased brothers ("her only ones," as the narrative parenthetically and pathetically informs us) occurs only once in the narrative of *The Bostonians*. At no subsequent point in the novel is any plot development, indirect discourse, or dialogic exchange reconnected to this particular element of family history in Olive Chancellor's interior meditations or social interactions, as they unfold. Nonetheless, it would be a mistake, I would argue, to assume that that brief aside within the flow of narration is either an unimportant contribution to character "biography" or even the stranded intimation of an alternate plot line, an undigested trace of the novel's origin as a magazine serial.[15] Rather, the brothers are the place in Olive's past where the story of the nation – in many ways the story of *The Bostonians* – is ruptured and becomes two: an irrecoverable unity followed by a caesura, a break reflected in the narrative contours of this novel, where the action seems to be a satirical reversal of the recent history of the United States. This paradigm of historical reversal – a mirror image of the course of the Civil War – suggests a difficult future without even agreement on the meaning of the past. Indeed, it is not only the meaning of the war that is subject to highly subjective pressures: Olive finds neither the history of the Tarrant family nor that of their particular milieu an acceptable past.[16] She idealizes Verena as a kind of miracle child, untouched by her environment.

The same strange refusal of the past occurs when Olive crosses swords with Basil Ransom during his campaign to occupy a stretch of territory in her virtual backyard, the mental country of rational progress, with the purpose of disturbing its community of assumptions and its teleological fables. Ransom's advantage is that he is largely aware of and in tune with his personal history, a point that Olive Chancellor cannot reach, as indeed she cannot reach the point of recognizing honestly her own desire for Verena, or admit to herself that she conspired to marry her shallow and irritating sister Adeline Luna off to her available Mississippi cousin.[17] For his part, he refuses to recognize the significance of slavery for the destruction of the South but remembers his family and his youth. Olive is more awkwardly placed: she can think deeply and passionately about the cause of women but continually tries to evade her own past. She is cauterized emotionally, cut off from the memory of her brothers as men that she has loved, and her silence causes the narrator to intervene to inform us of their fate. Her ambivalence about the motives for her invitation to Ransom causes her to become the victim of Basil's ironic refusal to be drawn into the kind of open ideological struggle that suits her personality. The conflict between the two cousins, whatever its real motivation, is fought successfully by Ransom on the level of coherent emotional investment, a context in which he deploys his forces with more assurance than his opponent can muster.[18]

Richard Terdiman in *Present Past*, his study of the psychic implications of modernity, discusses the way in which the phenomenon that he terms the "memory crisis" of the nineteenth century involves two separate but mutually influential developments: a spatial social mobility and expansion in productive energies that destroy the place/memory nexus, and a rise in the power of the nation-state alongside the strengthening of the ideology of bourgeois citizenship that, together, redefine the significance of history and memory.[19] The decades after 1865 saw a range of powerful upheavals across the United States that brought deep changes to economy and polity, and *The Bostonians* sets out to explore one such paradigm of crisis and change. Basil Ransom is not only an internal immigrant from the South (and his journey may be an early form of "white-flight" from Reconstruction rather than from the immediacy of defeat – the war has been over for at least nine or ten years before he migrates north), but he also poses, by his actions on the ideological and actual territory of New England reformism, a question in the direction of Olive Chancellor. That is, to what extent does her memory of the significance of her family's sacrifices in the Civil War enable her to understand the cultural legacy of national division and the political struggles to which she has devoted her life? To put it another way: if the excavation of historical fact leads to reproduction and – as the psychic analogue to a mnemonic act – the recovery of memory to interpretation, as Terdiman suggests in *Present Past*, then the question is whether Olive's consciousness of her brothers' deaths is merely the reproduction of that initial knowledge or a memory that can open the way to self-awareness and deeper understanding.

Ransom would appear to be at an analogous intersection of the potentialities of memory and historical recovery but responds with a kind of prickly quiescence. He is given neither to sentimental recollection nor to historical analysis of the conflict in which he has taken part. He does not idealize his past or by implication the secession of the Confederate states; nor does he participate, however, in any public repudiation of the political values that led to the disaster. In this he reflects a peculiarity of the consequences of the political transformations of the nineteenth century, in particular the effects of the Enlightenment on the fabric of social and cultural relations and languages. In the slipstream of major social and political transformations there can be found a "subterranean obstinacy of belief," as Terdiman expresses it, a force in the psyche that retains, or projects, the social values and restrictions of the past into a present in which they have already been, in terms of legal and social reality, eradicated. This obstinacy of belief represents not a turning away from the unreliability of individual memory toward an understanding of social forces and their processes of interaction but rather a hypnotic subordination to "a past we never chose [that] dominates the present that seems the only place given us to live."[20] One can easily sketch the polar extremes that Basil Ransom and Olive Chancellor might represent: the one obsessed with an irrecoverable past in which gender roles and sexual assumptions were unquestioned, and the other cut off from any past other than the one created by her current feminist beliefs projected backward into history. Indeed, the narrative dynamic of James's novel could be seen as an attempt to fight back against precisely that tendency to degenerate into caricature. *The Bostonians* explores, one could say, the potential for a kind of ethical irony – a distancing of the self and its capacities for intellection from the blind assumption of the ontological legitimacy of one's perceptions and desires – that, in an ideal world, would bring Basil Ransom to the realization that he needs to focus on understanding the inevitable clash of political interests over the question of slavery to explain his present situation, and Olive Chancellor to the recognition that she needs to open herself to her memories of her deceased brothers in such a way as to let them flow into her relations with Ransom, the nearest familial connection, as far as we know, to the context in which they died.

But Basil Ransom and Olive Chancellor, we should note, are not the only characters in *The Bostonians* concerned with problems of history and memory. The portrait of Miss Birdseye, in particular, is that of a woman who embodies a colorful autobiography of political involvement, as a former activist who traveled the antebellum South bringing Christian teaching and abolitionist vision to the African American slaves and also attempted to come between the Irish immigrants in the Boston slums and their alcoholic indulgence. The energetic commitments of her earlier life are contrasted with the soft, unworldly idealism to which she has declined in the Boston of the 1870s, although one imagines the two not being unconnected. The importance of Miss Birdseye can, perhaps, be measured by the fact she has an unstable dramatic presence in the text, promoted from object of pity to object of respect, possibly a result of the magazine serial origins of *The Bostonians*, in the sense that James's idea of the role assigned to that character in the narrative structure of the novel appears to have changed. The narrator's approach to describing Miss Birdseye shifts from one of patronizing hostility to respect and affection.[21] When we first meet Miss Birdseye, as Basil and Olive arrive at the elderly woman's house for the evening's activities, the narrator takes pains to introduce her to the reader as someone "whose charity began at home and ended nowhere, whose credulity kept pace with it, and who knew less about her fellow-creatures . . . after fifty years of humanitarian zeal, than on the day she had gone into the field to testify against the iniquity of most arrangements" (55).

This tone becomes less patronizing by far when the Mississippian and Miss Birdseye travel through the city on the streetcar together and vanishes entirely at the scene in Cape Cod when the old lady is dying. Indeed, the narrator appears to have been convinced by his accounts of his protagonist Ransom's experience of Miss Birdseye that he has been a little too quick to judge her at the earlier stage of events. The narrator – who is generally unpredictable in his readiness to intervene between the story and the reader – does not admit openly to any particular change of heart, but the death of Miss Birdseye is not played for satirical effect. Although she misreads the relationship between Verena and Basil – thinking that Verena has converted him to a feminist position – her impression is not the result of a complete ignorance. Rather, her enduring optimism sees a kind of national reconciliation in the two younger people, their friendship or love affair taking place under a rational New England sky, full of generosity and mutual respect. This optimistic view may not be quite as false as critics have tended to see it.

Ransom, despite himself, is affected by Miss Birdseye's death: "The impression of the simplicity and humility of her end remained with him, and he reflected more than once, during the days that followed, that the absence of pomp and circumstance which had marked her career marked also the consecration of her memory. She had been almost celebrated . . . and yet the only persons, apparently to whom her death made a real difference were three young women in a small 'frame-house' on Cape Cod" (389). Ransom identifies, perhaps, a certain stoicism in Miss Birdseye's history that unexpectedly matches his own attitude to events and fate. Although he dissembles to an almost embarrassing degree with the old woman, encouraging her misunderstanding of how he feels about the feminist performative campaigning that Verena is engaging in, nevertheless he does not regard her as stupid or gullible but rather sees her as someone whose idealism is of an earlier, more attractive variety than his cousin Olive's, more innocent and without defensiveness or paranoia.

Indeed, the urge to idealize from which Olive suffers renders her unable to see the real quality of social interactions and in particular drives her to identify conspiracy where she might have, more accurately, observed contingency.[22] The visit by Basil and Verena to Memorial Hall is retrospectively endowed with significance at a crucial moment much later in the narrative, as Olive recognizes with tragic clarity the threat that Ransom embodies for her world. She transforms the incident into a conspiratorial action of the most malign kind. After Verena has finally revealed most of the story, having kept it secret for a long time, Olive's tendency to paranoia takes charge: "The one grain of comfort that Olive extracted from the terrors that pressed upon her was that now she knew the worst; she knew it since Verena had told her, after so long and so ominous a reticence, of the detestable episode at Cambridge. That seemed to her the worst, because it had been thunder in a clear sky . . . [and] it imposed itself upon Olive that that occasion was the key of all that had happened since, that he had then obtained an irremediable hold upon her" (372). Olive's belief that she has discovered the "key" to the cycle of events is symptomatic. Certainly, Ransom's intention was to meet Verena at the Tarrant's house and introduce himself to her more fully. However, the excursion to Harvard was Verena Tarrant's suggestion (she had a friend there who worked in the library, among other things), and her conversation with Basil was marked, as we saw, by a distinct clash of attitudes. Unless we as readers decide that Verena is such a weak and malleable personality that she cannot be anything except a kind of feeble victim to Ransom's imperial masculinity – the position taken by Olive herself at one point, interestingly enough – then we must see the exchange in Cambridge as proceeding along a track dictated by a complex interaction of personalities. Ransom's reaction to the commemorative plaques and inscriptions in Memorial Hall is as unpredictable as Verena Tarrant's series of responses to the sudden visit of a Southerner who shows little likelihood of being brought over to the side of Boston feminism by force of argument. The drama of this scene in the novel results from, I would argue, the interpenetration of two intelligences that do not move in harmony but nonetheless show a willingness to engage each other.[23]

The engagement – using the term in awareness of its military as well as its socio-sexual meaning – takes place in and around Memorial Hall, however, a fact that has some curious implications. In an odd way, Verena could even be seen as standing in for Olive in this exchange. The names of Olive's two brothers might well be included among the names of those killed in action. As the sons of a prestigious Boston family they would, in the normal course of events, have gone to Harvard. It might have been a delicate project had James written Olive Chancellor a scene in which she visits the memorial herself and undergoes the sudden resurfacing of the memory of personal bereavement. But he did not do so. Instead, he chose to interweave the romance plot with the institutional act of Harvard's honoring of its dead students and teachers and to leave the memory of loss to the narrator's commentary. Basil Ransom and Verena Tarrant begin to search out and respond to each other not in some domestic environment or occasion of entertainment but inside the walls of a commemorative architecture erected to secure the memory of sacrifice in war. The Mississippi veteran and the Boston political mystic meet in the shadows of a building whose purpose is to give history the emotional force of personal memory, and to invoke the nation as the justification for loss. In this section of *The Bostonians*, Ransom seems to be testing where the parameters of the nation are drawn, for his own fate as for Verena's, against the background of Memorial Hall. He is not quite sure where his confrontation with the invocatory power of Memorial Hall will leave him, and Verena Tarrant senses this uncertainty in his state of mind.

Olive Chancellor is not completely wrong in her later convictions of conspiracy, because there is a strong element of design in Ransom's visit to the Tarrant house in Monadnoc Place. The occasional military tonalities that enter *The Bostonians* have given support to readings that see the novel as a satirical reversal of the Union forces' occupation of the defeated Confederacy, a kind of Reconstruction in a distorting mirror. Erecting a counternarrative to the feminization of the South – an act of retribution for the South's aggressively contemptuous attitude to the nonslave states during the political controversies of the 1850s – the novel offers a desexualized, intellectual Boston unable to resist the virile energies of the roving Confederate veteran.[24] The merging of sexual and martial tropes in James's novel, however, draws on a specific popular tradition arising from an incident during the Civil War.

As Ulysses S. Grant relates in his *Memoirs*, he replied on February 16, 1862, to General Buckner at Fort Donelson, in Tennessee, who was attempting to draw out as long as possible the inevitable capitulation of the Confederate garrison to Union forces. Buckner had sent Grant a communication proposing that delegated officers from the opposing commanders should meet and negotiate details of the surrender. Grant dismissed the suggestion and sent a curt message to his opposite number, demanding unconditional surrender and concluding with the famous line: "I propose to move immediately upon your works."[25] The subsequent victory at Donelson, coming at a lean time for the federal government, made Grant a household name while at the same time, unexpectedly, the final sentence in the letter to Buckner entered the popular imagination. There, various double entendres of "moving upon your works" were embraced with enthusiasm.[26] Lovers wrote it to one another, indulging in the pleasure of a racy comment that, even when it was used in a sexually suggestive sense, had the imprimatur of a mordant turn of wit by a successful military commander who had brought home a celebrated Union victory. Furthermore, the notion that the recipient of the remark was, in its original context, the Confederate garrison commander lent a force to Grant's message that – echoing back from its later appropriation by the popular culture – ascribed a kind of feminine passivity or receptivity to the Confederate side. The South was being feminized, and thus in the gender matrix of mid-nineteenth-century America socially humiliated, in a maneuver that seemed to reverse the politico-sexual paradigm of the 1850s.[27]

Basil Ransom, either consciously or unconsciously, appears to be on a mission to turn the rudder around once more. Early on in the narrative, Basil's move to New York is described as "making advances" (44) long before any interaction with Verena takes place. The comment belongs to the passage recounting Olive's thoughts as she considers whether she will invite him to Boston. It is not quite clear whether it is Olive or the narrator who imputes the character of a military maneuver to the journey north. It becomes an overdetermined, slightly ominous metaphor, but there is no reason to assume it is not being said with a sense of irony. Equally, Ransom's journey to the North is an ironic comment on the likelihood that any move from the paralysis of Mississippi to a hand-to-mouth law practice in New York City will be anything other than one more proof of the victory of the political, industrial, and administrative machinery of the Union. In the postwar United States, the choice for the former Confederacy is either to embrace the dominating social and economic structure of industrial capitalism or to suffer the continually increasing economic and cultural disconnect between the South and the rest of the country. Ransom's own migration suggests his ambivalence about where he stands on the available options.

In any event, Ransom has already abandoned his Southern home and does not appear to have any plans to return. Interestingly, there is no suggestion in James's novel that his protagonist is even aware that an event of major significance for the South – the final capitulation of Radical Reconstruction after the resolution of the Hayes–Tilden presidential impasse of 1877 – has taken place.[28] It can be a legitimate critical gesture to assume that the absence of an element of the historical background to a fiction is in fact an excluded presence that demands attention, but one should be cautious when applying it to *The Bostonians*. It is not only that James, as one might expect, is less interested in rendering a realism that draws its strength from the details of social history than in the mapping of a psychological conflict arising out of the merging of political conviction with deep-seated personality structures. It is also that the characters contain certain unresolved elements that do not cohere neatly to the benefit of any standard historical interpretation of the 1870s. There would be bitter feelings for Olive Chancellor in the sudden end of Reconstruction, certainly: her idealist conceptions of political virtue and the memory of her fallen brothers would coalesce to make it an obvious political defeat, but her feminism would dismiss its relevance with grim certainty. Likewise, if Ransom embodies an uncompromising but well-spoken refusal of Reconstruction politics, then he does so in the guise of a déclassé, transplanted intellectual who finds something attractively unproblematic in his bachelor lifestyle in Manhattan, complete with comfortable beer cellars and a casual acquaintanceship with ladies from the entertainment business. Indeed, New York's beer cellars might well have offered, as well as refreshment and company, a sympathetic environment for the expression of political opposition to the racial equality implications of Radical Reconstruction and a general dislike of the Republican Party.[29] There is something indolent about Basil Ransom, and something much more aggressively focused in Olive Chancellor. But within the context of the sexual narrative of the novel, no simple parallels should be drawn, I would argue, between the protagonists' roles in the dance of seduction and evasion on one side and the assignment (or assumption) of gender characteristics in the struggle over states' rights, slavery and abolition, and the meaning of the Union on the other. Indeed, precisely such an assignment of meanings opens the question of politics as culture, or politics displaced by culture.

As Alan Trachtenberg argues in his discussion of the "politics of culture" in postbellum America, gender became a key element of campaign polemic:

> Reformers and genteel intellectuals who stood above party battles invited the scorn of the regulars . . . couched frequently in images fusing anger at feminizing culture with sexual innuendo, the manly braggadocio of the stalwart: "political hermaphrodite,"

"miss-Nancys," "man-milliners." . . . In the images of both sides, reform above parties and loyalty within parties, the issue seemed to join culture versus politics, the realm of the feminine against the realm of the aggressively masculine. But this apparent bifurcation by sex and culture only obscured the more significant underlying development: high culture – the culture of the intellectual world – becoming more political in its motives, and politics more cultural in its methods and consequences.[30]

Basil Ransom is far from being a reformer or even genteel, in the sense in which Trachtenberg is using the terms, but he is definitely involved with the increasingly fraught interweaving of cultural energy and political motivation in Boston and New York (and across the country), and to a similar degree to Olive and Verena. Trachtenberg's point, that the apparently unbridgeable chasm between a male-dominated world of political power-broking and no-holds-barred electoral campaigning, on one hand, and a female milieu of moral education, domestic warmth, and culture, on the other, was illusory, suggests that all the principal characters in the narrative are invested in the deployment of cultural resources for their different purposes: Olive and her network of movement soirées, fundraisers, and solidarity events, Verena with her talent for hypnotic feminist prophesy, and Ransom in his intellectual journalism – with which he is begins to have some success. To put it baldly, if culture is feminine, then Ransom's creative energies fall under that rubric too.[31]

The Bostonians is thus, among other things, a novel about the inevitability of culture and the destiny of culture as the primary, all-enveloping language of political expression and social conflict. Whether the term *culture* is used in its normative or descriptive meaning is not of great importance. Both the institutions of culture (Harvard, for example, or the Boston reform movements) and the cultures that individuals give expression to (Ransom's formal chivalry; Miss Birdseye's Panglossian optimism) are deployed for specific objectives that mirror larger social developments. The novel enacts the process in which, politicized in a way that had not been seen before, national, sectional, and other groups work not only to achieve reforms or fight reforms, envision the future or invoke the authority of some particular tradition but also to control the psychic landscape within which these struggles are perceived

and judged. Where before the Civil War it was primarily Northern Abolitionists and Southern political representatives, for example, who fought
in the ideological trenches of the slavery debate, after 1865 popular attitudes, values, and moods were considerably more important across the
board. After the war – itself a kind of brutal universalizing of the implications of that debate – political ideas had to speak to the interests of, or at
least command the attention of, a more diverse polity than the republic
had seen before, including immigrant communities in the expanding
ghettos of the large cities, and the definition and management of the
boundaries of acceptable ideology (what people were to be allowed to
think) became objectives in themselves.[32] The increasing power of the
advertising industry, for example, caused the cultural products of its aesthetic transformation of desire and social identity to assume the weight
of ideas and convictions validated by knowledge or experience. In an
analogous movement, politics became more participatory in its theory
and emotional appeal but much less so in its existing forms. Again, Alan
Trachtenberg expresses it succinctly: "To say that the parties were sites
of cultural, rather than genuinely political, behavior is not to say that
they were politically feeble or irrelevant, but that their politics lay in displacing economic and social issues by appealing to cultural issues, in fos-
tering among voters an imaginary sense of participation and control,
while at once denying them the substance of politics."[33]

In an echo of the intellectual and social experiments of the 1840s, a
corrupt mainstream politics is opposed by a politics of reformist idealism
in the Gilded Age. The original text of that idealism had, however, gone
under the wheels of the massive scale and implacable violence of the Civil
War. What we are left with are Miss Birdseye and, more pointedly, an un-
trustworthy reminder of the least impressive characteristics of antebellum Boston activism in the person of Verena's father, Selah Tarrant. Or
rather, Tarrant's fuzzy, self-deluding ideas and unctuous salesman manner (which provoke such contempt on the part of Olive Chancellor) have
been reborn in the inspirational feminism of his daughter's performances. Her character and thinking are much more attractive than her father's, but they share with his the primary characteristic that they
embody a discourse whose governing principle can be expressed as follows: the more hypnotic the speaker, the more legitimate the political
message. In *The Bostonians* America has entered the era of psychic

politics, and none of the protagonists is untouched by it. Against this background, Miss Birdseye is almost a spirit from the Enlightenment – a courteous, feminine Thomas Paine.

The concept of a politics of the psyche or a "postrational" politics has been applied to the age of mass popular movements built around extreme, even paranoid, theories of ethnic exclusiveness and national destiny. This approach guides Carl Schorske's authoritative study of the interplay of culture, identity, and emotion in Vienna, the capital of the Austro-Hungarian empire, at the end of the nineteenth century.[34] My argument here is that the phenomena that Schorske describes are not limited, historically, to the last decades of the Habsburg dynasty or indeed geographically to Central Europe. What the concept of psychic politics suggests in terms of American social and cultural history, however, involves a different distribution of energies across a different social landscape. Nevertheless, the European model is illuminating in many respects. It reflects, for example, the odd parallel development to be observed in the United States between, on one side, the rise in reform politics and its public expression from the 1840s on, and, on the other, the interest in – and implications of – psychic abilities, mesmerism, and heightened states of consciousness. The belief in the significance of the irrational – or at least the legitimacy of phenomena not obviously explicable by scientific procedure – becomes a cross-thread within the broader fabric of a politics of rational reform. Indeed, the parallels between "the turn to the depths of psychology and to aesthetics," to use Michael Roth's formulation, in various strands of ethnic nationalism in Central Europe during the last quarter of the nineteenth century and a somewhat earlier, thoroughly American, manifestation of dissatisfaction and frustration with rational exchange and analytic debate, flanked by petit bourgeois class resentments and ethnic paranoia, might be more significant than often realized.[35]

The attitude expressed by Verena Tarrant with regard to her own talent for political oratory is complex. At one point in the narrative she tells Olive Chancellor that Matthias Pardon, the newspaperman, has promised her that he can guarantee positive effects in the real world from good publicity, orchestrated by him: "Producing a pressure that shall be irresistible. Causing certain laws to be repealed by Congress and by the State

legislatures, and others to be enacted" (159). The sober inventory of constitutional objectives stands in almost satirical contrast to the dynamic of
her dramatic performances, and the suggestion in this scene is that Verena expresses, and Olive understands, these objectives in a mutual spirit
of irony, both women having transcended the unimaginative level of seeing modifications to the legal and constitutional system of the United
States as a door to women's freedom. (Verena's attitude could also, however, be more of a companionable echo of the sarcasm that, she senses
correctly, will be Olive's reaction to Pardon's vision of the way the world
works than an expression of Verena's real feelings about constitutional
reform.) But Verena's spirit in public performance is something else
again. The language of "moving," the sense of an experience in which
the listeners imbibe the spirit of the monologue, rather than hearing the
arguments presented in the lecture, is the dominant motif in the descriptions of Verena's poetic delivery. Her talks begin "incoherently, almost
inaudibly, as if she were talking in a dream" (83). She is described as having the capacity to affect people, to move them – the familiar terminology of the revivalist meeting. The view of Ransom and a number of other
guests, seeing and hearing Verena for the first time at Miss Birdseye's
evening gathering, is that she is a kind of child seer, the otherwise innocent conduit through which something other than herself is transmitted.
The difference between Ransom and the others is that Ransom is deeply
hostile to the content of her "harangue" as the narrator describes it
twice within one paragraph (86-87).

The conclusion of Verena's presentation seems to be milder and more
circumspect than the term "harangue" would warrant. It is full of qualifying subordinate clauses and asserts its vision in a tone that is, if not
apologetic, then certainly diplomatic. Nonetheless, the outline of its
rhetorical posture is clear: the argument to experience and political theory is only of limited qualification, while the argument to vision is superior (or at least of equivalent status). As Verena says, she is a "simple
American girl" with little knowledge of the world and its demands. That,
however, is not the whole story: "But there are some things I feel – it
seems to me as if I had been born to feel them; they are in my ears in the
stillness of the night and before my eyes in the visions of the darkness"
(86). The republican constitutionalism and individual professional integrity represented by, respectively, Mrs. Farrinder and Doctor Prance

are being put on notice by this phraseology. Neither of the women has been overimpressed by the visions from the darkness that Verena advances as her source of knowledge and motivation, but, equally, anyone who believes in the power of these visions is likely to feel, as manifested in Olive Chancellor's attitude toward Doctor Prance, that those who do not so believe are simply closed-minded, egoistic, and in the end hostile. The politics that are built on visions seen on the edge of sleep are those that inspired the Austrian poet Hugo von Hofmannsthal to identify, in a memorable formulation quoted by Schorske, a new use of language – in many ways exhibiting a clear analogy with a new kind of poetry – aimed at the awakening and deployment of mass emotions and desires that were hermetically sealed against the rational and liberal virtues of the bourgeois nineteenth century: "Politik ist Magie. Welcher die Mächte aufzurufen weiss, dem gehorchen sie."[36] [In a slightly amended translation from Schorske's: "Politics is magic. The one who knows how to summon the powers from the deep will be the one whom they obey."] Whether Verena Tarrant's performative talent is being exercised in the service of righting a social wrong (campaigning for votes for women, for example) is not at issue here: rather, the arc of her development as a practitioner of inspirational feminist preaching departs from the minutiae of political campaigning and the formation of effective coalitions to appeal to sacrificial desires and instinctive loyalties buried in the subconscious of the audience. And the audience grows as the narrative progresses, until a large public auditorium is filled to capacity with an excited, impatient crowd hungry for drama and emotional release.

The final scenes of the novel, in the Music Hall, have been the subject of a number of critical readings of *The Bostonians* concerned with the relationship between the public and the private environments, and with the convergence of political passion and mass entertainment.[37] The New England cultivation of the power of the secular public lecture had its apotheosis in the lyceum circuit that, after the 1870s, had been bypassed by the more ambitious, nationally organized Chautauqua movement. The lyceum itself had begun to decline in importance after the end of the war, partly because of public agencies' taking on many of the educational and archival roles that the body had originally occupied itself with. Somewhere between the worthy programs of the Chautauqua summer schools, seminars, and cultural projects (William James regarded them as an enervating "middle-class paradise," as Trachtenberg comments)[38] and the rise of modern mass entertainment in the large cities, there was a space to be filled. The exponential growth in the communication and transport networks after the Civil War, as well as the expansion of a literate but not necessarily broadly educated middle class, had created an audience that was, on one hand, eager for knowledge and expansion of horizons and, on the other, largely removed by time and demography from the combination of moral idealism and intellectual seriousness represented by, for example, Ralph Waldo Emerson, George Ripley, Theodore Parker, and the Unitarian rebels of the 1830s and 1840s. What James suggests at the conclusion of the novel is, I would argue, that the "Boston" lecture, once a delicate equation balancing intellectual curiosity, moral appeal, and scholarly knowledge, has become primarily a mass-cultural experience, a hypnotic flow of tension and release, assertion and submission, in which the emotional drama of the performance dominates.[39] Verena's appearance is now a commodification of personal vision for public consumption and a subordinate element in the broader reality of hard-nosed competition among the national print media – personified by Matthias Pardon. She has become an experience, enmeshed in her own capacity for playing an audience's sensibilities back to it as an aesthetic product.

It is not only Verena's relationship with the audience that takes on a certain negative atmosphere, however, but also the physical surroundings in which she is about to make her major debut. The immense Music Hall impresses Basil Ransom with its ominous grandeur, suggesting images of high culture and obscure revolutionary violence. Ransom finds himself entertaining thoughts of being a lone assassin: "There were two or three moments during which he felt as he could imagine a young man to feel who . . . has made up his mind, for reasons of his own, to discharge a pistol at a king or president" (414). Ransom's reverie involves, interestingly, the phrase "for reasons of his own." The privacy of motivation, as James recognizes, is the last and most effective weapon in the hand of the assassin. If an act of violence has political consequences but does not emerge from any other political idea than a nihilistic vision untranslatable for any purposes of rational negotiation, the established authorities suffer an additional blow in that they are deprived of the one thing they require to provide an explanation for the act. John Wilkes

Booth's assassination of President Lincoln is, in contrast, perfectly explicable on every level and could even be seen as an act of guerilla warfare similar to the operations of the irregular units on both sides of the
Civil War. Despite the obvious parallel between Booth and Ransom as
Southerners, this past event does not embody the action that resonates
in Ransom's mind in the theater. Rather, his image of the young man
who "had made up his mind" is, I think, a displaced threat aimed at
Olive Chancellor. Ransom believes that the event itself is putting Verena in danger, or is at the very least exposing her physically before a
sensation-hungry crowd. He perceives emanating from the audience
something of "the ferocity that lurks in a disappointed mob" (416). As he
observes the Music Hall filling up with the audience before the performance, Ransom finds himself playing with the notion of an act of inexplicable violence being directed at a head of state. Ransom's thoughts
appear to be less a glance backward to the homegrown assassination of
Abraham Lincoln in Ford's Theater than a prescient gaze forward to the
more exotic anarchist murder of President McKinley by the young Leon
Czolgosz at the turn of the century. In line with the politics of the psyche
that, as I argue, leave nobody untouched, Ransom finds himself quite
easily sliding from his romance-plot intentions into imagining the possibility of a violent and definitive gesture in which a young man alters the
future of the world in a momentary blur of uncompromising action.[40]

In the final moments of *The Bostonians*, however, Ransom simply
walks out the door with Verena, with no obvious threat of physical injury
on any side, although the brutal impact of psychological and emotional
defeat on Olive is rendered with an icy clarity. It is as if she has been psychically assassinated by Ransom, a man who had "reasons of his own." At
the climax of the narrative, it becomes somehow unimportant whether
Ransom has in reality sought to harm Olive Chancellor, or not: his campaign has been successful and has left Olive with the task of facing those
forces to whom she was going to "sell" Verena and her inspirational tal-
ents.[41] Although Olive's resilient self-control is in many ways still intact,
it is clear that she is afraid of the audience to which she will now have to
announce the cancellation of the evening's program, even if her fear has
more to do with public humiliation than mob violence.

The question of the audience remains largely unanswered. The narrator feels it necessary to tell the reader, perhaps somewhat too casually,

that Ransom is relieved to know that "even when exasperated, a Boston audience is not ungenerous" (433). Although the shifting of focus from the intellectual satire of Boston reformist drama to the romantic comedy of Basil and Verena's flight governs the final narrative turn of *The Bostonians*, it could be argued that the defusing of the implications of a mass gathering based on visionary politics and a powerful mise-en-scène happens a little too quickly. The narrative balance seems to be predicated on a less fraught and threatening experience than the one the protagonists have just undergone. The sudden retreat into the private manifested by Ransom's final securing of Verena seems too lightweight to counter the subterranean movements of aestheticized political theory that are, unmistakably, growing in importance. These last moments of the novel do offer, however, one interesting exchange that takes place as Basil and Verena exit the Music Hall together, hearing as they go the noise of the increasingly impatient audience. Ransom announces that they will leave for New York City and get married the following morning:

> "And what will the people do? Listen, listen!"
> "Your father is ceasing to interest them. They'll howl and thump, according to their nature."
> "Ah, their nature's fine!" Verena pleaded.
> "Dearest, that's one of the fallacies I shall have to woo you from. Hear them, the senseless brutes!" (430)

There is a complex and ironic clash of ideas in this passage. Verena is concerned that the basically humane instincts governing the individuals in the restless audience should not be obscured by their temporary collective insanity; Basil, however, intends to make it clear to Verena that their collective behavior is by no means an aberration provoked by the circumstances of the public event but a consequence of the absence of precisely that center of natural goodness that she believes in but Basil Ransom does not. This dueling between two opposed ideas, however, is not merely the reflection of a parallel clash of personality and attitude; it is a metonymic representation of two major controversies in American cultural and political history, both of which bear upon the narrative shape of James's novel.

The passage, in New England intellectual life, from the bleak predestinarianism of Puritan theology to the belief in human progress and the

sense of an innate, moral guiding light identified with the Unitarian revolution of the late eighteenth and early nineteenth century, as Barbara
Packer suggests in the *Cambridge History of American Literature*, not
only took much time – at least a century and a half – but also required a
long series of maneuvers involving challenge, resistance, and resolution
between sites of authority and the pressures of individual experience.[42]
Nor was it a complete revolution: there were a large number of faithful in
the traditional churches who would still, well into the middle of the nineteenth century and beyond, feel more at home with Jonathan Edwards's
Great Christian Doctrine of Original Sin Defended (1758) than they
would with William Ellery Channing's *Moral Argument against Calvin-
ism* (1820). To regard the social world as anything other than irretriev-
ably fallen from God's grace remained anathema for many. Nonetheless,
the strength of liberal Boston in particular grew consistently over the
century, and Verena's indulgence regarding the true "nature" of the audience is, if anything, a mainstream attitude in that local context. The
tones of an earlier, more doctrinaire New England ideology are more obvious in Olive Chancellor's rhetoric, in which the displaced energies of
Puritan striving reappear in the single-minded focus on political struggle, flanked by an uncompromising idealism, that marks her character.

The Southern states, in contrast, had little patience, and often much
contempt, for the rigor and exclusivity of the New England moral sensibility, particularly when it came to political interventions on the issue of
slavery. These states fought to resist and neutralize any political idea or
policy, from the shaky Missouri Compromise of 1820 to the savage constitutional and political skirmishes of the 1850s, that might have even a
slight effect on the right of states to maintain the economic system of
slavery. But, more significantly, the South fought to ridicule and delegit-
imate any assumption that the founding documents of the United States
give any purchase whatsoever to abolitionist principles. As one historian
comments:

> During the founding period, many good Americans could indulge
> themselves with the expectation that the progress of history, of it-
> self, would resolve the contradiction between the principles of the
> Declaration of Independence and the slavery compromises of the
> Constitution. But by the late 1820s and early 1830s, the necessity

forced itself onto the minds of Southern statesmen that they had to make a choice: Either the existence of slavery would have to be affirmed as something good and desirable (in which case the principle of equal natural rights would have to be rejected), or the nation would have to be formally rededicated to the principles of the Declaration (in which case slavery would need to be, in Lincoln's words of a later time, "put on a course of ultimate extinction"). Southern statesmen such as John C. Calhoun made their choice and began openly to repudiate the founding principles.[43]

It was a strange configuration: although without empathy with or cultural feeling for the influential strain of New England theological rigor that saw predestination as Calvin's gift to the Reformation, the South began to chip away at the natural rights theory of the Declaration of Independence with the same unbending hostility that Jonathan Edwards would no doubt have shown, had that embodiment of eighteenth-century Puritan intelligence lived to see the European Enlightenment's shadow on the window of the American Revolution. Ransom's promise to Verena Tarrant, that he will convince her eventually of the nonexistence of any human "nature" that can be assumed to be rational and good, is both a resurgence of the old antebellum South's campaign against those assumptions of American national principle whose implications it regarded as disastrous, and a somewhat comic reappearance, on an evening in Boston, of the hostility to any such assumptions that once characterized the original religious beliefs of New England. For a brief moment, James permits the more-or-less unreconstructed Southerner Ransom to use the oldest of Puritan theological principles against Verena, a woman so affectionately and yet hyperbolically described (with a weave of irony around every misinterpreted sign on the old woman's part) by Miss Birdseye earlier in the novel as "a daughter of New England" who will win over her recalcitrant lover and future husband to the progressive camp with a combination of graceful femininity and moral authority (358). But, in doing so, James also knows that his protagonist is acting perfectly within the actual script of American cultural history as a representative of Southern political theory. The new dimension that has opened up is that Basil appears to have every intention, ultimately, of bringing Verena around to his position. No other objective, indeed, occupied the South more intensely in 1878, and for many subsequent years.[44]

Ransom represents what might be called the counternarrative of Southern cultural memory. This counternarrative was, at the time *The Bostonians* is set, well on its way to becoming a prime example of mystical, postrational politics, which moves in a synergic relationship with the emotions and presuppositions that swim below the surface of established public discourse. The politics of the Lost Cause was the former Confederacy's contribution to this supranational phenomenon. There were, however, two distinct strains of advocacy under this broader rubric: the Inner Lost Cause and the Outer, or National, Lost Cause. Thomas Connelly and Barbara Bellows argue with regard to the origins and style of the first type:

> Any direction to which southerners could turn brought only entrapment in guilt and doubt. The puritan ethic had taught them the relationship between success and God's grace while basic southern piety stressed God's personal closeness and intervention in man's affairs. The new evangelism in effect preached that one's feeling of inner peace was the only evidence of salvation, while the increasing popularity of Darwinism and pragmatism extolled the survival-of-the-fittest institutions and the relationship between achievement and merit.
>
> Confused, and not a little angry, the postwar generation of southerners fought back with almost grotesque assertions of their moral superiority.[45]

The collision of a historical and ideological demoralization with passionately held tribal convictions is likely to produce a peculiar and indeed neurotic relationship to the social environment. This posture, however, was not universal, and the South also produced a subtler and more flexible approach to restoring its sectional autonomy: the postwar construction of the character of Robert E. Lee (foreshadowed in Herman Melville's poem "Lee in the Capitol," as I discuss in Chapter 2) for consumption outside the South in particular was a prime locus of this activity: "The new breed of southern writers found a skillful weapon in Social Darwinism. At once Lee was the epitome of romance and tragedy, as was the entire Confederacy. He remained the cavalier, bred in an idyllic society capable of producing superior men. Yet this same romantic environment that taught Lee the higher virtues of honor and duty became his undoing. Lee was ultimately "no less tragic than romantic, trapped in an environment of agrarian capitalism and slaves."[46] Like the cultural trope "Robert E. Lee," Basil Ransom cannot explain his past more effectively than as the natural response, on the basis of social concepts of loyalty and duty into which he had been born, to the tragic implications of secession as an inescapable moment of political crisis. He accepts the grim irony of his position and thereby embraces the minimalist and fatalistic conservatism of his comment to Verena: "We are born to suffer – and to bear it, like decent people" (237). And, in fact, to do that is to avail oneself of a more powerful narrative than the narrative of social reform and constitutional nationalism embodied in many Northern accounts of the war. Or, to change the emphasis somewhat, Ransom's alternative paradigm in *The Bostonians*, reflecting the South's increasing ability after the Civil War to dominate the national imaginary, offers a set of values described more accurately by gemeinschaft than gesellschaft.

Although Ferdinand Tönnies's terminology, "community" and "society," proposes a more rigid bipolar structure than cultural historians are comfortable with today, the two concepts are remarkably apposite for a discussion of the collective self-images of the former Confederate and Union sections of the nation, respectively, in the later nineteenth century and beyond. As Ernest Gellner formulates the issue:

> The cult of community and specificity receives enforcement from the entire Romantic tradition and its claim that the best, or even the only, truly human elements are to be found in the non-reasoning aspects of life. Reason is defied twice over: by the love of the *specific* rather than the *universal*, and of the *passionate* rather than the *calculating*. Love, or passion . . . is enlisted in the political arena: political confrontations are presented as the conflict of life with sterility, of vitality with disease, a disease which masquerades as reason and compassion.[47]

The import of Gellner's comment on the politics of reason and unreason for this study is that *The Bostonians* embodies a conflict between two kinds of American national sensibility: one sees a productive contingency in social relations, imagines all citizens as partaking in an experiment that could, if nurtured and steered, bring about (for example) a more open and fair distribution of power and influence between the sexes in the public as well as in the private sphere, while the other, a largely defensive but articulate Southern nationalism that is concerned with writing a narrative of tragic choice into American cultural memory, seeks to block any suggestion of reformable social institutions with an assertion of the incurable mendacities of human nature and the unpredictability of any and all consequences.

Basil Ransom's concept of community is, it should be said, more the ideal of the modern nuclear family than that of the social hierarchy of the plantation, and Olive Chancellor is clearly a woman as passionate in one context as she is calculating in the other. Nevertheless, the lines of battle in *The Bostonians* bear a noticeable similarity to those between social and political modernity and the resistant forces of local ideology and approved tradition. Edmund Burke's "little platoons," the visible and tangible weave of relationships with family and friends, are what Verena is being deprived of by her career as an inspirational lecturer, in Basil's view of things. He offers Verena, in a patronizingly jocular way, her own married household as a substitute arena: "My dear young woman, it will be easy; . . . the dining-table itself shall be our platform, and you shall mount on top of that" (379). Ransom imagines Verena as a victim of modernity: her heart belongs at home but is being hawked out in the anonymous streets of Boston by people who want to use her for purposes of social engineering. In contrast, however, to the more Central European experience sketched out in Gellner's vision of stubborn ethnic authenticity in a life-or-death struggle with silver-tongued cosmopolitan liberalism, the clash of cultures in James is an American one, and – as with Schorske's account of the rise of the political irrational discussed earlier – we must make some adjustments to the model in order to bring out its significance for the discussion of *The Bostonians*. But the model retains its potential. The life-or-death struggle between the Confederacy and the rest of the country had, in the eyes of many of its participants across the broadest spectrum of activity, precisely that quality of (for the South) a desperate fight for home, family, and local specifics against (for the North) the determination not to permit the violent dismantling of one of the two principal political achievements of the Enlightenment, the American Union. In particular, the idea of a battle over what constituted government and political identity and pitted, in Hugo von Hofmann-sthal's terms, the powers from the deep against the legacy of the Enlightenment, is closer to the reality of nineteenth-century America than is often admitted.

There is at the same time, however, a different configuration in James's novel. The irrational seems to be distributed more generously across the political landscape in the United States, and conversely the intellectual force of the Enlightenment is subject to many strange local pressures, from the social theory justifications for slavery in the South to the mystical idealism of Boston reformers, legacies for Basil and Olive, respectively. Moreover, the struggle manifest in *The Bostonians* may possibly be more shadowboxing than genuine. That is, the conflict between Basil Ransom's mordant conservatism and Olive Chancellor's revolutionary ambition is at least as much about who secures the fruits of modernity as it is about the legitimacy of modernity itself. Indeed, the effective pursuit by Southern writers of the National Lost Cause appears to be reflected elegantly in the characters and narrative arc of James's novel. As the South succeeded in using writing, and the weapon of narrative pathos, to enlist the reader's sympathies, as Paul H. Buck once put it, on the side of the Confederacy without that reader's realizing what was happening, so does Ransom succeed not only in winning the game but also in showing that culture is the open field on which successes can be achieved that might not be obvious even to those who have already secured the political victory.[48]

If the politicization of culture is a marker of modernity, then the effective use of cultural energies as a political weapon must partake of modernity, even if the ostensible purpose is to resist its encroachment. Just as psychic politics, as argued earlier, draws into its flow all who are engaged with it even if they perceive (or claim to perceive) it as merely a means to a specific end, the dialectic of modernity does not permit a cost-neutral use of its forces against itself. Modernity is not only an abstract historical period but also a particular map of social relations and a particular dynamic of political interaction. In any conflict, the posture one adopts becomes a figure not only of the combative attitude that one is expressing but also of the shape of the force against which one is directing that expression. As a responsive defense maps unavoidably the configuration of the attack it is seeking to block, Ransom's largely unspoken but uncompromising

skirmishing reflects and indeed mimics the enemy's assumption of superior morale, in the person of Olive Chancellor. The style and structure of
Ransom's campaign against modernity in the shape of the gender politics
of the Boston feminist avant-garde involve two elements: the infiltration
of an ironic narrative of Southern existentialism into a space occupied by
New England reformist dynamics, and the construction of a countermodernity that uses, cleverly enough, much of the cultural velocity of
modernity to establish its presence. Ransom's countermodernity comprises his essays, one of which is rejected by a journal with the comment
that his ideas appear to be about three centuries out of date and that
"doubtless some magazine of the sixteenth century would have been very
happy to print them" (198).

Ransom responds to the jibe by considering that perhaps he is ahead
of his proper time. Whether he is ahead or behind is never revealed in the
course of the narrative – nor is it in any way a testable hypothesis. What
is clear, however, is that Ransom's use of anachronism to draw attention
to a particular intellectual or textual intervention is ultimately successful. Although dismissed by the editor of the journal who found his article
unsuitable, Ransom begins to infiltrate his ideas through the world of
magazines with a kind of cocksure belief in their own maverick status,
and his contribution eventually finds a home. Once the article has been
accepted, of course, the resentful anachronism appears transformed into
the quality of originality: "The essay in question is the most important
thing I have done in the way of a literary attempt, and I determined to
give up the game or to persist, according as I should be able to bring it to
the light or not. The other day I got a letter from the editor of the *Rational Review*, telling me he should be very happy to print it, that he
thought it very remarkable, and that he should be glad to hear from me
again" (359). Ransom comments that the essay contains many of his fa-
vorite opinions – the ones he has expressed to Verena Tarrant. The use of
the word "literary" is interesting here: Ransom is presumably using it
in the broader, nineteenth-century sense of belles-lettres, to include
everything from autobiographical reminiscences to reviewing to essays
on scholarly or other themes. Nonetheless, at the earlier stage in the
novel when Ransom's attempts to get published are not achieving any
success, the narrative gives the distinct impression that he has been
writing something like undiluted political philosophy. It appears that the

identical text has now been accepted, suggesting that his willingness to revise and resubmit his work as a literary essay has borne fruit.

To find the appropriate form for the opinions one wishes to express is one thing; to find a form that appeals to an audience and to use that form to communicate opinions that secure agreement from an audience that is not sure what it is agreeing to is the achievement of the Southern writers of the late nineteenth century. Ransom, at the conclusion of *The Bostonians*, has won Verena and moved into the realm of magazine journalism and the public communication of the day. Part of his success with Verena is the certain fascination he exerts on her and Olive as a stoic, conservative Southerner and the playing of their different responses to his advances. Similarly, part of his newfound success in the literary world can be traced to the curiosity value of his "sixteenth-century" opinions. In an atmosphere of reform, somebody interrupting to shout that there can be no such thing because human beings themselves cannot be "reformed" is at least going to attract some attention.

Conservatism need be neither pious nor transparent, and there is no reason to believe that Basil Ransom would be any the less an ironic author than he is an interlocutor. To shout, "There cannot be reform!" will, as mentioned already, certainly attract attention: what is not certain is the motivation for the shout. Just as displaying anachronistic views during social intercourse in an insouciant manner can be both an expression of one's unpopular, or at least maverick, status and a satirical comment on the sensation value of that position, so, likewise, will the construction of an authorial personality contain both the elements of that personality and an ironic commentary on them. To apply this point more bluntly to Basil Ransom: you cannot profess a sixteenth-century weltanschauung if you are not in the sixteenth century. What you can do is turn intellectual history into cultural artifact and then market the thought and language of a past era, in the shape of a lovingly crafted archaism, to the taste and demands of the present. That is precisely what the reconciliationist writers of the National Lost Cause managed to do with astonishing success – and some of this process happened on the pages of the same journal in which *The Bostonians* first appeared.[49] For all their attempts to hold back the cultural implications of the modern, they used the most advanced networks of media publication and distribution in post-Civil War America with intelligence and confidence. Nothing reveals Basil

Ransom's ironic modernity so clearly and poignantly as the successful appearance, in a journal called the *Rational Review*, of his "sixteenth-century" ideas.

I conclude this chapter with a brief discussion of the comic, or farcical, elements of *The Bostonians* and, in connection with these, the spectrum of ironic possibility suggested by the novel's ending. These two topics have implications for any reading of *The Bostonians*, and the question of the confidence to be placed in the narrator's final remarks is complicated by the degree of closure to be attributed to the ending. The trope of reconciliation is pervasive (after all, James uses the intersectional marriage motif unapologetically), but it has the potential to suggest radically different conclusions. One conclusion I call history *repeated as farce* and the other *radical uncertainty*. The closure of comedy, I would argue, is diametrically opposed to the uncertainties of irony, and James's novel, it appears, wants to encompass both these tropes. Gary Handwerk comments that "irony is nothing more than a question designed to draw another subject into discussion of who and where one is."[50] In *The Bostonians*, this question is posed by the interactions among the central characters, including Olive Chancellor, as they move through a set of confrontations that complicate and alter the relationship between their desires and reveal their different capacities to engage in the kind of ironic intersubjectivity that a changing social environment demands.

The dialogue between Basil and Verena in Memorial Hall, for example, is a complex play of formal gallantry, ironic conversational back-and-forth, and gentle sarcasm; its setting, however, is a place where the invocation of memory has been set in stone and glass as a collective, profoundly nonironic, gesture of commemorative duty. This juxtaposition is sharpened by the fact that Olive Chancellor, whose brothers both fell in the service of the Union, would be the most appropriate audience for Ransom's walk to face the former enemy within the architecture of their memorialization. Nevertheless, it is Verena, who presumably was a young child during the Civil War and appears to have no visible connection with any particular trauma or loss arising out of the conflict, who is able to understand and help those, like Basil Ransom, still negotiating the pressures of memory and history. In contrast, the tortured realization on the part of Olive that the walk to Memorial Hall ("that baleful day in

Cambridge") was the crucial embryonic moment in the relationship between Basil and Verena is a mixture of skewed recognition and blindness. It is the event that Verena wished to conceal from her, and she eventually finds out about it, but more than that it is the event at which Olive herself should have been a major participant. If Olive had been able to confront Ransom with the mourning of her brothers' sacrifice as both an irreplaceable loss and a parable of her own political consciousness and ideals, the novel seems to say, her sense of judgment might have remained in operation, her tendency to jealous paranoia held in check, and her readiness to see her position subject to ironic relativization (such as that shown by Doctor Prance) maintained. Had she admitted to herself, for example, that she wanted to invite Ransom to Boston for some more substantial reason than that, as she says evasively, her mother would have approved of the gesture, then perhaps the course of events, the road from Memorial Hall, would have turned out differently.

Olive Chancellor, to sum up, lacks the understanding of intersubjectivity and the capacity for irony that Verena manifests on key occasions. Far from being a lightweight personality and equipped only with the shakiest of intellectual weaponry, as Olive believes, Verena has a strong sense of her own as well as others' realities and an ability to articulate complex ideas in graspable images. Indeed, she might be the only individual who is not touched by the dangerous energies of the psychic politics of which she is such an effective transmitter. Where Ransom sees in the crowd a savage animal that is only waiting for the chance to break loose and go on the rampage, Matthias Pardon sees it as a part of the ever-growing audience for his ego and source of the profits of the corporation that employs him, Olive Chancellor sees it as a mass echo-chamber for the performance of feminist passion, but Verena sees it as a collection of human beings. Despite Ransom's patronizing response regarding the "nature" of the crowd in the auditorium and how he plans to educate Verena to the truth about such nature, Verena's comment retains a note of cheerful common sense and practical goodwill – and of intelligence too.

What I am saying is that it is by no means a foregone conclusion that Verena's marriage to Basil represents the final capitulation of New England reform traditions, feminism, and sharpened political consciousness to a reactionary fantasy of wifely subservience or a gothic reconstitution of the patriarchal structures of the antebellum South. The much-quoted last few lines of the novel, as Basil and Verena leave the theater and Ransom discovers, when they reach the street, that Verena is weeping, and in particular the narrator's rather distant and almost coy prediction that "with the union, so far from brilliant, into which she was about to enter, these [tears] were not the last she was destined to shed" (433) can be interpreted several ways.[51] This is the radical uncertainty: the passage can be read, as it often is, as a gloomy foreshadowing of an unhappy marriage that is to come; it can be read as a parable of the reintegration of the South into the nation; it can also be read, more modestly, as a comment on the likelihood of Verena's shedding more tears later. Since we cannot really be certain, I would argue, about the significance of the ones she is weeping outside the Music Hall, we have even fewer grounds to assert the meaning of any she may produce in the (potentially) long future of their marriage. She may well be crying with joy watching her daughter graduate from Barnard College; she may be overcome with emotion the first time she and Basil see the Grand Canyon; she may be weeping with despair when the news comes that Basil went down with the *Lusitania*. We cannot know, but as characters in fiction also live in the world of wider social relations reflected in that fiction, the reader may assume that they must be subject to the vicissitudes of that world, and the shifts in those relations. There is no reason, therefore, to believe that the final sentence in *The Bostonians* means anything other than what it says. And the ironic, almost arch, tone of the narrator becomes, at that moment, a signature tune played one last time, and fading.

That signature tune is important, however, to hold the line on the uncertainties of the text. The narrator's distance from both the reader and the characters in the novel, sometimes seen as a weakness, can also be regarded as a vote to reserve judgment. Although the door to the future is open, there is no guarantee of any particular quality to Basil Ransom's and Verena Tarrant's lives in that future, because the burden of history is not – or is only partially – removed from them. *The Bostonians* is, as I have been arguing, a novel of cultural memory: the recollection of war and loss; the politics of historical legitimacy; the need for commemoration. It is also a novel of sexual interaction. The introduction of gender into the discourse of national re-integration, or the "culture of conciliation," as Nina Silber has termed it, opens up the possibility of casting the politics of the post–Civil War and post-Reconstruction United States against the backdrop of a struggle between the social weight of the heterosexual union and the secret satisfactions of woman-centered friendships. It also permits the re-enactment of the movement from politics to culture, from the male-gendered language of political theory to the feminine one of narrative seductions.[52] But, as Homi Bhabha has remarked in a slightly different context, the nation as a narrative strategy embodies an ambivalent dynamic, and even if Ransom's "writing" is more seductive, and has more conviction, than Olive Chancellor's, he cannot secure its ontological boundaries indefinitely.[53] As the stories through which the nation understands its condition are not infinitely stable, neither is *The Bostonians* a text that offers a high level of narrative security. The road from Memorial Hall does not lead back to the memory of the prewar South, or into the pastel future of romantic comedy. With Verena, Basil Ransom will have to live with uncertainty, which is the plainest term for of the narrator's farewell message.

The South succeeded in controlling narration in the late nineteenth century, thus proving, casually and ahead of time, the truth of some late twentieth-century literary theory by using that advantage to manage the nation, or at least the inner workings of the national imaginary. But, as happens with many such victories, the asymmetry of historical forces translates the achievement into a different political form from the one expected. In this instance, the struggle against the aggressive modernity of the Union, in an ironic maneuver, has to deploy the tools of American cultural modernity to that end. The injured masculinity of the defeated Confederacy moves into the female-gendered world of writing to attempt to recapture its self-respect. The struggle for social reform shades into the politics of the postrational. The validity of memory and the power of commemoration are both contingent, potentially open to relativization by way of social exchange and emotional interaction.

The Bostonians knows these things and knows also that an ironic national reconciliation is to be preferred to a sentimental one. There are even moments in the novel when the reader might be convinced that the characters know it too. As Basil Ransom responds to Verena Tarrant during their walk to Memorial Hall, when she asks whether he has left the South and relocated to New York City for good: "Given it up – the poor, dear, desolate old South? Heaven forbid!"

He means, of course, yes.

4

Bierce and Transformation

However, other forces at play in the Civil War signalled something far more potent than combat's cost in lives: that the very nature of combat did not fit, and could not be made to fit, within the framework of soldier expectations. Forces of change and novelty made themselves felt less dramatically and drastically, but they slowly chipped away at soldiers' resolve, and their results were over time more dispiriting. Ultimately they led many to the realization that they could not fight the war they set out to fight. The engine of change was technological modification. An advance in weaponry overthrew the efficacy and then the moral meaning of the tactics soldiers wished to employ, robbing of significance the gestures they had been determined to make.

Gerald F. Linderman, 1987

Man's vestiges were nowhere to be found,
Save one brass mausoleum on a mound
(I knew it well) spared by the artist Time
To emphasize the desolation round.

Into the stagnant sea the sullen sun
Sank behind bars of crimson, one by one.
"Eternity's at hand!" I cried aloud.
"Eternity," the angel said, "is done."

Ambrose Bierce, "Finis Aeternitatis," 1892

THE FICTION WRITER who seemed to be haunted by the memory of the Civil War to a greater degree than any other of his generation was Ambrose Bierce. For Bierce, this condition was not a matter of a contaminated political legacy or the fear of a morally dysfunctional national imaginary such as that which overshadowed Melville's *Battle-Pieces*. Rather, it was rooted in something we have come to grasp, almost to be casually familiar with, in the twentieth and twenty-first centuries: the persistence of a traumatic memory of combat experience within the psyche of the individual veteran. The stories that Bierce began to publish in the late 1880s and that finally appeared in the collection *Tales of Soldiers and Civilians* in 1892 are unique in late nineteenth-century American writing. They speak of a painful excavation of items of consciousness from a quarter of a century earlier, and a merciless, almost nihilistic representation of contingency, violence, and unresolved conflicts of character and environment. These narratives stand as a crafted rebuke to the many sentimental accounts of the war that presented, directly or indirectly, a model in which a terrible national division had now been mutually transcended. That model of memory and commemoration was centered on reconciliation between "the Blue and the Grey" and gestured toward the intersectional celebrations of various anniversaries of the war in which both Union and Confederate veterans would take part, culminating in the fiftieth anniversary of the Battle of Gettysburg in 1913 – which was, coincidentally, the year Bierce disappeared and presumably died. Bierce's stories are almost completely free of any representation of the Civil War as a political struggle about ideas, no matter what such ideas were about or how they had changed or shifted. Partly for this reason, it often appears that the absence of politics in Bierce's fiction, rather than enabling a notion of reconciliation, renders it moot. His narratives have long since left the cozy exchange of veterans' stories behind and confront the insoluble difficulties of reconciling memory and time, history and experience. Furthermore, although Bierce's contribution to the new literary realism, a mode that would include fiction and reportage by Stephen Crane, Harold Frederic, William Dean Howells, and Richard Harding Davis, was unique in its detached objectivity and precision, his own status within the moving parts of American literary history has always been somewhat fragile. This state of affairs has more than one explanation, including the lack of a finished novel or even a novella, as well as the distracting effect of the patchwork quilt of war stories, stories of the supernatural, poetry, satire, and journalism that, together, make up his collected writings, but it does seem that a certain grudging acceptance of Bierce at the fringe of the canon, but no nearer, has been the modern academic consensus.[1] His influence and prestige may have been higher among fiction writers than among critics and may be more substantial outside the United States than at home.

For example, a few years ago, Robert von Hallberg published a series of interviews with writers and intellectuals from the former German Democratic Republic (GDR). Among the interviewees was the fiction writer Katja Lange-Müller, who in the course of her exchange with von Hallberg made the following comment: "As is the case with all great comedians, [Kafka's] material is very existential. But I'm quite certain that Kafka was not understood by many people in the GDR, because you don't joke about such things. Kleist was understood no better for what he is, because he was taken too seriously. Ambrose Bierce was also not understood. You're not allowed to think things like that."[2] Whatever about his currently assigned status in the American canon, Bierce finds himself in elevated company here at least. To be in a tradition, albeit the minority one of being misinterpreted in East Germany, that includes Kleist and Kafka suggests that there are contexts in which Bierce's work attracts significant attention and greater critical respect than it often has in American literary studies at home. It is also worth noting that Lange-Müller sees the lack of understanding as an important element of the literary history she is sketching out. To be the subject of misplaced or evasive critical judgments by professionals, too, is part of the grim comedy of the Kafkaesque and Biercean destiny. Lange-Müller's remark opens up a more important question, however, regarding Bierce's work. That question, reflecting the hierarchy of canonical reputation and its implications for engagement with a particular author's work, concerns the justification, in a world of limited time, for spending it on reading, critically exploring, or teaching Ambrose Bierce. Toward the end of this chapter, a brief comparison of the different evaluations of Bierce on one side and Stephen Crane on the other suggests some important things about how the cultural memory of the Civil War has been interwoven with the cultural history of American fiction-writing.

The operative critical consensus that Bierce's claim on our time – in all senses of the phrase – is limited, has a certain superficial credibility. A standard biographical reading of Bierce will begin by emphasizing that his fictional writing was informed by an understanding of war that he learned during his four years, both as an enlisted man and as an artillery officer, in the Union army between April 1861 and June 1864 (when he received a dangerous head wound at Kennesaw Mountain in Georgia). The account will proceed to note that Bierce's journalism was an extended polemic against the corporate barons of the Gilded Age culminating in the relentless campaign in 1896, under the banner of Hearst's *San Francisco Examiner*, against the railroad magnate Collis P. Huntington.[3] Little of Bierce's work would open a view onto the troubled intersection of language and psyche discoverable in Poe, for example.[4] Nor do Bierce's narrative snapshots of men under fire seem to resonate with the force and elegance that Crane – who, born in 1871, never experienced actual combat as a Civil War soldier – achieved in *The Red Badge of Courage*. And even in the more rarefied atmosphere of Lange-Müller's comparison, Bierce cannot match the deeper, more complex notes that emerge in Kafka's fiction, where social reality and acts of communication are transformed into something chaotic and, at times, malevolent, and where the intimidated consciousness of a new kind of victim-protagonist is brought into existence. Nonetheless, the recognition that Bierce's narratives have won – again, as noted, from fiction writers rather than literary scholars – suggests that the issue of time, particularly the justification of time devoted to reading him, is not as clearly beyond discussion as his subcanonical niche implies.[5] I raise this issue not only because a foreign response to Bierce can be intriguing and maybe illuminating in and of itself, or because the different graphs of his reputation inside and outside the United States imply their own, literary-historical ironies.[6] And the comments by Lange-Müller point to aspects of Bierce that were quietly overlooked by ideological readings of his work in that particular German context and even within the tradition of American critical responses to his work.

More precisely, I want to argue that Bierce explores the limits of narrative as a mode of expression (Bierce's narratives have something of a fable about them, but also something of a psychoanalytic hypothesis), and he is repeatedly confronted with the impossibility of reconciling the implications of traumatic events with either historical accounting or the claims of memory. The characters in the various narratives will not be reconciled with the destructive ironies they live through, or are crushed by, and some of the stories go further to challenge the notion that the act of narrative itself can be understood as a mode of reconciliation between the language of the expressible and the inarticulate traces of past experience. That is, neither a claim to establish historical truth nor the creative truth of subjective recollection can offer any guarantee that writing consists of anything other than frantic attempts to impose an order of significance on the passage of time – and time is, above all, the medium through which history and subjectivity slowly converge, as loose ends are trimmed and memory is trained to retain, or edit out, the appropriate data. Indeed, in a formulation that Bierce would have enjoyed immensely, Michel Foucault once observed that truth is "undoubtedly the sort of error that cannot be refuted because it was hardened into an unalterable form in the long baking process of history."[7]

Bierce's Civil War narratives have a distinct, and at times almost obsessional, concern with matters of time and error and are infused with a gothic logic that is an exploration not so much of the uncanny as of its unavoidable transformation after contact with American stoicism. In the story "Parker Adderson, Philosopher," for example, the eponymous protagonist is a Union spy who has been caught during the night by a Confederate unit and condemned to death. He manages to surprise and disconcert the Confederate general by responding to his approaching execution – which he believes will take place at dawn – with the strained insouciance of a self-confident high school student called into the principal's office for a disciplinary infringement.

> "You admit, then, that you are a spy – that you came into my camp, disguised as you are in the uniform of a Confederate soldier, to obtain information secretly regarding the numbers and disposition of my troops."
>
> "Regarding, particularly, their numbers. Their disposition I already knew. It is morose."[8]

Adderson refuses all possible religious solace, turning down the general's offer of some time with the chaplain with the remark, "I could hardly secure a longer rest for myself by depriving him of some of his" (*CSS*, 337). Adderson discusses possible anthropological explanations of the human fear of death, advancing the theory that primitive man had "not enough intelligence to dissociate the idea of consciousness from the idea of the physical forms in which it is manifested" (*CSS*, 338). He considers theological speculation about an afterlife in the same spirit, regarding it as just one more example of man's creating a narrative to explain and mitigate what he does not and cannot know.

In contrast to Adderson in his equanimity and philosophical acceptance of his upcoming execution, General Clavering is distracted and given to making random comments about dying, remarks seemingly directed more to himself than to the prisoner. At a certain point, the story takes a sudden and violent turn when the general calls in a staff officer, a captain, and instructs him to have a firing squad fall in, and to execute Adderson immediately. Adderson's behavior is transformed: he becomes petrified with fear, pleading that he thought he was going to be shot at dawn. General Clavering points out that Adderson had made that assumption; he himself had said nothing to that effect. Without warning, Adderson attacks the general with a knife, and the captain, drawing his sword, intervenes in the brawl to rescue his commanding officer. The consequence is that Adderson kills the captain with the knife, the captain injures the general, accidentally but fatally, with his sword, and Adderson, "begging incoherently for his life," is dragged out to the parade ground and shot. As the sound of the firing squad echoes through the night, General Clavering comes to consciousness, murmurs, "How silent it all is" and "I suppose this must be death," and then dies himself (*CSS*, 340).

Apart from the twist that Parker Adderson, described in the title as a philosopher and revealed in the text to be a master of the epigrammatic comeback, meets death without the slightest note of stoicism or philosophical repose, while the general, who states openly that he would not like to die, passes away in an almost beatific moment of spiritual relief, there are some curious elements at this point in the narrative. The primary complication comes at the moment when Clavering orders Adderson's immediate execution by firing squad. Why his imperturbability and, the reader might assume, courageous self-control in the face of death at dawn should crumble in such a dramatic way when Adderson is confronted with the prospect of death in five minutes is open to a number of interpretations. Psychologically, he does not seem to be concerned about spiritual preparation, but it is possible that we should read his dismissal of religious consolation as less than earnestly meant. Neither is it clear whether Adderson's calm fatalism is connected to some tactical military advantage of which he is aware – it is within the bounds of possibility that he imagines that he might be able to communicate with the Union forces before morning, but it is not suggested in the text that any great significance would come of either failing or succeeding to deliver his intelligence. (Indeed, Adderson's remark about the moroseness of the Confederate troops suggests that the Union forces are aware already of the low morale on the other side and are planning appropriately.) Nor is it obvious why Adderson seems to prefer death by hanging (the method he believes will be used for a dawn execution) than by firing squad, other than that it will give him more time to create a narrative of the situation for himself.[9] The question of time and narrative may, in fact, offer the most convincing solution: having exercised some psychic control over the situation and having apparently taken over the helm in the dialogue with General Clavering, Adderson is suddenly paralyzed by terror at the realization that he never had any real control at all.

He, however, is not the only one who lacks control over the situation. The result of the desperate fight in Clavering's tent leads to the death of all three characters. The havoc takes on a melodramatic shape when it is revealed that it is the staff officer, rather than the prisoner, who has killed the general with his sword. Adderson does not recover his self-control, however, after the incident and remains a cowering bag of nerves until he is executed a few minutes later. The narrative "Parker Adderson, Philosopher" concludes with a paradigm that has savagely reversed almost every expectation that it raised at the outset. One could sketch the organization of the story and the possible moments of peripeteia, or dramatic reversal, as follows: Parker Adderson knows he is going to die; he reveals himself to his captor as a man of courage and self-discipline, almost treating his death with a satirical levity; in contrast, General Clavering is clearly haunted by thoughts of his own mortality. Adderson is surprised by the announcement of his immediate execution, having assumed that he had a few hours left to live; he grabs a knife and attacks the general and is, in turn, attacked by the captain; in the confusion, ultimately all three die. There is a parallel between the sudden transformation of Adderson's character, and indeed of the reader's assumptions, and the randomly destructive outcome of the fight in the tent. Adderson's sudden collapse into abject terror, which has the psychological force of an act of revelation in both the narratological and the theological senses of the word, generates a kind of corrosive disappointment, as if one has been subject to a fraudulent advertising campaign about the reserves of courage and self-discipline in human beings. Likewise, the deaths of the general and the staff officer in the struggle with Adderson seem geometrically wrong, more unexpectedly random and destructive than appropriate for a short story with the balanced narrative composition of this one.

The boundaries of psychological realism and dramatic construction, assuming some mutual understanding between literary artist and reader, are bent by the dynamic of "Parker Adderson, Philosopher" in a way that suggests a profound suspicion at the heart of Bierce's conception of fiction. If adept readers know that the expectations set out by the story (for example, Adderson will remain witty and composed, and the general will achieve some self-knowledge or insight through his interlocutor) will be challenged or reversed in some form, the scale and violence of the peripeteia seem to be designed to abuse and humiliate such expectations, rather than merely confront them with new possibilities. Indeed, the performance of authorial control by Bierce – the detached and well-modulated narrative voice, the expertly constructed dramatic scene and action – seems designed to throw the chaos of the events into a sharper profile. Even if there is an element of narrative coherence between Clavering's premonitions of his own death and the actual event at the conclusion of the story, the way in which that event is set in motion by the suddenly panic-stricken Adderson overshadows that coherence with a sense of the fraudulence of any stories about character, if "character" can be defined provisionally as the narrative of individual moral identity.

If the matter of time, or time left remaining, is the axis on which the narrative turns or reverses, it can be broken down into, on one side, the moment of Adderson's existence as a prisoner with the expectation of execution and, on the other, the moment of execution itself. This is revealed suddenly as being outside his existential scope, a result of his having inferred mistakenly that he knew and thus controlled, at least as a psychological fiction, the decreasing temporal gap between the first moment and the second. As Frank Kermode has expressed it in his classic study of the meaning of time and endings for religion, culture, and literary works, we are always trying to humanize the movement of time, naturalizing it into the English language, for example, by means of the quasi-onomatopoeic phrase *tick-tock*. *Tick* is "our word for a physical beginning," Kermode comments, "*tock* our word for an end."[10] The bipolar sign contains two distinct elements that operate under different pressures: the first sets a potential duration in motion, but the second, the *tock*, gives the duration meaning by bringing it to a close. We cannot perceive or comprehend any such duration without the closing element that organizes the gap between the two. The problem is that the arrival of the next *tick-tock* means that the unit has becomes a system, and now there is another, more problematic, duration to be crossed between the *tock* of the last closure and the *tick* of the new opening: "The fact that we call the second of the two related sounds *tock* is evidence that we use fictions to enable the end to confer organization and form on the temporal structure. The interval between the two sounds, between *tick* and *tock* is now charged with significant duration. The clock's *tick-tock* I take to be a model of what we call a plot, and organizes time by giving it form; and the interval between *tock* and *tick* represents purely successive, disorganized time that we need to humanize."[11]

For Parker Adderson, the knowledge of the duration between his potential execution and the moment of its arrival allows him some authorial management of his approaching death. He acts as if he were in a narrative space after a *tick*, with a fatal but recognizable *tock* expected in a few hours. The plot of his capture and execution is well-structured and subject to the checks and balances of fictional organization. The general's sudden order to take Adderson out to the parade ground and shoot him comes as an unforeseen and violent disruption of the story, knocking the paradigm out of kilter and making clear that the duration of his witty and sardonic exchanges with Clavering had been the "successive, disorganized time" between *tock* and *tick*, rather than the formally composed narrative of a courageous spy facing the consequences of his work with calm acceptance. In the contingent, meaningless duration that turns out to have been Adderson's real location, the philosopher is no longer the ideal figure whose intellectual resources are capable of facing execution at dawn but the incoherently moaning creature terrified of dying. It would appear that the individual announced by the author before the narrative proper begins, "Parker Adderson, Philosopher," exists only in the ideal world of the title rather than in the fictional execution – in both senses of the word – of the story. As the plot unfolds, the name becomes an ironic, indeed sarcastic, comment on the meager consolations of philosophy – and the fragility of self-discipline – when execution by firing squad is, in disregard of the cultural procedures that Adderson mistakenly assumes to be inviolable, suddenly three short minutes away.[12]

The story entitled "One of the Missing" explores a different, but equally important, aspect of the time-plot and the dynamic of contingency. In this narrative, unlike in "Parker Adderson, Philosopher," the central motif is less the eruption of chance into a situation in which elements of drama and character appear to be in some kind of paradigmatic balance and more the irrelevance of drama and character within an evolutionary process of almost biological anonymity. Set in the Kennesaw Mountain area of Georgia, this story centers on the confluence of events that lead to the critical intersection of the lives of a Union soldier on a scouting assignment, Jerome Searing, and an unnamed Confederate artillery officer. Searing hides in a deserted farmhouse and observes a column of Confederate troops withdrawing from their positions. He cocks and aims his rifle, hoping to pick off an enemy solder in the rear of the column:

> But it was decreed from the beginning of time that Private Searing was not to murder anybody that bright summer morning, nor was the Confederate retreat to be announced by him. For countless ages events had been so matching themselves together in that wondrous mosaic to some parts of which, dimly discernable, we give the name of history, that the acts which he had in will would have marred the harmony of the pattern. Some twenty-five years previously the Power charged with the execution of the work according to the design had provided against that mischance by causing the birth of a certain male child in a little village at the foot of the Carpathian mountains, had carefully reared it, supervised its education, directed its desires into a military channel, and in due time made it an officer of artillery. By the concurrence of an infinite number of favoring influences and their preponderance over an infinite number of opposing ones, this officer of artillery had been made to commit a breach of discipline and flee from his native country to avoid punishment. He had been directed to New Orleans (instead of New York), where a recruiting officer awaited him on the wharf. He was enlisted and promoted, and things were so ordered that he now commanded a Confederate battery some two miles along the

line from where Jerome Searing, the Federal scout, stood cocking his rifle. (*CSS*, 266–67)

Both the narrative moment and the shifts of tone and emphasis in this passage are worth examining closely. The intersection of character and plot has been whittled down to an arithmetical sequence of predetermined events, from the birth of the child somewhere in the eastern reaches of the Austro-Hungarian empire to the American battlefield at Kennesaw Mountain in the state of Georgia, a sequence that is a kind of absurdly telescoped picaresque story. There is no purpose, in a sense, to the life of the anonymous artillery officer other than to "be there" for the moment when Private Searing climbs into the upper floor of the damaged plantation house. Analogously, there is no purpose to Searing's biography other than to provide the complementary element in the paradigm, to be the victim of a badly aimed Confederate artillery shell that ploughs into the house, causing the building to collapse on Searing and creating the morbid setting for the conclusion of "One of the Missing," in which Searing undergoes a psychically fatal experience.

The narrative voice, in contrast, is speaking from somewhere outside the immediate theater of action. It can take both the middle range and the long view, not only surveying the local area with the eye of a military scout but also encompassing the biographical history of one of the two characters with a panoramic, perhaps even global, sense of scale. The narrative voice can also, as manifested in the latter half of the story, enter into the micro-processes of Searing's mind as he seeks to reverse the helpless and dangerous position he has landed in. In the quoted passage, however, it is also concerned with its own expressive modulations and its authority over the actions represented. The procedures mirror those of the epic chronicler, particularly at the beginning of the passage, in which an appeal is made to a muse or other deity for the authority to tell the story, or speak the poem. In this narrative the invocation is more parodic, however, and the parody returns us to the underlying tone of the authorial voice. "But it was decreed" and the "Power charged with the execution of the work" are both conscious (but mild) archaisms that act as performative markers, emphasizing the storyteller's legitimacy and his control over the material he will be relating. Indeed, the echoes, in an American context, are not only of traditional opening gambits of epic narratives but also of the predestinarian thread in evangelical Protestantism that was a major component of the family atmosphere in which Bierce grew up and that often survived in the fabric of emotion and belief even where it had been somewhat diluted theologically.[13] The secular and sacred intonations begin to break up, however, in the course of the passage, revealing another voice beneath with a quite different register and vector of intention.

The use of the term "that wondrous mosaic" might give pause: the question of the narrator's attitude to what he is describing raises its head, partly because the phrase rings a warning bell as being just too positive and celebratory in the context of a war story (even for a reader not familiar with other Bierce fiction). The "harmony of the pattern," later in the sentence, has a similar dubious effect. As the narrator moves into the story of the "birth of a certain male child in a little village at the foot of the Carpathian mountains," the sense increases that there is a line of rhetoric moving parallel to the cheerfully compressed account of the facts of someone's biography. Though it is possible that there is something intrinsically comical or deflating about references to villages in the Carpathians, the juxtaposition of this remote area with the Georgia mountains strikes a somewhat uneasy note in the text. As the passage proceeds, the "Power" seems to be less a familiar figure from Reformed Christianity, a Puritan deity whose will, no matter how difficult to understand, demands obedience, and more of a cosmic junior executive who involves himself, as if carrying out a project authorized from higher up, in the task of managing the fate of two unimportant individuals, one of whom is going to suffer distinctly from this special attention. The observation that the disciplinary problems that this unnamed character experienced caused a speedy emigration, and that his being "directed to New Orleans (instead of New York)" led to his being recruited by Confederate rather than Union forces, may be little more than a sardonic reversal of the postwar Southern jibe that the North had solved its recruitment problems by filling its ranks with streams of recent immigrants from continental Europe, whereas the South had been defended by native-born (and racially superior, went the implication) white stock. Whatever the real direction of the remark, it undoes even more effectively the initial rhetorical fabric of the passage. The narrator's subsequent comments are now, without a doubt, marked by a sharply sardonic twist: "Nothing had been neglected – at every step in the progress of both these men's lives, and in the lives of their contemporaries and ancestors . . . the right thing had been done to bring about the desired result. Had anything in all this vast concatenation been overlooked Private Searing might have fired on the retreating Confederates that morning, and would perhaps have missed" (*CSS*, 267). What is not clear, however, is the theological location of the narrator. His attitude, that of ironic elevation over the events of the story, is unmistakable, but it is not obvious whether he believes that God, fate, or some other distinct supernatural force intervenes in the flow of the universe to direct, over long stretches of time, the precise intersection of two lives at a point in history, at a time and place on the globe, as one of an infinity of possible intersections and outcomes, or whether this is merely an ironic deflection of the understanding that the universe is entirely accidental in its configuration and no intersection or outcome is any more than a sequence (albeit an unimaginably long one) of blankly random events. A universe ruled by an inscrutable divine will, or a universe lacking any divine intention or presence at all, is the choice offered.

The second half of "One of the Missing" draws in the scope of the narrative radically, from generations of time and thousands of miles from continent to continent into the narrowest imaginable dimensions: the consciousness of Searing, trapped under the rubble of the house with his loaded and cocked rifle jammed into a position where the trigger is unguarded and the barrel pointed at his own head. This is where the throbs of pain "tick off eternities" and the sight of the muzzle of the rifle, a few inches from his face, eats away at his mental balance. During what appears to be several hours, Jerome Searing at times drifts off into a half-conscious state, and at times struggles against nervous collapse, and tries again and again to move his limbs. Finally he succeeds in grasping a piece of board and attempts to get some leverage with it to move the rifle. Unable to do this, he finally manages to press the piece of board against the trigger. The weapon has already been discharged, however, and no explosion comes. The final segment of the narrative draws away from Searing in the wreckage and recounts how Lieutenant Adrian Searing, the private's brother, hears from his position in the Union lines the faint sound of the collapse of the plantation house and receives the order from his chain of command to advance. Lieutenant Searing determines the time to be eighteen minutes past six. When the troops reach the Confederate positions they confirm that a retreat has taken place. They discover a dead body in the wreckage of the house:

> It is so covered with dust that its clothing is Confederate gray. Its face is yellowish white; the cheeks are fallen in, the temples sunken, too, with sharp ridges about them, making the forehead forbiddingly narrow; the upper lip, slightly lifted, shows the white teeth, rigidly clenched. The hair is heavy with moisture, the face as wet as the dewy grass all about. From his point of view the officer does not observe the rifle; the man was apparently killed by the fall of the building.
>
> "Dead a week," said the officer, curtly, moving on and absently pulling out his watch as if to verify his estimate of time. Six o'clock and forty minutes. (*CSS*, 273-74)

The actual time elapsed between the collapse of the building and Searing's death from shock, if that is what it was, has not been several hours but a maximum of twenty-two minutes. Searing's body is assumed to be that of a Confederate soldier, and his time of death to be about a week earlier.

The obsessive meditation on time that this narrative embodies is, as suggested earlier, very different from the psychic destructuring that appears suddenly to overturn the textual assumptions of "Parker Adderson, Philosopher." Here, in "One of the Missing," the narrative parameters arising out of the intersection of action and character are compromised at an early stage of the story by the authorial manipulation that moves in to designate the fate of Searing as the result of either a random historical process or a manifestation of a divine will whose obscurity is prima facie evidence of its dislike of humanity. The biographical description of the Confederate artillery officer's journey from Eastern Europe to America is itself a condensed narrative of pawns on a large chessboard-like universe. In contrast to the speeded-up time of that part of the narrative, the experience of Searing trapped under the rubble is of time slowed down until its component elements seem no longer to form a continuum but to separate into discrete, painful units. Searing does not know that only minutes pass after the shell hits the house (and the last shred of intentional motive is removed by the fact that the artillery officer was firing at a completely different target and missed), as indeed the artillery officer does not know, and will never know, how his whole life has been subject to a kind of anonymous teleology that does not redeem time so much as elevate it to the level of contingency. In Frank Kermode's paradigm, Searing is suffering the duration between the *tick* of violent ejection from his sniper's perch on the roof and the *tock* of closure (whatever that closure may involve), a duration that expands indefinitely within his consciousness, threatening never to come to completion. The artillery officer, in contrast, is an unwitting object of the destructured *tock*; *tick* of sequential but unconnected events. For the officer, his story is the process of time itself in terms of its mechanical teleology: nothing that has happened to him is of the slightest importance beside the necessity of his being there at Kennesaw Mountain at the time foreseen – or simply, at the time. Even those, such as Searing's brother, who live in "normal" time are subject to professional insecurity about time – he and the other officer continually check their watches – and are likely to make wrong judgments about, say, the time of death of the soldier they discover in the rubble.[14]

As soon as a child begins to think about time, writes Robert Coles in his study of irony and the maturing of consciousness, he is connected to generations of philosophical investigation that go back at least to Genesis.[15] Bierce's treatment of the passage, or passages, of time in his story has its origins in a long tradition of speculative explorations of the subject, and in one in particular that has had a significant influence on western thinking and culture. At the beginning of the Christian era, Saint Augustine approaches the subject of time in his *Confessions*:

> What, then, is it that I measure? What has become of the short syllable, which I use as the standard of measurement? What has become of the long one, which I measure? The sound of both is finished and has been wafted away into the past. . . . So it cannot be the syllables themselves that I measure, since they no longer exist. . . . It is in my own mind, then, that I measure time. I must not allow my mind to insist that time is something objective. I must not let it thwart me because of all the different notions and impressions that are lodged in it. I say that I measure time in my mind.[16]

The philosophical desire to question time and the theological impulse to preserve the mysteries of God from useless prying are polar tensions in

Augustine's text. Christian doctrine will assert that because only God can exist in nontime, any attempt to transcend human time trembles on the edge of the sacrilegious, as informed Christians know that the universe of nontime can be only sketchily implied in human conceptual exercises but not truly understood. Nonetheless, there are areas of consciousness that, at least subjectively, complicate the linear progress of syllables that arise, make themselves heard in a present that cannot be experienced other than as a theory of the discrete moment of existence, and fade into the past. One of these areas is memory, for which Augustine's model is recollecting and reciting a psalm. The psalm is the manifestation of a paradigm of expectation and memory required to recover the text, learned and memorized at an earlier date, and move it once more from the future that is in the present of expectation, through a present that cannot be isolated, and once more into the past that is the present of memory.[17] Augustine's choice of the recitation of a sacred poem, the result of a creative act, to illustrate his understanding of the work of memory serves the purpose of making his thoughts more concrete for his audience. Moreover, the vertically integrative process of the recitation becomes a kind of allegorical metonymy: the relationship of the individual components of the psalm to the whole psalm are a parallel to that of a man's actions to his whole life, and one man's life to the history of mankind. His example, however, also raises the question whether the response of the sayer to the psalm, or of the audience to the recital, is anything but continuous and unchanging. Augustine recognizes the power of the psalm to move and delight the faithful Christian but is somewhat wary of conceding significance to anything like expressive power or aesthetic judgment (although the very idea of parts and wholes does admit of something like an internal harmony of composition, at least).

Time and measure, nonetheless, are clearly matters of the mind. As Augustine says, it appears that time is merely an extension, although of what he does not know: "I begin to wonder whether it is an extension of the mind itself."[18] Human beings are both trapped within in time and, crucially, capable stepping outside of the flow to perceive time that has not happened and time that has, because our minds are active sites of our rational faculties and capable of grasping a weak impression of the mysteries of God. In using the syllable, the act of saying, and by extension the coherent "saying" of a text of a certain structure and duration as his

examples, Augustine suggests that language is the gateway to understanding the passage of time. Furthermore, provided the scope of the experience is controlled, he regards the orally recorded and remembered
text, the psalm, as an authorized tool for emotional release and meditative calm. What he is inclined to treat with suspicion is the use of language to create a pleasurable experience in and for itself. The argument
about the validity of aesthetic criteria and the experience of art, a resilient and long-lasting one in Christian theological and cultural thinking, remained at different levels of intensity into the middle ages and
beyond, and the use of language or narrative structures to create a different sense of time presented a specific problem of moral probity and artistic responsibility. For example, the Renaissance intellectual Scaliger,
writing in Italy in about the middle of the sixteenth century, makes the
following observation – and, despite the jocular tone, is expressing
something about which he has strong feelings: "Disregard of truth is
hateful to almost any man. Therefore, neither those battles or sieges at
Thebes which are fought through in two hours please me, neither do I
take it to be the part of a discreet poet to pass from Delphi to Athens, or
from Athens to Thebes, in a moment of time."[19] Although Scaliger was
concerned about dramatic composition, performance, and audience reaction, the matters that occupied him found their echo when prose fiction began to assert its vitality and potential in western literary culture.
The epistolary novel of the eighteenth century was, among other things,
an attempt to create a temporal verisimilitude in which the experien-
tially confirmed sense of reading a letter that has taken a reasonable and
limited amount of time to write, irrespective of the duration of the
events described in that letter, would be recreated in the reader's interaction with the fictional text. The implied temporal boundaries of the
letter would legitimize the fictional text in a way that an unmediated narrative of events would not.

The writer of fiction became aware of a subtler trap than the one the
dramatist had to deal with. If he or she constructed a framework for narrative around the real time of that narrative, it was tantamount to increasing the level of artifice in the work to buttress its claims to
authenticity (as the epistolary authors had done). If, however, the
author abandoned the various tools and methods for securing such authenticity, then the freedom to move back and forth across expanses of

time, collapsing longer periods and expanding shorter ones at will, de-
creased the visibility of artifice but heightened the artificiality, or fictive
quality, of the text. Since prose fiction first made its presence felt as a major component of various national cultures, authors have always had the
possibility of stepping forth from behind the narrative techniques of literary storytelling and admitting that they have complete and unchallenged
power to structure all aspects of their fictional worlds, including the matter of time, as they think fit. At the same time, however, the imperative
that demanded adherence to an inherited contractual duty to the prospec-
tive reader (to maintain an illusion, for example) was and is still very
much in evidence. A history of texts from Laurence Sterne's *Tristram
Shandy* and Nathaniel Hawthorne's *Scarlet Letter* to Ian McEwan's
Atonement reveals writers juggling conflicting and powerful forces: desire for verisimilitude, display of narrative authority, pleasure both in artifice and in artifice exposed, and pressure from the social or economic
context in which the book will be read. Different authors at different periods, working with different genre options, have responded to these challenges with a wide range of traditional and experimental techniques. In
Bierce's fiction we see, as Cathy Davidson emphasizes, a style of writing
that is clearly separating itself from the literary norms of American culture during the Gilded Age, but with Bierce a tradition of critical misreading has unfortunately set in: "We still strive to read Bierce as a failed
realist or as a naturalist with an incongruously macabre sense of humor . . . [and] automatically apply the definitions of his age to his
work."[20] What marks out Bierce's stories as working to a different literary
agenda from the conscientious realism of William Dean Howells, the im-
pressionism of Stephen Crane, and the psycho-moral investigations of
Henry James is the central trope of the irony of memory in a desacralized
world. Bierce's stories – unlike the naturalist fiction they occasionally re-
semble in atmosphere – reveal little interest in the conspiratorial details
of social life or the dichotomy between interior drive and the pressure of
social expectation.[21] Like the work of later practitioners such as Jorge
Luis Borges (who had to write against the assumptions of high modernism rather than the pruderies of late nineteenth-century American
realism), Bierce's fictions are ironic fables, in which the ironic configuration is not primarily constructed around, say, a particular juxtaposition
between a character and an event within a narrative, although many such

juxtapositions can be found in his work. Rather, the more complex ironies emerge from a voice that suffuses the narrative in its totality and tries to make significant all that it remembers. This ironic voice is formed out of the process by which a narrator's understanding of his power over both the characters and events of his fiction is compromised by the – open or covert – admission to the reader that such power is only a metaphor for a power over time that humanity does not possess.

In "One of the Missing," Bierce displays his authorial power by switching from the telescoped time of the Confederate officer's biography to the unending time, or twenty-two minutes, of Private Searing's life after the collapse of the building. The continual checking of their watches by Lieutenant Searing and the other officer is a military requirement to identify precise moments as a way of imposing order on a flux of unpredictable events. Nonetheless, despite the measurement of time that is meant to embody precision and order rather than the distortions the imagination can engender, the narrative ends on a cluster of misunderstandings: the Union soldiers "seeing" the wrong uniform, and the officer misjudging the time of death. These misperceptions echo the random concatenation of events that led to the moment when the Confederate artillery officer from the village in the Carpathians brings about Searing's death unknowingly by firing at a different target. Where "Parker Adderson, Philosopher" might be Bierce's attempt to show time as crucial for character to achieve expression, and the destruction to the psyche if the presumption of available time is removed, "One of the Missing" involves a more casual and foregrounded play of authorial autonomy, in which time is removed from the level of character to that of open narrative manipulation. In that narrative the deployment and display of artifice is, to repeat, both a sophisticated authorial technique and an admission of inadequacy in the face of a universe that is not subject to human narrative control. In "Parker Adderson, Philosopher" real time, so to speak, is taken away from the prisoner: he assumes several hours of life remain but discovers that he has only a few minutes left. This realization brings his "character" (in both senses of the word) to the point of disintegration, and beyond. In the other story, time is already an illusion that can be spent or hoarded by the authorial voice, stretched out, contracted, or turned into the motif of continual watch-checking for reassurance. Both narratives, however, know that human beings are obsessed with time and epistemologically trapped within its passage. Assimilated as we are to the *tick* and the *tock*, the ironic posture of Bierce's narrator is that he needs time to relate the story, as we need time to read it, but that he cannot offer any redemptive moment that will validate our time, as indeed the characters in the narratives are not offered any such moment, either. Something in Bierce remains starkly conscious of the a profound loss of redemptive potential in the flow of memory, as if the memory of war had now become truly a pathology more than anything else.

The streak of Calvinist predestinarianism found in many of Bierce's war narratives acts as a countervailing influence to the sense of indeterminacy that marks the passage of events and the attempt to narrate such events. In the story "One Kind of Officer," the interweaving of both principles, or sets of criteria, defines the narrative, and the question of their relative utility for interpreting the universe and the significance of experience is posed at a high pitch of literary intensity. The ultimate stability of the ironic voice, or voices, of the narrator and supranarrator; the struggle to identify and accept the actions of a superior Power, or divine, eternal plan, as Bierce uses the terms at different points throughout the stories; the invocation of the random event and the indeterminacy of experience and communication: all these elements are locked into a narrative structure that evinces, paradoxically, a precise architecture and an epistemological uncertainty.

"One Kind of Officer" is divided into six subsections, each with its own title: the opening section bears the title "On the Uses of Civility." The first sentence of the story is a categorical statement made by a senior officer to an individual clearly junior in rank to the speaker: "Captain Ransome, it is not permitted for you to know *anything*." The passage continues:

> "It is sufficient that you obey my order – which permit me to repeat. If you perceive any movement of troops in your front you are to open fire, and if attacked hold this position as long as you can. Do I make myself understood, sir?"
>
> "Nothing could be plainer. Lieutenant Price," – this to an officer of his own battery, who had ridden up in time to hear the order – "the general's meaning is clear, is it not?"

"Perfectly."

The lieutenant passed on to his post. For a moment General Cameron and the commander of the battery sat in their saddles, looking at each other in silence. There was no more to say; apparently too much had already been said. (*CSS*, 289)

The opening dialogue of "One Kind of Officer" contains, as in the form of an orchestral overture, some of the motifs and structures that will be deployed throughout the rest of the narrative: the question of knowledge and the right to possess it; the insecurity of apparently unambiguous communication; the relative weights assigned to formal authority and personal animus. The tone effected by the title of the first section, "On the Uses of Civility," suggests that the attitude of the narrator is one of ironic removal from the emotional content of the story. In fact, the series of titles for the six different sections suggest a level of control situated above that of the narrator, as if there were, higher up in the ladder of authority, an "editor" or similar entity who is concerned with structuring the narrator's memory of things in accordance with quite different criteria.[22] The readers' attention is drawn to the term *civility* in order to focus, with the detachment of an anthropological study, on the last gesture made in the scene. As Captain Ransome's elegant but slightly overdone salute to the general upon the latter's departure reveals, in the military it can be "one of the important uses of civility to signify resentment" (*CSS*, 290).

The next section, entitled "Under What Circumstances Men Do Not Wish to Be Shot," consists of a description of the dismal state of affairs in which the Union forces – to which the three officers mentioned in the opening section are attached – find themselves. The landscape they are moving in is being battered by rainstorms and the troops are struggling through mud and a gray fog that covers everything. "An army has a personality," the narrator asserts, and in this collectivity resides a "wiser wisdom than the mere sum of all that it knows" (*CSS*, 291). What the collectivity knows remains somewhat obscure, however, because the weather conditions and general environment in which the maneuver is taking place are blurring perception and intelligence. Beyond their immediate location is "the dubious region between the known and the unknown" (*CSS*, 291). The defensive earthworks where Ransome's battery has dug itself in are facing north, angled away from the Union forces' eastward-pointing positions to insure a clear field of fire, and Ransome appears to be holding the outermost perimeter of the army's left flank. The somewhat indeterminate designation of Ransome's position is followed by the third section of the narrative, which carries the enigmatic title "How to Play the Cannon without Notes." In this passage, Ransome is isolated, a figure in an enveloping mist that has distorted and blanked out the visual environment with a wet, gray curtain. The captain is approached by a sergeant whose normal size is distorted by the fog. He is carrying a message from Ransome's subordinate Lieutenant Price and delivers it to Ransome in a dialogue marked by attempts at communication on one side, and withdrawal from it on the other. Sergeant Morris reports that the advance units have heard enemy activity in the fog, that an attack appears to be imminent, and that Lieutenant Price requests instructions. Ransome's reply to each sentence spoken by Morris is a monosyllabic affirmative that does not reveal whether or not the captain has grasped the significance of the news he has heard, or how he intends to respond to it. The sergeant finally receives orders from Ransome to Lieutenant Price, instructing him to have the battery open fire.

"To Introduce General Masterson" has as its centerpiece an exchange between General Cameron and the divisional commander, General Masterson. Cameron is asked about the positioning of his battery and comments that he wishes it were as well commanded as it is well positioned. General Masterson is a little surprised and suggests that Ransome is a good officer. The following dialogue ensues, Cameron beginning:

> "He is too fond of his opinion. By the way, in order to occupy the hill that he holds I had to extend my flank dangerously. The hill is on my left – that is to say the left flank of the army."
>
> "Oh, no, Hart's brigade is beyond. It was ordered up from Drytown during the night and directed to hook on to you. Better go and – " (*CSS*, 294)

The two officers are interrupted by the noise of artillery fire. The whole field is beginning to come alive, as units prepare for a possible engagement. There has been one originating action at the root of all this activity. As the narrator has it, "scarcely five minutes had passed since Captain Ransome's guns had broken the truce of doubt before the whole region was aroar: the enemy had attacked nearly everywhere" (*CSS*,

294). The subsequent section, "How Sounds Can Fight Shadows," begins with a scene at the battery, which is maintaining a solid barrage in the direction of fog. The gunfire is causing a displacement of the fog but substituting waves of smoke from the detonations. The sound of cheering comes from out of the fog, "inexpressibly strange – so loud, so near, so menacing, yet nothing seen!" (*CSS*, 294–95). Vague figures are seen in the mist, and the battery keeps up its barrage and the smoke decreases visibility even more. Lieutenant Price approaches Ransome, and the two appear (the narrator does not make the reader privy to the dialogue) to have an argument. Ransome ends the conversation with the words "Lieutenant Price, it is not permitted to you to know *anything*. It is sufficient that you obey my orders" (*CSS*, 295). Immediately after this, a few of the attackers try to penetrate the Union lines, and some close-quarter fighting takes place in conditions of near-zero visibility.

The sixth and final section of the narrative is entitled "Why, Being Affronted By A, It Is Not Best to Affront B." The division commander, General Masterson, arrives at the dugout occupied by Ransome's battery and is immediately aware that something is wrong. The gunners are silent and embarrassed. Looking over the parapet of the earthworks Masterson sees the corpses of soldiers killed during the skirmish and realizes that they are not Confederate but Union troops. He challenges Captain Ransome to explain why he has been firing on his own side. Hart's brigade had been stationed to the left of Ransome's position but was not visible in the fog. Their approach to link up with the main force had been taken for a Confederate assault. Ransome, however, rather than expressing at least a minimum of shock and remorse for his (tactical) error, concedes that he knew that the oncoming soldiers were Union men. Confused and angry, the general demands an explanation, but Ransome's response is to refer him to General Cameron. Masterson informs Ransome that General Cameron has been killed. The men are gathering slowly around the officers, aware that Ransome has now become the accused: "It was the most informal of courts-martial, but all felt that the formal one to follow would but affirm its judgment. It had no jurisdiction, but it had the significance of prophecy" (*CSS*, 297). The captain asks for Lieutenant Price to step forward. He does so and immediately informs the general that he attempted to make Captain Ransome aware of the true state of affairs but was treated in a contemptuous manner and ordered back to his duties.

Ransome asks Price whether he knows about the orders under which he, Ransome, stood as battery commander. Price says that he knows nothing. The story concludes with the following passage:

> Captain Ransome felt his world sink away from his feet. In those cruel words he heard the murmur of the centuries breaking upon the shore of eternity. He heard the voice of doom; it said, in cold, mechanical, and measured tones: 'Ready, aim, fire!' and he felt the bullets tear his heart to shreds. He heard the sound of the earth upon his coffin and (if the good God was so merciful) the song of a bird above his forgotten grave. Quietly detaching his sabre from its support, he handed it up to the provost-marshal. (*CSS*, 298)

In a sudden embracing of action, quite opposed to the passivity that he has shown up until now, Captain Ransome preempts the expected order from the general to surrender his officer's sword and removes it and hands it over himself to the military justice authority in attendance.[23]

The narrative of "One Kind of Officer," in its entirety, requires some careful separation of the levels of fictional operation. The tone of the title itself is neutral and appears to promise very little. The title might be seen as an invitation to identify which officer-type each character with a commission, Cameron, Masterson, Ransome, and Price, represents. This role is not immediately obvious, because all officers, with the exception of Masterson, are involved in a sequential act of assimilating and transmitting orders, orders that become gestures of personal animosity (whether correctly perceived as such or not) buttressed by the hierarchy of military authority. As the narrative progresses, the position of Captain Ransome as the central character suggests that he is the "one kind of officer" concerned, but it is not unquestionably clear at any point, not even at the conclusion, that he is indeed the sole referent of the title. The six subtitles for the individual numbered sections of the story are more interesting. Where the main title is neutral, even bland, the section titles are consciously arch, lyrical, or evocative: "On the Uses of Civility," "Under What Circumstances Men Do Not Wish to Be Shot," "How to Play the Cannon without Notes," "To Introduce General Masterson," "How Sounds Can Fight Shadows," and "Why, Being Affronted By A, It Is Not Best to Affront B." This inventory of titles suggests that their relationship to the narrative is largely oblique and ironic, and even the modestly literal

title of section IV has a note of distance: General Masterson is being introduced for some reason that the general might not be happy about. Moreover, the titles and the division into sections that they mark appear to be
designed to break up the primary narrative rather than mesh with it. The
individual components of the story become uncoupled from one another
and orient themselves around their subnarrative divisions rather than
any narrative totality that the story may be striving for. The effect of this
structural move is to create a gap that has to be crossed between one section and the next. Where traditional chapter divisions in novella or novel-
length texts are broadly inserted when a specific line of action or exchange
has reached a kind of "natural" conclusion, and the reader passes with a
sense of completion to the next chapter opening, the narrative division
Bierce introduces into "One Kind of Officer" foregrounds an intentional
discontinuity. The story is transformed from a flow of narrative into a
series of tableaux.

The tableau vivant is a form in which an illusion of the relationship between image and time is performed by the static positioning of living human beings in a visual and spatial context often designed to recreate an
existing painting or sculpture. The aesthetic of the tableau is connected,
in a sense, with the impossibility of the individual tableau-participant's
being able to represent the stasis of the work of art. For human beings to
remain still enough for the tableau to be perfect, a kind of suspension of
time would be necessary – the kind of suspension that is a staple of science fiction stories in which an alien force or an object with special powers is capable of stopping the movement of time in the universe for all
except the protagonist. The memorable scene in Edith Wharton's 1905
novel *The House of Mirth*, for example, in which Lily Bart's success as
the key figure in the tableau organized for the guests at the upper-class
house-party is a compliment to her acting abilities and an ironic comment on her inability to make the progress of time and the process of aging stop, is a testimony to the power and the pathos of the tableau as a
socially exclusive aesthetic requiring the leisure time and resources of
the propertied upper-middle class.[24] Although the setting and atmosphere of Bierce's narratives are far removed from Wharton's bourgeois,
fin-de-siècle New York, the two authors' different uses of the tableau
converge on a remarkably similar objective. The tableau enacts, in "One
Kind of Officer," a structural gesture analogous to that made, at the level

of character development, by the scene in *The House of Mirth*: at the root of the tableau is the desire to suspend the passage of time, and the impossibility of that suspension.

To attempt to suspend the passage of time in Bierce's narrative is to suspend the inevitable moment when General Masterson discovers that Ransome's battery has slaughtered large numbers of Union troops (Hart's brigade, deployed to the left of what Cameron thinks is the outside left flank of the army), and that Ransome knew that it was not the enemy out there in the fog. Each tableau in the story is individually loaded with meaning, but exists only in its own context of realization. To dissolve the individual scenes into a unified narrative flow would be, in contrast, to write a story in which the events would appear as a sequence formed by the seamless interweaving of a beginning, a middle, and an end. The prevention of this consolidation of elements is the task of the editor, the voice with intervention authority above that of the narrator, who in turn has already placed himself at an ironic distance from the action and personae of the story. The editor is imposing, or at least proffering, a set of clarifications of the flow of events. The style of these section titles does not mesh with the tone of the narrative voice, itself marked by ironic detachment. Rather, these titles are both enigmatic and explanatory, but that combination is destined to be unstable, indeterminate. The visual scene, as described by the narrator, is cross-threaded with a pattern of motifs, all of which emphasize the lack of available intelligence – in both senses of the word – and the passivity of the figure of Ransome in particular. Manifested in an increasingly dense and suggestive language, the images begin to thicken ominously: the silence of General Cameron and Captain Ransome after their acrimonious exchange; the all-enveloping fog; the painfully slow progress of the various army units through the mud, moving as if they were "at the bottom of a white ocean of fog among trees that seemed as sea weeds" (*CSS*, 291); Ransome's immobile posture and blank expression as he sits silently on his horse (again, the sense of a tableau) shortly before ordering Price to have the battery open fire; the disintegrating communication structure of the Union forces and the play between obscurity and knowledge woven into a kind of grotesque pastoral, a fable about the fragility of understanding as the sounds emanating from the surrounding woods are subject to the fatal misinterpretation that they mean an impending attack; the "dim, grey figures" approaching out of the fog who are not

Confederates, despite the apparent color of their uniforms, but Union soldiers; General Masterson, who wants some "light" shed on Ransome's "incomprehensible conduct" (*CSS*, 296).

Illumination and knowledge are, however, tools of psychological conflict and negotiation in "One Kind of Officer." The exchange between Cameron and Ransome and that between Ransome and Lieutenant Price are to all intents and purposes identical: each senior officer says to his respective junior that the latter is not permitted to know anything. The last word is emphasized in both statements, closing off any further discussion with the finality of military authority. In neither exchange, however, does the narrator (exercising his textual authority) inform the reader about the preparatory remarks that lead up to the observation that has caused the problem. With Cameron and Ransome, we enter the narrative only at the moment General Cameron makes his arrogant response to Ransome. In an odd parallel to this opening narrative gambit, the reader is not made privy to the exchange between Ransome and Price later in the story, in "How to Play the Cannon without Notes." What the narrator, or the narrator and the editor together, have chosen to excise is the most important moment in the narrative: what was said between the parties to cause the reaction it did. Although the reader can speculate that Price is, in fact, telling Ransome that they are firing on a friendly force – as he later testifies to General Masterson – it is less obvious what Ransome has tried to tell Cameron. We do not know whether Ransome knew for certain that Union troops were stationed farther out on his left flank and tried to inform Cameron of this fact, or whether he merely suggested that the general's orders to fire at anything that moved might be a little dangerous, because of the prevailing visibility. Whatever the narrator's loyalties may be, and those are not necessarily in plain view, the disruptions and uncertainties that are the result, at key moments, of editorial intervention are even more suggestive of a posture unfriendly to the most likely reading (or misreading) of "One Kind of Officer." The editor has, perhaps, his own theory about what the reader should and should not know.

What we might not know, to put it bluntly, is the truth about Ransome. Although the narrative does everything short of hanging a sign around his neck to identify him as a suffering hero caught in the tragedy of his own rigorous sense of honor, the configuration achieved by Bierce in this story is that we experience nothing of Ransome's inner life other than what the vaguely adjacent narrator is able to tell us from the outside looking on. The fact that the exchange between Cameron and Ransome engenders the resentment that is passed on from Ransome to Price is less interesting than the fact that the resentment is ultimately passed on to the men in Hart's brigade who are mown down by artillery fire from their own side. The stubbornness, if that is what it is, of Ransome's reaction, the mental posture reflected in the immobility of his physical presence, is not clearly defined in the narrative. It is, however, suggested pointedly by the editor's arch section title "Why, Being Affronted By A, It Is Not Best to Affront B"; had the contemporary label "passive-aggressive" been available to the narrator of this story, it might well have been applied to Ransome. The kind of aggressive passivity, however, that brings about such wanton destruction, and indeed continues it after having been directly informed of its victims, could be described as pathological. Ransome's action or inaction throughout the narrative may not be a result of his attempt to bring the reality of his orders home to the short-tempered General Cameron but rather a signal pointing to Ransome's egoism and complete disregard of any consideration other than his own offended pride. The question of ego becomes more than speculation at the conclusion of the story when Ransome, after Price's report to Masterson, feels only the reality of his own existence and the seemingly unjust fate he is about to undergo. Ransome hears "the murmur of the centuries breaking upon the shore of eternity," the "cold, mechanical, and measured tones" in which he imagines the firing squad ordering his execution, and "the song of a bird above his forgotten grave" (*CSS*, 298). These images are all evocative of the popular caricature of a "poetic" sensibility, in which the artist's exaggerated sensitivity becomes a touchstone for all other ethical or social considerations. Ransome's response to the affront from Cameron is to make a bloody artwork, to construct a brutally dramatic poem out of a mixture of resentment, fog, and an artillery barrage. Indeed, the crucial moment of the exchanges between the officers is the withdrawal of authority to "know *anything*": this high-handed denial (on Cameron's part) of Ransome's need and (on Ransome's part) of Price's need to receive military status-derived factual knowledge provokes, in each instance, a response to the perceived slight in a form that juggles information, interpretation, and performance to reveal the epistemological gaps in the original statements of authority. There are, however, orders of difference between Ransome with his savage enactment of ironic misunderstanding – using his artillery as a rhetorical tool – and Price with his well-timed, laconic demolition of Ransome's defense of his actions and evasion of responsibility for the massacre. Ransome's reaction to the affront is that of a psychopath: one kind of officer.

If Ransome's reaction indeed reveals such a pathology, then the relationship between the narrator and the intervening editor becomes a little clearer. The narrator has been impressed by Ransome's demeanor and accepts his theory of the events. He has misread Ransome's responses and his silences, possibly even identifying with him, whereas the editor has a different interpretation. The narrator's flowing prose can only buttress the "Ransome" story, but the editor can at least force some reconsideration of the sequence of events by dividing the story up by means of his bland and occasionally deflating section titles. The editor may not, in fact, be completely certain of the truth of the case and may realize that anyone's recollection can be as subject to distortion as the shapes were in the fog, but he can at least resist the narrator's desire to give the story a formal coherence and poetic elegance. Because the reader is denied both the foreground to Cameron's dismissive remark and the actual substance of the dialogue between Ransome and Price, neither the narrator nor the editor can prove what happened evidentially, but the editor can at least set some markers of ambiguity in the text, suggesting that the narrator's account is open to question. The sense of this series of tableaux, which is the achievement of the editorial intervention on the body of "One Kind of Officer," is to challenge the logic of historical narratives of explanation and the tendency to aesthetic evocation of the movement of time. The narrator is working with his memory of the events to form a narrative of the incidents that will make sense of the sequence of human reactions, Ransome to Cameron, Price to Ransome, Ransome to Masterson. The editor does not necessarily believe that this narration is anything like the truth of the matter. Neither, however, will any future military justice report on the case be necessarily any more authentic. The court-martial proceedings implied in the final few sentences of the story will no doubt be structured around the same principles of authority and military status that caused the events to happen in the first place. "One Kind of Officer" challenges the restrictive, official version of historical events and the tendency to elevate memory into an aesthetic of transformation directed at the past. As the editor of "One Kind of Officer" knows intuitively, the truth of Ransome's act remains an enigma that disrupts the rational parameters of historical explanation and the poetic of recollection.[25]

The three stories I have been exploring represent the complexity of Bierce's fiction when it attempts to get to grips with the difficulty that time presents for both memory and history, even within the fictional narrative itself. The room to maneuver available to the narrator, or to the implied author, is greater than that available to the characters in the fiction. In Bierce, a sardonic narrator will always have the ironic drop on his characters as they try to make sense of their experience. This authority enables the narrator to maintain a certain distance from the action, and to put that action into the context of a global distrust of the legibility of motive and the applicability of any theological or philosophical criteria to the flow of events. To put it broadly, once irony has opened up the gap of signification, it is very difficult to get it closed again, since a narrative resolution must include, to some degree, the reconciliation of meanings. In "One Kind of Officer" there is a striking gap between the deployment of authorial confidence and the text's inability to bring opposing interpretations to resolution. This absence of resolution might be seen as a crippling inadequacy, but as Kierkegaard, who in his *Concept of Irony* (1841) had certain objections to uncontrolled surges of irony, explains:

> For irony, everything becomes nothing, but nothing can be taken in several ways. The speculative nothing is the vanishing at every moment with regard to concretion, since it is itself the craving of the concrete, its *nisus formativus* [formative impulse]; the mystic nothing is a nothing with regard to the representation, a nothing that is nonetheless full of content as the silence of the night is full of sounds for someone who has ears to hear. Finally, the ironic nothing is the dead silence in which irony walks again and haunts (the latter word taken altogether ambiguously).[26]

That Bierce finds himself, again and again, embracing the ironic nothing is less a comment on the nothing in his stories than on the fact that the kind of contingent, disorganized time in which his dramas take place – once again, the gap between *tock* and *tick* – is indeed the dead silence in which irony returns to haunt its speaker. Interestingly, Kierkegaard's translators point out in a note that his taking the word "altogether ambiguously," as he asserts at the end of the paragraph, arises from the fact that the word *spøge*, in Danish, means both to "haunt" and to "jest."[27] This happy convergence of meanings is no longer present in the English *spook,* unfortunately, but even a vague suggestion, in the wake of a translation, of the nature of the ghost of irony dogging Bierce's fiction is welcome. Both authorial voice and ontological jester, it returns again and again to "spook" any attempt to tease intimations of a Christian redemptive epiphany out of the text. Although Kierkegaard's concept of the ironic nothing involves an emptiness that is eerily free both of the possibilities of creation and of the silence that makes one listen even more closely, it could be (for Bierce) the kind of silence that is indeed dead but has been caused by the closing down of the meretricious promises of language and narrative – promises that might fool the reader into ascribing a redemptive dynamic to the act of fictional creation. The ironies of narratives such as "Parker Adderson, Philosopher," "One of the Missing," "One Kind of Officer," and many others (including the memorable "Occurrence at Owl Creek Bridge") create a Kierkegaardian dead silence that is haunted by the echoes of the irony reverberating into infinity and by the admission that time can be reversed only by authorial fiat, and that that is only one more fiction.[28]

At the outset of this chapter, I raised the possibility that Bierce's fiction could be seen as a kind of psychological testing procedure in which the reader's desire for the integration of the elements of the narrative into a paradigm of moral realization is confronted with a refusal to invoke any such significance, or at least an ironic evasion on the part of the implied author. In that connection, Bierce's counterdefinition of the word trial in *The Devil's Dictionary* is suggestive:

> Trial, n. A formal inquiry designed to prove and put upon record the blameless characters of judges, advocates, and jurors. In order to effect this purpose it is necessary to supply a contrast in the person of one who is called the defendant, the prisoner, or the accused. If the contrast is made sufficiently clear this person is made

to undergo such an affliction as will give the virtuous gentlemen a comfortable sense of their immunity, add to that of their worth. In our day the accused is usually a human being, or a socialist, but in mediaeval times, animals, fishes, reptiles and insects were brought to trial.[29]

The narratives can be seen as miniature trials (or courts-martial) in fictional form. The ambiguity here is that good arguments could be made for the writer's seeing himself either as the defendant, the prisoner of the narrative, or as one among the row of judges, lawyers, and upstanding citizens. If he is a defendant, Bierce would seem to be disclaiming any authorial power and suggesting that it is unwise to invest authors with the capacity to perform narrative with the object of displaying right conduct. Rather than Walter Benjamin's description of the storyteller as "the figure in which the righteous man encounters himself," for example, Bierce as storyteller would be the figure in which the citizen-reader encounters a dark laughter at the moment he wishes to see his righteousness confirmed.[30] If, however, he is a judge, Bierce is admitting that the author has the authority to assign responsibility, condemn or release a character, and by implication ease the tension and unhappiness that the story has triggered in the reader's psyche. But he is also a judge who refuses to take part in a process whose only purpose is to ritualistically renew the declaration of one's own blamelessness. He departs the narrative before the moment of delivering the verdict. He does not want to merely pronounce guilt, innocence, or any intermediate status, because that will not do anything except assert that a trial is a system that concludes in asserting such distinctions. As his brief but accurate historical comment highlights, trials once had little to do with human responsibility or conscience, since even animals were brought to trial to alleviate the feelings of the injured party. The irony of Bierce's narrative art is designed precisely to prevent his fiction from becoming that kind of social palliative, to prevent its being taken for granted, and he is prepared to resist energetically and uncompromisingly any such assimilation to others' political or theological world views. This particular aspect of his work is close to what Kierkegaard, among others, identifies as the way in which the whole of existence becomes "alien to the ironic subject and the ironic subject in turn alien to existence."[31]

Kierkegaard's ambivalence regarding the more apocalyptic effects of irony can be found in statements such as the following:

> The ironist . . . has stepped out of line with his age, has turned around and faced it. That which is coming is hidden from him, lies behind his back, but the actuality he so antagonistically confronts is what he must destroy; upon this he focuses his burning gaze. The words of Scripture, "The feet of those who will carry you out are at the door," apply to his relation to his age. . . . The irony establishes nothing, because that which is to be established lies behind it. It is a divine madness that rages like a Tamerlane and does not leave one stone upon another.[32]

One of the possible explanations for the peculiar and indeterminate position Bierce occupies is that his ironies are too detached and, in a way, too destructive for the fabric of American fiction. Against the backdrop of a culture, and I am speaking here of the late nineteenth and early twentieth century, that had, for all its commitment to leisure and entertainment, a Puritan distrust of play, Bierce's fiction appears to provoke with a kind of morose but exultant refusal of American civic teleology.[33] It simply will not commit itself to the process of establishing things, the placing of one stone on another. Or, to put it another way, Bierce's narratives are aimed, in a somewhat hostile manner, at readers who "obviously expect literature to present us with a world that has been cleared of contradictions. If we try to break down the areas of indeterminacy in the text, the picture that we draw for ourselves will then be, to a large extent, illusory, precisely because it is so determinate. The illusion arises from a desire for harmony, and it is solely the product of the reader."[34] In Wolfgang Iser's analysis the operating definition of modern literature involves its desire to confront the reader with the unavailability of authorized meaning, even at the price of the kind of security and trust that the realist novel had created between author and reader, and that had enabled the novel to assert its predominance in the hierarchy of literary texts in the first place. In that modernist paradigm the reader is continually trying to corral the narrative into his or her set of inherited expectations, while the text remains ironic, awkward, evasive, or disingenuous – always, for its part, trying to slide out from under the sequence of interpretations that the reader is producing.

Indeed, as Cathy Davidson shows, Bierce's influence on younger colleagues, and those whose careers began after his had long since ended, is incontrovertible.[35] One reason goes back – as we saw in the discussion of Augustine – to the original religious conception of time as that outside which redemption must be secured. Literature, because it can play with both the passage of time and the reader's emotional needs within the flexibility of language, printed text, and narrative structure, offers a simulacrum of redemption. As in the work of many modernist and especially postmodernist writers, the irony in Bierce's fiction is born out of the knowledge of this aspect of literature and aims at dismantling the reader's illusion about the value of any such simulacrum. As one critic has remarked, however, such apparent honesty and rigor can be a kind of "narrative seduction" that could "merely mask another form of reader recruitment, a seduction of a different kind."[36] It is not that there is no narrative persuasion in Bierce's stories but rather that the recruitment bonus appeals largely to those who are already open to the dismantling of inherited authorial assumptions. The authority, the seduction in another sense, is embodied in the invitation to join the implied author in the chilly isolation of his ironic vision.

The commitment to an ironic perception of existence means that a possibly therapeutic experience of reconstruction in which Bierce could give unconstrained expression to a poetic of – partially – redeemed memory remains excluded by the thematic and structural procedures of his fiction. Bierce refused to embrace what one might call the secularmystical dimension of both individual and collective memory of the Civil War, as embodied in Walt Whitman's image of the war dead and their timeless relief in "When Lilacs Last in the Dooryard Bloom'd":

> I saw battle-corpses, myriads of them,
> And the white skeletons of young men, I saw them,
> I saw the debris and debris of all the slain soldiers of the war,
> But I saw they were not as was thought,
> They themselves were fully at rest, they suffer'd not,
> The living remain'd and suffer'd, the mother suffer'd,
> And the wife and the child and the musing comrade suffer'd,
> And the armies that remain'd suffer'd.[37]

Although there is some implication in Bierce's narratives that death might be a relief from the malice of the universe, his theological speculations are in many ways a conscious inversion of Whitman's lines and the vision that the religious believer and the nonbeliever might be likely to concur in, if for different motives: the believer because it is in its essence a statement of Christian belief, and the nonbeliever because Whitman's invocatory language and the images of undifferentiated dead are a spur to national reconciliation after a brutal and long drawn-out conflict. If the dead are, metaphorically, at peace, then the responsibility of the living is to secure on a new basis the peace of the nation. In "Lilacs" there is the sense of a meaning given by something outside time (if not an absolute transcendental significance) to the memory of death and suffering in the storms of contingency.

In bleak contrast, the most important fiction by Bierce involves the presentation of a story of unredeemed and unredeemable time to the reader, who must in turn dedicate some of his or her time to read those texts. The questions of investment, reward, and the cultural status of the work are inescapable for any act of reading, it is true. But the answers are what make the relationship between the critical fortunes of Ambrose Bierce and those of the younger writer Stephen Crane, which I discuss in the final section of this chapter, one of considerable importance for American cultural memory.

As I suggest at the beginning of the chapter, Ambrose Bierce's literary reputation has always been a fragile affair. Taking an optimistic view of Bierce's position, one could assert that, with his "Occurrence at Owl Creek Bridge" one of the most anthologized of American short stories, and his grim sketches of men under conditions of chaos and uncharted violence a unique contribution to war writing, his work has gained a minor but identifiable stature. But Stephen Crane, a colleague and competitor in the 1890s fiction industry, is rather better positioned as the author of an unchallenged classic of American prose narrative in the shape of *The Red Badge of Courage* (1894-95). The internal coherence and cultural resilience of Crane's novella seem to establish beyond doubt that *Red Badge* is the early modernist masterpiece, the transformation of naturalist observation through the prism of an individualized, interior psychological landscape. In contrast, Bierce's achievement even in the best of his short fiction could be regarded as trapped unproductively and morbidly between the limited range of Gilded Age realism and the mechanical procedures of the late nineteenth-century popular short story.

This assessment may be connected, however, to the most significant biographical difference between Bierce and Crane: Bierce had personal experience of combat during the Civil War while Stephen Crane, born in 1871, did not. There is a major and problematic complex of trauma and memory at work in Bierce's writing, a concern that is not so significant for Crane – somewhat to Crane's benefit, perhaps, since *Red Badge* is perceived thereby as the more imaginative work, the one that actually transforms the imagined experience of combat into the achievement of modern American fiction. To further enhance the perceived structural and psychological inadequacies of even Bierce's best work – the engineering of the climaxes and resolutions, and the apparent lack of depth – his experiential connection with the Civil War can work to his disadvantage, implying a lack of imaginative charge and a dependence on personal recollection. In stark contrast, too, to the Biercean refusal of the redemptive arc, *The Red Badge of Courage* embodies a rising vector of consciousness, gathering in velocity until it launches itself from the platform of the final passages of the novel. Rather than the continual rainstorm of Bierce's "One Kind of Officer," which makes an ominous impressionist painting of the landscape, the "trough of liquid brown mud under a low, wretched sky" in Crane's novella becomes the primeval slime that retreats to permit Henry Fleming's spirit to soar upward in a showy confirmation of his spiritual arrival.[38] The ending of *Red Badge* re-injects clarity as a retrospective measure into even those parts of the text that have been obscure and disconnected on the journey there. As the horizon turns golden in the dawn following the battle, the young Fleming has the whole world of meaning in the palm of his hand.

Whether one's favored definition of *postmodern* tends more toward Frederick Jameson's model of a cultural shadow-play marked by, among others, a peculiar reduction in the level of affect, Jean Lyotard's rejection of master-narratives, or even Ihab Hassan's critique of a disruptive literature of silence, one element in common is a suspicion of the casual assumptions of realism and the transcendental subjectivities of modernism. In *The Red Badge of Courage*, the claim to modernist canonicity is rooted in two elements. The first is the dramatic psychological subjectivity – that is, the degree to which a subjective vision dislodges the representation of a mutually accessible reality from its previously governing position. Crane has become the American author who, with a wave of his creative wand, turned the Civil War from lived, and indeed painfully lived, collective experience into a metaphor of transformation through individual testing, an exclusively male rite of passage that helped move the gauge of American fiction from the realm of social affections to the arena in which male subjectivities determine the shape of the world. As the well-known passage goes: "He felt a quiet manhood, nonassertive but of sturdy and strong blood. He knew that he would no more quail before his guides wherever they should point. He had been to touch the great death, and found that, after all, it was but the great death. He was a man."[39] The second element is the assumption of a core of narrative irony in the novella. This assumption became rather important for twentieth-century Americanist criticism, because it rescued Crane and his text from its dual burden of a hypersubjective naturalism and a callow appropriation of war-as-rite-of-passage. The presence of an ironic gaze behind the ostensible preferences of the narrator was not necessarily what the first generation of readers of *Red Badge* would have perceived, however, but even assuming that such a rhetoric of irony is present in Crane's text, it would have to be a very different phenomenon from that which pervades Bierce's writing.[40]

Crane's protagonist, Henry Fleming, is distinguished from the unlucky figures portrayed in many of Bierce's short stories by the enthusiastic individuality of his narrative presence. He is going to have experience, that experience is going to mean something, and meaning will survive the ending of the narrative. Indeed, the message between the lines at the conclusion of *Red Badge* is that (with a reassuring narrative clap on the shoulder) "the kid's gonna make it, the kid's gonna be alright!" One might have said the same for Crane's future career, but that would turn out to be a somewhat more tragic progression. The question is whether the rite-of-male-passage dynamic in the novella was something that Ambrose Bierce approved, or failed to take note of, when he first responded to *Red Badge of Courage* with the (possibly apocryphal) comment that Crane had "the power to feel" and was "drenched in blood." But an important subsidiary query is whether it is likely, or not, that

Bierce observed any ironic potential in Crane's narrative.[41] It is certainly possible that he did see it but did not quite trust the ironic charge surrounding the protagonist's psychological journey to be a sufficient counterweight to the story's transformational fantasy. Bierce's opinion had changed anyway, by 1896, when he commented in his column that there could be only two worse writers in America, "namely, two Stephen Cranes."[42] But no matter what the status of Bierce's preferences, the irony of Crane's fiction is less the kind of defensive posture against trauma and bereavement I have been discussing in this book, less a struggle with loss, memory, and the inadequacy of language, and more like an aesthetic shadowing on the text that can be simultaneously potentially significant and of no great account.[43]

War Is a Force That Gives Us Meaning, the title of a 2003 book by the *New York Times* reporter Chris Hedges on people and their beliefs in, around, and after violent conflict, is eerily accurate as a description of the symbolic argument of *Red Badge*, a work that is a remarkably unambiguous example of the way in which culture works to assimilate war into a reified human behavioral normality. As Hedges expresses it: "Tragically, war is sometimes the most powerful way in human society to achieve meaning. But war is a god, as the ancient Greeks and Romans knew, and its worship demands human sacrifice. We urge young men to war, making the slaughter they are asked to carry out a rite of passage. And this rite has changed little over the centuries, centuries in which there has almost continuously been a war raging somewhere on the planet."[44] Hedges argues that, inevitably, an abyss opens between lived reality and projected image, between the memory of war and the creative mythologizing of it, and concludes: "The tension between those who know combat, and thus know the public lie, and those who propagate the myth, usually ends with the mythmakers working to silence the witnesses of war."[45]

I would speculatively reinterpret Bierce's comments on Crane, therefore, after the runaway success of *Red Badge*, as evidence of a sour-grapes attitude as the older writer sees the younger stealing his theme and his inspiration and as a realization that the mythmaker was, in American literary history, on his way to displacing and even silencing the man who had done a certain amount of witnessing. Bierce may well have recognized in Crane the writer who was going to do what he, Bierce, could not and perhaps did not want to do. In its broad ambition, *Red Badge* is at once a novel about the transformation of "animal sweat and blister" into knowledge and maturity and a cultural allegory that transforms writing about the Civil War – a modest activity that numbers of people had engaged in over the previous thirty years – into the creation of modern American literature. To so create is to collaborate on a significant collective task that mirrors the American claim to transform the raw materials of the continent into national economic, social, and cultural value. The ruling trope in Bierce's fiction, however, is a negative version of that: the absence or impossibility of transformation.

The question of transformation haunts the literary memory of American wars from Nathaniel Hawthorne's short story "Roger Malvin's Burial" to Anthony Swofford's Gulf War narrative *Jarhead*. The creative vitality of writing seems to sail arrogantly over the static inventory of death and guilt: it appears to want to even redeem it. Crane as the early modernist stands at the switching point where the narratives of American war became infused with the new energies of modernist literary art. But in its divided loyalty to the trauma of memory and to the poetics of recollection, the writing of war can sound a counterintuitive note that predicts later literary and critical reversals: for example, the eclipsing of modernism by a postmodernism that can embrace happily premodernist styles and thought. In many ways, Bierce's handling of the same raw fictional material as Crane's is an early (and perhaps premature) iteration of what became the implicit postmodern critique of modernism: that the master-narratives of psychic interiority, aesthetic autonomy, and imaginative transformation were neither as convincing nor as unassailable as modernists and their readers liked to believe. In an eerie moment of confrontation with a natural desire for narrative significance and, simultaneously, the recognition of its implacable absence, Michael Herr describes, in his account of an American war a century later and an ocean away, a scene suffused in a pure Biercean spirit. In *Dispatches*, Herr writes of a failed interview with a Special Forces soldier in Vietnam about his experience:

> "Patrol went up the mountains. One man came back. He died before he could tell us what happened."

> I waited for the rest, but it seemed not to be that kind of story; when I asked him what had happened he just looked like he felt sorry for me, fucked if he'd waste time telling stories to anyone dumb as I was.[46]

In the Biercean world, this soldier's attitude to narrative and audience would be completely comprehensible; in the Cranian world, this particular soldier would be an unproductive entity, not the most likely candidate for the transformative dynamic that makes art out of experience.

"The present-eternity contrast," writes John Lynen in his study of time in American literature, "defines experience in a manner which bears directly on the writer's problem as to how perceptions, events, and ideas are to be arranged on the page."[47] Although writing is an act that both invests and consumes time, the long question, stretching from Zeno through Augustine to Henri Bergson's *Time and Free Will* and beyond, of how humanity lives in time and understands it, cannot be resolved at the level of the fictional narrative. Equally, the fictional narrative cannot escape from the question of time and its passage, and it deploys many strategies and constructs to negotiate even a provisional autonomy for itself. There are in Bierce trace elements of a Puritan dislike of the poetic elaboration of experience, and an equal dislike of a claim implicit on the part of the aesthetic to embody values that mimic the redemptive structures of Christian theology. These traces come out, in a manner that clearly foreshadows the fictional play of writers such as Borges, in the unwillingness to deploy narrative authority in a way that disguises such authority and gives the reader the comfort of an unquestioned contractual relationship with the author – the relationship Stephen Crane appears to offer. The text offers a present that demands the audience's time, but its implacable movement into the past, into memory, does not in and of itself reconcile the time given with the significance produced; nor, indeed, does it reconcile the fictionality of fiction with the desire that words on a page represent the truth of some matter, even if it is only the emotional reality of our responses to narrative. Neither the memory of modern war nor the act of writing embodies a significance that transcends the contingency of its happening, the indeterminacy of language, or the divergent rhetorics of history and memory. In Ambrose Bierce's fiction, as in the work of other writers on war, irony is the form that memory has to live with. Indeed, his own definition of "recollect" points to the kind of rubric, one of creative manipulation of dark matter, under which his fiction was produced: "To recall with additions something not previously known."[48]

5

Paul Laurence Dunbar

MEMORY AND MEMORIAL

> I heard the last
> Traffic unmeshing upon Boylston Street,
> I halted here in the orange light of the Past.
>
> *John Berryman, "Boston Common: A Meditation*
> *upon The Hero," 1942*

> The American people have always been anxious to know what they shall
> do with us.
>
> *Frederick Douglass, "What the Black Man Wants," 1865*

FROM THE DOUBLE-EDGED approbation of William Dean Howells's introduction to Paul Laurence Dunbar's first substantial collection of poetry, *Lyrics of Lowly Life*, in 1896, through Langston Hughes's confidently ambiguous reference to a "major (albeit minor) poet" in his 1966 essay "Two Hundred Years of American Negro Poetry" to Henry Louis Gates Jr.'s tentative recruitment of Dunbar to the ranks of "signifyin(g)" African American artists who set out to undermine European aesthetic paradigms in his 1988 study *The Signifying Monkey*, a certain line of perhaps subconscious evaluation of Dunbar emerges repeatedly. The implication of these critical assessments is of an artist both creatively self-confident and shyly obedient to public taste, indubitably a major figure and realistically second-rate, committed to black self-expression and hopelessly in thrall to Anglo-American literary models.[1] Such internally divided responses have generated a set of critical question marks, more unspoken than anything, about the value of Dunbar's work; much writing on his poetry and fiction is inclined to give with one hand and take back with the other. By that, I do not mean to imply that the history of Dunbar scholarship and critical judgment has been a set of one-dimensional approvals or rejections but rather to suggest that, for whatever reason, Dunbar's voice within modern American literature has often been muffled rather than sharpened by the debate over his work. At times, Dunbar has been the victim of some peculiar interpretations or, at least, of readings that lack a certain sense of proportion.[2]

The discussion in this chapter focuses on Dunbar's engagement with the memory of the Civil War and Emancipation and on how his poetry bears the marks of the broader struggles around American national and cultural identity taking place during the final years of the nineteenth century. In the context of Dunbar's poetic objectives, I read the technical accomplishment and lyric virtuosity of his poetry as a refraction of an ironic self-reflexivity in his work, for example, in his sonnet on the black soldiers of the 54th Massachusetts Volunteer Infantry regiment and its commander, Colonel Robert Gould Shaw. Two initial theses run as follows: Dunbar's work is capable of standing up to a great deal of critical scrutiny and embodies a specific moment of proto-modernism in American poetry characterized by a discontinuity of form and theme; Dunbar's aesthetic achievement constitutes an attempt to create an African American poetic voice that is simultaneously recognizable as a key component of the American national imaginary. Tragically, the divergence of the collective memory of Dunbar inside the African American community, where affection and respect for his poetry persisted, from that within mainstream American culture, which forgot him, embodies the potential for failure that has often haunted such acts of poetic synthesis. That divergence is more than a little disconcerting because of the wide, cross-racial popularity of Dunbar's poetry during his lifetime.

Furthermore, the status of Dunbar's poetry has been compromised by a tendency among critics to separate it into two parts – the so-called dialect poems on one side and, on the other, verse in Standard English deploying a Victorian diction structured by a traditional meter – as well as by a long-standing unease, among some African American scholars and writers, about the politics of Dunbar's literary achievement.[3] The counterargument I want to make here is a crude one, to some extent, but I

believe it is necessary: the inflexible labeling of Dunbar's poems is an unproductive approach to this author and, furthermore, hinders all critical
evaluations of the poetry as a complete body of work. The level of technical accomplishment (rhyme, stanzaic form, metrical structure, verbal
play) is, if anything, greater in the dialect poems than in the traditional
lyrics. Beyond that, however, several poems in both groups show evidence of experimentation at unexpected moments. On the first point, the
technical accomplishment and the skill evident in these poems' vocal authenticity are entirely related to the way in which the dialect is structured
and shaped by the use of ballad and folksong rhythms from a number of
sources including African American as well as British and Irish folk traditions.[4] The well-known poem "Accountability" offers a good example:

> We is all constructed diff'ent, d'ain't no two of us de same;
> We cain't he'p ouah likes and dislikes, ef we'se bad we ain't
> to blame.
> Ef we'se good, we need n't show off, case you bet it ain't
> ouah doin'
> We gits into su'ttain channels dat we jes' cain't he'p
> pu'suin'.[5]

Part of the effect of this poem is the disharmony between the resonance
of the title, "Accountability," with its clipped tone and its echo of the political demands of the Progressive era, and the verbal music of the poem
itself with its consciously evasive, folksy philosophizing as the speaker
seeks to justify some action whose precise description is deferred until
the last two lines of the poem.[6]

The dialect is a curious balancing act between vocabulary such as
"constructed," "channels" and "pu'suin'" (sometimes with standard
pronunciation, sometimes not), and nonstandard grammatical formulations like "we'se." This is not a simple dialect poem, therefore, but
rather a complex interweaving of the folk rhyme (for example, the riddle
or proverb) from the British and Irish traditions, the popular American
comic song tradition, and the caustic wit of rural African American culture, and it lays claim to a legitimacy as both folklore performance and
contemporary composition. The structure echoes the old "Fourteener"
ballad, with the sense of an oral narrative riding the long expansive lines

and the presence of an indispensable caesura as a breathing space and hinge in each line.[7] The metrical structure foregrounds the poem's African American conversational rhythms – although there is a self-referential note, as if the speaker is exercising a monologue he has long since internalized – while also sketching out a formal claim for the text, the assertion of its status as an aesthetic construct within a broad tradition of verse in English. In doing this, I would argue, Dunbar provides an early signal of the desire of poetic modernism to integrate nontraditional language types (fragmentary conversation and dialogue, extraneous texts, and the like) into its expanded range of poetic resources. Indeed, quite apart from any discussion of his poetry's proto-modernist moments, Dunbar's work manifests itself, from his earliest publications, across an impressive battery of registers, from comedy to elegy, and from Tennysonian lyric to political allegory. The range of poetic voices that Dunbar speaks through suggests a restlessness, an authorial posture that does not want to stand still long enough for any misreading to take place or false assumption to be made. It would be difficult to reduce the spectrum of voice, theme, and style represented by such diverse poems as "Accountability," "Robert Gould Shaw," "A Corn-Song," "A Border Ballad," and "The Secret" to any single-focus critical paradigm.[8]

"A Corn-Song," in particular, suggests a relationship to a strain of modernism expressed in lyric poetry and identified by Graham Hough as combining both a "self-conscious modernity" and an "awareness of what is passing . . . far more acute than the awareness of what is to come."[9] Hough's description of the peculiar sensibility of early modernist verse, poised uneasily between an disenchanted cultural past and a future dominated by scientific rationalism, sees the experiments of Baudelaire and Rimbaud, for example, as embodying an associative rather than discursive orientation to classical forms even as they dismantle the traditional poetic models from within. He offers Rainer Maria Rilke's "Herbsttag," with its interweaving of oddly decentered images and studied melancholy, as a good example of the way in which a traditional motif – a fall day in the country – can be made strange, giving rise to less familiar but nonetheless convincing psychological and cultural resonances:

Wer jetzt kein Haus hat, baut sich keines mehr.
Wer jetzt allein ist, wird es lange bleiben,

wird wachen, lesen, lange Briefe schreiben
und wird in den Alleen hin und her
unruhig wandern, wenn die Blätter treiben.
[Whoever has no house by now, will not be building.
Whoever is now alone will long remain so,
rising to read, to compose long letters,
to walk restlessly up and down the avenues
amid the whirling leaves.][10]

Hough identifies a restlessness and insecurity on the part of the poetic voice, commenting that the modernist lyric is "a poetry of unorthodox celebrations and chance epiphanies."[11] "Herbsttag" is exemplary: there is nothing in the text to establish with any certainty how the poetic "I" responds, or expects the reader to respond, to the encroaching season. Indeed, that very uncertainty may be the originating moment of the poetic act or, to put it another way, it announces the emergence of a new language of memory in which memory is no longer a site of Wordsworthian creative recovery but is instead an unpredictable quantum of energy in the mind. Such moments are reflected in two American examples. The first is found in the closing lines of Robert Frost's "After Apple-Picking":

One can see what will trouble
This sleep of mine, whatever sleep it is.
Were he not gone,
The woodchuck could say whether it's like his
Long sleep, as I describe its coming on,
Or just some human sleep.[12]

As in the German of Rilke's poem, the language and the cadences are more fluid, words looking out for a rhythm rather than passively reflecting the formal discipline of standard poetic expression, while simultaneously admitting the pressure and attraction of that discipline. The metaphor of autumnal decline is no longer a convention in a symbolic language of season. Instead it represents an opening, a release of the metaphor itself from the poetic status into which it has been locked. The uncertainty of the speaker's position is underscored by the vestigial presence of prelapsarian communication with the woodchuck – a fellow creature, after all, who knows something about seasons – but that is now merely the memory of a loss.

The second American example is Dunbar's poem "A Corn-Song," which appeared originally in the 1895 collection *Majors and Minors*. This poem has a number of interesting characteristics, including the polyphonic irony of its composition. For the moment, however, I focus on the final stanza, in which the field-hands return home:

> And a tear is in the eye
> Of the master sitting by,
> As he listens to the echoes low-replying
> To the music's fading calls
> As it faints away and falls
> Into silence, deep within the cabin dying.
>
> > Oh, we hoe de co'n
> > Since de ehly mo'n;
> > Now the sinkin' sun
> > Says de day is done.[13]

This is neither a disingenuous pastoral elegy for plantation days nor a one-dimensional dialect lyric of any kind. Rather, it foreshadows the movement reflected in the Rilke and Frost poems ("A Corn-Song" is the earliest poem of the three) where a metaphor begins to resonate in a way that emphasizes the instability of the boundary between genres of experience, between expression and representation, as the speaker himself becomes an observer of ambiguous status within the structure of the poem. The master is listening to something that he, oddly, appears to understand. But he may not want to understand it, because that would destroy his self-confidence – the assumption of justified privilege that enables him to enjoy listening to the folk chants of the slaves – and also reveal to him his poverty of spirit, his separation from natural cycles of physical work and relief. At the deeper level of implication, however, the chain of motifs of evening, exhaustion, hierarchy, and fertility cannot be directed in their metaphoric resonance by the observer who retains authority over the poem. "A Corn-Song" opens out at its conclusion to set the possibilities free: that the master's tears can be anything from an emotional response to a powerful vocal performance to a recognition of the inhumane logic of economic exploitation under slavery, and that the poem is committed to the evocation of the sensual, aesthetic experience rather than a resolution of its social implications. Dunbar achieves this focused ambivalence by a self-assured deployment of his lyric inventiveness and, more important, an expert reworking of the cultural legacy of the black South.

"A Corn-Song" echoes the passage from Frederick Douglass's second autobiography, *My Bondage and My Freedom*, in which he discusses the power and poignancy of the slave songs he remembers from his youth:

> In the most boisterous outbursts of rapturous sentiment, there was ever a tinge of deep melancholy. I have never heard any songs like those anywhere since I left slavery, except in Ireland. There I heard the same wailing notes, and was much affected by them. . . . I have sometimes thought, that the mere hearing of those songs would do more to impress truly spiritual-minded men and women with the soul-crushing and death-dealing character of slavery, than the reading of whole volumes of its more physical cruelties.[14]

One of the points Douglass wants to make here is that a set of miscommunications and misunderstandings were in play: the master often failed to read the attitudes of the slaves correctly, for example, and the songs themselves represented a clear message of suffering, but only for those whose spiritual sensitivity and maturity would enable them to hear it. The structure of "A Corn-Song" represents Dunbar's attempt to rehearse these contradictory pressures within a single pastoral poem in which the binary field-hands/master equation is triangulated by the presence of the poetic observer.[15]

As the folklorist Roger Abrahams describes them, corn songs (particularly in Virginia and Maryland, but also in the Carolinas and Georgia) were part of a ritualization of the annual corn-shucking duties in which the work was carried out under the fiction of a voluntary activity, with much singing and competitive activity between the teams of slaves. Corn shucking often took place at night under torchlight, which lent a dramatic and exotic ambiance to the event, and accounts by white and black reporters (including some former slaves) transmit the sense of a special time associated with pleasurable memories. Abrahams argues that the corn-shucking ceremonies represented, beyond any particular individual's experience of them, a kind of enactment of mutual cultural misunderstanding, as songs, gestures, habits, and lifestyles jostled – sometimes easily, sometimes not – against each other in plantation society: "The practices emerged as forms of active resistance, not in the sense that they attacked the system but rather in the ways in which they maintained alternative perspectives toward time, work, and status . . . this event, the corn shucking, meant something quite different to the black participants and the white observers. To white onlookers, the event was an entertainment verging on the spectacular; to the slaves, it was an opportunity to celebrate together."[16] Abrahams explores the putative origins and antiphonal structures of the corn songs, sung by the corn shuckers under the leadership of a dominant community figure, suggesting that African folk customs and styles merged with the existential facts of the American South and the English language to produce an African American folk poetry that was flexible, ironic, celebratory, and subversive. He writes: "The songs collected in connection with the corn shucking bespeak the Afro-Americans' excitement in working, competing, eating, and dancing together. They also continually comment upon the world the slaves saw around them, poked fun at the actions and attitudes of certain planters and other powerful whites, and expressed their shared anger at the agony they found in being 'sold off to Georgia,' and other inequities."[17] Dunbar grasped the potential of that cultural memory and deployed it. The achievement of "A Corn-Song" is twofold: first, the integration of the tradition of corn songs from the rural South allows a poetic composition that counterbalances the English lyric with the poetry of the African American slave (and in connection with a ritual that had some of its roots in old seasonal practices from rural England); second, the antiphonal structure of the poem echoes that key element of the Southern corn song but transforms it into a proto-modernist statement of poetic ambivalence that, among other things, contains a nostalgia for the past that is genuine and, at the same time, ironically destabilized.[18] The reader should be, as a consequence, unsettled and forced to question whether the poignant, elegiac tones of the poem can be accepted and enjoyed, or not.

Dunbar is no more willing, in this poem, to reassure the reader of the stability of his or her position than Rilke or Frost would be. What the three poets are prepared to offer the reader is an invitation to consider that poetry is no longer bound by convention, even as it makes use of all conventions that suit it. A fundamental challenge is launched in these three poems, and it is similarly directed in all three. That challenge is to the parameters for the reading of lyric poetry.[19] The contemporary reader was asked to understand something that went against the grain, as far as the cultural assumptions at the turn of the twentieth century were concerned: that the structure of poetic expression involves subordinating the selection of formal parameters to the needs of the individual poem. Form, that is, in Dunbar, Rilke, and Frost is rendered contingent, or informal, in the process of composition. Poetic measure, to put it another way, no longer embodies for these poets the largely unquestioned authority it once did – and nor should it for the readers, was the implicit message.

In the moment that it is no longer a reflection of traditional authority but a contingent poetic tool, prosodic choice has assumed a different status. The poet and his or her application of selected forms are now the poles of an equation in which two uncertain elements are establishing their temporary relationship. The relationship is temporary as the poet has relinquished the authority of traditional forms (even as he or she deploys them) and the forms themselves refuse to guarantee the poetic text any particular stability. The poetic speaker, also, may lack any certainty about his status within the structure of the poem. The roots of this state of affairs may well be located at a somewhat earlier date than the period we usually identify as early modernism. David Simpson in his study of irony in English Romantic poetry, for example, argues that an earlier generation of writers experienced a sea change in aesthetic assumptions: "It can be said that the Romantic writer confronts the business of communication in a new and more urgent way, in that he is preoccupied with the potential gap, not only between his own meaning (if he is aware of it) and his means of expression, but also between the resultant 'text' and its reader."[20]

In the first chapter, I advance the example of Lowell's Commemoration Ode to argue the late arrival of key elements of Romantic poetics in American writing. Here I would add that the persistence of the issue of poetic authority into the modernist era is at least a sign – if at times a misleading one – of the difficulty of making sharp-edged periodic

distinctions in literary history. In Dunbar's poetry we can find a specifically American struggle with the authority of form: he is, in Simpson's
words, "preoccupied with the potential gap" as he brings the inherited
weight of English poetic expression to bear on a range of experiences
outside the parameters of that tradition. Dunbar is, as it were, condemned to enact in his work the impossibility of the task to which his creative energy has been committed, a condition that is reflected in both
Rilke's and Frost's poems.

The poetic "I" in "Herbsttag" and "After Apple-Picking" and the implied speaker in "A Corn-Song" are all speaking their poems in a way
that sketches out Rilke's, Frost's, and Dunbar's position as one that is
subject to larger forces and pressures they may not fully understand and
cannot always resist and reveals (in Dunbar) a further difficulty that the
speaker is unwilling to commit to one position or to select one poetic language that would restrict his freedom of movement. Indeed, all three
poets are struggling with the languages available to them, but only Dunbar faces the problem of justifying the poetic speaker's position as the
poet's position. I would argue that the speakers of "Herbsttag" and "After Apple-Picking" enjoy, despite the experimental tones of the texts in
question, a certain stability of lyric voice, a locus of experience identifiable and respected as such within each national culture, whereas Dunbar's fragile speaker is left trying to maintain three angles of vision – the
master, the field hands, and the implied observer – within the equilibrium of "A Corn-Song." Despite the agility he shows, Dunbar is always
in danger of having his weave of poetic voices misunderstood as vaudev-
ille, or denigrated as mimicry. As at the corn-shucking ceremonies
themselves, race and misreading go together. The experience of other
black poets confirms that even more informed and supportive reviewers
could, unconsciously or not, communicate between their lines a certain
surprise that the creative act had actually taken place.[21]

In Dunbar's "A Corn-Song," the gap that emerges between the different registers of the poem is a forewarning of the potential gap between
the poem and any interpretive reading it may provoke. Indeed, "A Corn-
Song" embodies a possibility that there is a deeply ironic moment at the
compositional center of this poem. Paul de Man, in his essay "The Concept of Irony," argues that the implications of the Romantic theorization
of irony begun by Friedrich Schlegel in "On Incomprehensibility" have

their apotheosis in Walter Benjamin's theory of the necessary destructive effect of irony that has reached the stage of undermining literary form itself. The ironization of form demystifies the work of art in an act of self-reflexive negativity in which the formal properties of the work reveal the ideology of the work from within its own compositional integrity.[22] Benjamin, in his first critical work, "Der Begriff der Kunstkritik in der deutschen Romantik" (The concept of art criticism in German Romanticism), advances the claim that irony as the "permanent parabasis" of all metaphorical dynamics of language means that form itself becomes the last stage of the progress of ironization, in which it seeks to ultimately dismantle the legitimacy of the work of literary representation as, for example, modernist authors such as Joyce, Kafka, and Faulkner pushed out the boundaries of fictional prose and exposed the novel's claim to be a stable form to which each individual literary project had to subordinate itself. By "parabasis" Benjamin means that the truly ironic text is one that exists as a kind of permanent digression from an assumed principal text that has been assimilated by its digression, as if, for example, a footnote were to swallow the entire work to which it was originally appended, or the description of a painting on a gallery wall assume more importance than the painting itself. Benjamin writes: "This type of irony (which originates in the relationship of the particular work to the indefinite project) has nothing to do with subjectivism or with play, but it has to do with the approximation of the particular and hence limited work to the absolute, with its complete objectification at a cost of its destruction."[23] De Man paraphrases Benjamin as follows: "The irony is the radical negation which, however, reveals as such, by the undoing of the work, the absolute toward which the work is under way."[24] I would paraphrase both de Man and Benjamin by arguing that the position of being a poet and the act of doing poetry are both subject to a potential ironic subversion in that the value of the form of a poem is sometimes inversely proportional to the stability of its (or its author's) cultural credit. In "A Corn-Song," the three crucial elements – the field-hands' song, the master's meditation, and the poetic voice behind the other two voices that organizes the poem – cast a questioning light on each other's position and presence and also point up the difficulty, the impossibility even, of the governing poetic speaker's task of holding this configuration in a steady state. That problem, which would trouble neither Frost nor Rilke, troubles Dunbar. Thus, in addition to being a poetic text of remarkable formal agility, "A Corn-Song" can also be seen as the ironic echo of a struggle to achieve a cultural validation that will inevitably be refused.

The "approximation of the particular and hence limited work to the absolute" may, however, have a sharper meaning for African American poetry. One manifestation of the gap between form and meaning is the sense of verbal expression itself as being two-sided, a victory over the silence into which the memory of slavery and the meaning of the Civil War for black Americans had been forced and, simultaneously, a solipsistic gesture of protest aimed without any real consequence at the new rigor of the color bar and the sinking threshold for racist violence that marked the 1890s. Dunbar's poem "Robert Gould Shaw," written to commemorate – and also to question the commemoration of – the 54th Massachusetts Volunteer Infantry regiment and its commander, and their disastrous attack in July 1863 on Fort Wagner, a Confederate fortification in Charleston harbor, embodies some powerful elements of this split phenomenon. In this poem, the reader senses an irony of authorial position that carries all the markers of a bequest from an earlier poetic tradition (which it is, to some extent) but that is far more an allegory of the failure to make poetry the tool of social repair. This repair has something to do with the racial configuration of American society at the century's end and much to do with the value of literary expression in that particular cultural environment. The rapid industrialization and urbanization of the United States after the Civil War had an unavoidable and, to an extent, traumatic impact on culture and education, as well as on political alignments, demographics, health, and the rhythms of daily life. The commercial expansion of print media had brought benefits to writers (increased outlets, wider distribution) but also the uneasy realization that they seemed to have no chance of escape from an America in which not to be marketable was as grim a prospect as being a craftsman whose skills were no longer needed on the factory production line. As new and aggressive magazines like *McClure's* changed the media marketplace, leaving behind longer-established, more literary journals such as *Century Magazine* and *Harper's*, a different kind of writing was demanded. "Muckraking" came of age in this period. Questions of fictional realism haunted writers and reviewers. Poetry, also, was in the process of undergoing radical, and unforeseeable, transformations in its social and cultural status.[25]

This process of change brought, as part of its complex web of some-times contradictory results, the increasing commodification of literary production and a more passionate defense of literature as the location of a kind of irreducible difference that had to be protected. It was a murky and volatile period that, as Frank Lentricchia reminds us in his sketch of an alternative history of modern American poetry, managed to be the crucible of both Frost's "localism" and Pound's cosmopolitan "para-noia."[26] The dissatisfactions that sound from under the surface in the work of a number of poets from the 1880s to the early years of the twenti-eth century – such as Emma Lazarus, Stephen Crane, Edwin Arlington Robinson, William Vaughan Moody, and Dunbar himself – would be-come, for a slightly younger generation, the active trigger that initiated a break with the formal parameters of the dominant modes of nineteenth-century poetry. Dissatisfaction provided one motive at least for the jour-ney to a more open creative future. Despite the often overanxious adherence to traditional poetic models exhibited by poets working in this period, Dunbar and others permit energies to emerge in many of their poems that belie the familiar formal designs that purport to offer the audience an unthreatening confirmation of expectations.[27] A certain un-easy posture can be inferred from the poetry of the American fin-de-siècle that will face the choice of either returning to traditional stability or risk-ing the gymnastic leap to a new state of affairs.

Even more than their white colleagues, however, black writers at the end of the nineteenth century found themselves in a sharply ambiguous position: on one hand, an increasing number of successful fiction writers and poets, and politically active scholars like W. E. B. Du Bois, were mak-ing their mark in the United States and abroad; on the other, that very success seemed to become a marginal, even invisible reality when mea-sured against the wave of lynch "justice" that marked the latest attempt in the southern United States (and not only there) to terrorize the African American population into submission and political quiescence. For artists such as Pauline Hopkins, Charles Chesnutt, Paul Laurence Dunbar, and James Weldon Johnson, the transformation of both individ-ual and collective experience into literature could not avoid putting the very concept of transformation into question: was the response, at times even the recognition, provoked by black authors sufficient to outweigh the resistant ideological mass that was white America at the turn of the

century?[28] It was easy to fall into the attitude that the literary work of art
was little more than a plaintive gesture by the minority of a minority in
the face of dismissal by, and even contempt from, the society at large.
Radical white writers may well have had to withstand the new class hostilities of industrial America and live with their political choices, but the
limited sense of national belonging that even the children of recent immigrants from, for example, Eastern Europe enjoyed was often, for
African Americans, the experience of an insecure status, physical, social, and historical. To create a vision of how black American history
could be made meaningful was an exceptionally difficult, perhaps impossible, task. As David Blight, with an ironic side-glance at the black folklore that had made white authors such as Joel Chandler Harris, author of
the Uncle Remus stories, into national figures, expresses it: "The future
beckoned, but the past remained a heavy weight to carry. Forgetting
might seem wise, but also perilous. To face the past was to court the
agony of one's potential limitations, to wonder if the rabbits really could
outwit the foxes or whether some creatures in the forest just did have history and breeding on their side."[29] In this passage, Blight asks indirectly
whether the cultural resources of African America were up to the task of
carving an acceptable niche for black thought and expression in the
changing social map of the United States. If even the symbolic capital of
folklore can be pirated by southern whites, what is left of a cultural history to exploit? This question becomes, for poetry, entangled with the
implications of what has been described as the "big blank in American
poetic history" between roughly 1890 and 1913.[30] Dunbar faced this
problem as he worked on "Robert Gould Shaw." The poem, published
originally in the *Atlantic Monthly* in October 1900, represents a complex
response to the gradual but unmistakable burial of the emancipatory
history of the Civil War experienced by Dunbar's generation. It is an
echo chamber for the arguments about race and memory of a fraught
period in American cultural history.

"Robert Gould Shaw" is a sonnet in the Petrarchan mode, comprising
an octet based on an interrogation of the ghost of Colonel Shaw and a
sestet that provides a kind of response to the query the poem has set in
motion.[31] The rhetoric of the first part of the poem is dominated by two
questions:

"Why was it that the thunder voice of fate . . . ?"

and

"What bade thee hear the voice and rise elate . . . ?"

by which Shaw, who was killed alongside his black troops in the attack on
Fort Wagner, is asked to account for his decision to leave the comforts of
life in his socially secure Boston family circle to go to war. His decision to
accept an assignment to the 54th Massachusetts, the first designated
African American regiment to be levied in the United States (although
all its officers were white), is also queried: why this extra sacrifice to
"lead th' unlettered and despised droves," as Dunbar calls the black soldiers and noncommissioned officers? The structure of the poem brack-
ets the questions between two types of "thunder," the thunder that
embodies the "voice of Fate" in the opening line of "Robert Gould
Shaw" and the "thunder at the gate" that closes the octet. The second
thunder is, clearly, the sound of weaponry that formed the backdrop to
the slaughter at Fort Wagner. The first "thunder voice of Fate" is at a
higher level of metaphorical abstraction – the motif suggests the moral
weight of the Puritan tradition sounding within Shaw's mind – but is
then transformed by a grim poetic maneuver into the fatal experience of
artillery fire at the close of the octet. Dunbar's skill, working as he is with
a delicately balanced and tightly constrained form, is in the invocation of
the link between the inexplicable motive that drove Shaw toward his fate
and the reality of his death in combat.

The difficulty of responding to the questions involves the way in which
the rhetoric of the poem deploys image and syntax. Although the questions, marked by "Why" and "What," carry the speaker's assumption that
they are legitimate and can, at least potentially, be answered, the grammar
of the poem is countered by the anchoring motif of the first eight lines. The
"thunder" in its dual manifestation is, apparently, a calling that cannot be
resisted – therefore the questions are to some degree misplaced – and it is
located outside the normal parameters of human consideration, because
the thunder of the guns at Fort Wagner subjected the men of the 54th
Massachusetts to the extreme resolution of martyrdom. Neither Shaw nor

his troops could oppose – nor could they perhaps fully understand – the calling that brought them to die together for a purpose that, Dunbar implies, was deeper, more resonant, than political victory or constitutional change. Questioning of, or resistance to, what fate has planned is presumptuous, and the two questions posed by the speaker are not meant to be crass attempts to elicit a rational gloss on a mystical or sacred experience. Rather, the peculiar achievement of the first eight lines of the poem is to interweave two complexes of thought about a response to a calling: the first is the merging of the individual testing that Shaw undergoes with the journey to the fatal but glorious "manhood's home" that the black soldiers make; the second complex involves the way in which the desire to ask and the knowledge of the inadequacy of any answer inform each other.

The final sestet of "Robert Gould Shaw," however, throws the momentum of the opening off-course:

> Far better the slow blaze of Learning's light,
> The cool and quiet of her dearer fane,
> Than this hot terror of a hopeless fight,
> This cold endurance of the final pain, –
> Since thou and those who with thee died for right
> Have died, the Present teaches, but in vain!

The questions posed in the octet are not answered in any obvious way here. The process at work is more like the construction of an alternative to the movement of journey and sacrifice invoked earlier. This alternative carries a significant negative charge, because the speaker suggests that the call, the thunder of destiny, should not have been followed. In a poetic statement that echoes the opening stanzas of Lowell's Commemoration Ode, a life of scholarly effort and intellectual pleasures is juxtaposed with military service in a cause dignified by political and moral values that link a particular community to the losses sustained by its members. The "slow blaze" of scholarship and the "cool and quiet" of the academic environment are counterposed to the extremes of heat and cold associated with the doomed attack on the Confederate positions and the sacrifice of the regiment. The syntax is curiously ambiguous, however, setting up a shifting temporal frame and a doubled referential direction for the motifs of "hot terror" and the "cold endurance."[32] The

terror and endurance would seem to belong to the experience on the battlefield of 1863, but the use of "this" in lines eleven and twelve obscures,
productively, the temporal relation between the elements of the sentence and suggests that the current state of affairs in 1900 is not only an
ironic comment on the idealism of Shaw and his men, now betrayed by
the racist political culture of the United States, but something stranger.
The poem's syntax becomes an analogue of the moment when the fight is
understood to be "hopeless" and the prospect of victory collapses into
"final pain." Or, to put it another way, it is one thing for the attack on
Fort Wagner by Robert Gould Shaw and the men of the 54th Massachusetts to have been hopeless from a tactical military point of view, and
quite another for it to have been hopeless because its configuration of
courage and self-sacrifice was fated, from the outset, to be an absurd
marginal note in an American history defined by the impossibility of
racial equality.

The questions posed in the first section of the poem have apparently
been answered, but now the "thunder" that moved Shaw to enlist and the
gunfire that met the charge of the black regiment can be seen as random
elements of experience, without the potential for integration into a
higher level of significance. Rather than being a call from tradition and
conscience, the "voice of Fate" is an inauthentic announcement that
should have been examined more closely, and even refused. The speaker
is therefore disinclined to provide any response in the latter part of the
poem that would buttress the idealistic choice described in the opening
lines. The evasion of the final sestet – the kind of evasive action that did
not, unfortunately, form part of the doomed attack on Fort Wagner,
which was an ineptly planned charge across exposed terrain – brings the
reader to the uncomfortable realization that the poem is less a celebration
of the courage of Shaw and his troops than an expression of sympathy
with the consequences some people suffer as a result of wrong decisions
made for the best of reasons. The pathos of the opening section of the
poem has been answered with a feint that leaves the initial line of thought
spiraling off into the unknown. Why the "thunder voice" called Shaw
from his Harvard classroom, and what drove him to embrace the unusual
and unpopular assignment to command the first African American regiment (attitudes in the North to the recruitment of black soldiers ranged,
generally speaking, from neutral to hostile) are questions for which any

answer has lost its relevance. And it is not only a matter of Shaw himself: the arrival of the soldiers of the 54th Massachusetts at "manhood's home and thunder at the gate" poses the question, what might their alternative have been? If Shaw's sacrifice and that of his men have been compromised by the "hopeless fight" and the "cold endurance of the final pain" that are taking place in 1897 (the year the memorial was unveiled) and 1900 as a distorted mirror-image of 1863, then the last section of "Robert Gould Shaw" is an uncompromising noncelebration of the historical experience that is the object of its poetic meditation.

There is another way, however, of looking at the implications of this poem. In particular, the act of Shaw and his men needs to be extracted from the corrosive situational irony of the context of Dunbar's performance of his text: a solemn commemoration of the contribution of black soldiers to the war effort at the middle of the single worst decade for black Americans since Emancipation. One way might be to see the voices that moved Shaw to choose his designated fate as indeed authentic, and to regard the quasi-biblical paradigm of divine call and human obedience as a functioning metaphor within the poem. But here the call is not quite divine in a Christian sense; rather, it is mystical in the sense of an intuition of fate. The voice of fate is the original message, as it were, that comes to Shaw and cuts across the pattern of his life, bringing him to a decision that, despite its lack of distinct religious imagery, nonetheless echoes the narratives of Christian martyrdom. In any event, the paradigm of call and obedience has to attempt to integrate the opposed lines of argument that define the poem. This is not to say that "Robert Gould Shaw" is without irony – I will indicate presently where I think it is located – but that the irony is not merely in the recognition of the futility of the original sacrifice against the backdrop of American racism. The call, the "thunder voice," is less a sacred message than a communication that appears to define the self as it demands the response that, in its act of responding, begins to fill that self with meaning. It is an existential enigma in which Shaw is called to make possible the discharge of a duty to meet the impossible demand. To use the term *existential* in the context of the American fin-de-siècle is to open up the possibility of accusations of both anachronism and misinterpreting the unique nature of the American experience. Nevertheless, the growth of a theory of a different kind of knowledge, one distinct from the Enlightenment metaphysical or positivist episteme, is a useful backdrop to readings of Dunbar and other African American writers. The phenomenological revolution, beginning with Edmund Husserl's *Logical Investigations* in 1900, wanted "to demonstrate how the world is an *experience which we live* before it becomes an *object which we know* in some impersonal or detached fashion" (emphasis in original).[33] The idea of a movement of consciousness within an environment of recalcitrant and often hostile "reality" operating at the molecular level of existence offers curiously illuminating parallels between the works of authors such as Paul Laurence Dunbar, Langston Hughes, and Richard Wright on one side of the Atlantic, and Husserl, Martin Heidegger, and Jean-Paul Sartre on the other.[34] Indeed, with his elaboration of the *call of conscience* Heidegger in particular offers a language, a terminology of vocation and reception, for reading "Robert Gould Shaw" and its implications in a way that avoids the trap of categories such as "Dunbar's verse" within a purely American cultural history, with their suggestion of incurable poetic limitation.

As Heidegger develops the argument in chapters 56 through 58 of *Being and Time*, the call of conscience is a summons to find the meaning that cannot be found in the social reality through which the self wanders, and that, if the summons is received, discloses itself as an interior communication of Da-sein (being-there) to itself.[35] Heidegger discusses the call as a voice that should not be confused with an "utterance": the call "does not say anything, does not give any information about the events of the world" (252) but calls from the process of realization of Da-sein itself. The summons has to be grasped, so goes Heidegger's argument in this section of his work, as a calling forth of the authentic self to its "potentiality-of-being," the understanding of which is more authentic the more the call of conscience is heard as a call (although it may be as much a silence as an utterance) meant for you, and "the less the meaning of the call gets distorted by what one says is proper and valid" (258). What is to be avoided is a kind of bad faith in which "the they" (Heidegger's term for, among other things, exterior social existence) defines Da-sein according to the needs of prevailing norms, or the like: "the call . . . is drawn by the they-self into a manipulative conversation with one's self and is distorted in its character of disclosure" (253). The refusal of the ontic (scientific or positivist) criteria of "the they" should be understood in those terms, and the "disclosure" or revelation of meaning will be granted only to those who have understood the summons as a call that comes from you and that, against the odds, reaches you. Shaw rejects the academic life and destiny offered by his social background for a "calling" that is – in another iteration of New England spiritual history – a sacred trope of duty with respect to instructions emanating from beyond the authority of human society and, in the nonreligious terminology of the poem, an acceptance of "the voice of Fate." His choice parallels, with a remarkable accuracy, the contours of summons and response that Heidegger sets out in *Being and Time*: "The call is precisely something that *we ourselves* have neither planned nor prepared for nor wilfully brought about. 'It' calls, against our expectations and even against our will" (254).[36]

How to respond to the summons that comes against one's expectations is sketched by Heidegger in the shape of a precognitive grasp of the need to, in a sense, liberate oneself by way of surrender to the call: "When Da-sein understandingly lets itself be called forth to this possibility, this includes its *becoming free* for the call: its readiness for the potentiality-of-being summoned. Understanding the call, *Da-sein listens to its ownmost possibility of existence* . . . it means solely the readiness to be summoned" (265). It is worth noting, to repeat a point made above, that "Robert Gould Shaw" is marked by the unwillingness to name precisely the message that the young Harvard student received or to explain his motivation. The poem may be unable to do either because it is about readiness to be summoned rather than the translation of that summons into the language of "the they." The sonnet enacts, particularly in the oblique relationship between the octet and the concluding sestet, a certain evasiveness regarding motive and justification that seems to be looking for a dimension of poetic language that this poem – with the best of intentions – cannot really provide. Echoing a similar phenomenon in "A Corn-Song," there is a fault-line in the poem that results from an unresolved tension, I would argue, between the technical accomplishment revealed in the mastery of the petrarchan sonnet form and the poem's more open, process-oriented, and dangerous thought. Indeed, the juxtaposition of Heidegger's and Dunbar's texts throws into relief the fact that the rise in phenomenological and existential philosophy in the early twentieth century was accompanied by the movement to understand poetry as not only a literary form but also a radically different kind of knowledge, essentially the opposite of rationalist philosophy and academic philological scholarship. Poetry employs a mode of knowledge that forces a choice, rather than describing a segment of reality. The question of choice, so crucial for the existentialists, is significant in "Robert Gould Shaw" to a degree that matches the intensity of Heidegger's exploration of its meaning.[37]

To sum up: the less obvious but more important question this poem is asking is not whether the sacrifice of the 54th Massachusetts was a pointless gesture but whether, if they had known that their struggle and their death would not bring equality and an end to racism, Shaw and his men would have made the same decision, would have taken the same path that they took at Fort Wagner. The answer the poem offers is that to commemorate their actions on that day is to offer at least prima facie evidence that they indeed would have so chosen. This sketching of an existential choice that, in the final analysis, allows no evasion, represents a very different analysis of the significance of the Civil War from the usual ascribing of the North's victory to a combination of manpower resources and a superior level of industrialization. Indeed, in "Robert Gould Shaw" Dunbar has written a tragic commemorative statement about the battle at Fort Wagner that is far closer in spirit to the kind of Southern narrative that I discuss in Chapter 3 with respect to *The Bostonians* than it is to the apologetic rationalism that proved so culturally ineffectual in the struggle over meanings and values that took place in the decades after the war ended.[38]

The question of irony remains, however, even if the superficial juxtaposing of past sacrifice with present-day reality is not the only site of the poem's ironic charge. I suggest that the matter of poetic form must be addressed when exploring the self-reflexive operations of this text. The irony of form is, as noted in the previous discussion of "A Corn-Song," a process that removes the text from all attempts to stabilize its existence as a reliable constant within a particular cultural and ideological order. This degree of ironization represents, even if all previous uncertainties, disharmonies, or ruptures between language and meaning have been resolved within the boundaries of the text, a type of uncrossable barrier between the contingent work and the absolute ideal toward which the particular text is reaching.[39] With respect to "Robert Gould Shaw," the use of a poetic form that, particularly in the metrically rigorous Petrarchan variant Dunbar chose, speaks of the authority of literary tradition, rhetorical elegance, and emotional balance in order to capture the implications of a dramatic, bloody, and possibly useless event in recent American history is the crucial and distinctive poetic maneuver (which could even be regarded as either quixotic or tending toward bathos). Walter Benjamin in his essay, however, appears to mean something more diffusely universal than a traditional model of metrical organization and instead is referring to a structural relationship of language (or another vehicle) that operates beyond or below the level of authorial choice and direction. Although there is some ambiguity in Benjamin's formulation, he makes his position clear that, contrary to any idea of the work of art as a revelation of the mystery of individual creative genius, the work embodies, if anything, the transcendental order of the ideal work itself – the "invisible work of art" that exists beyond the borders of its visible, contingent alter-ego.[40]

With "Robert Gould Shaw," nonetheless, Dunbar has constructed a sonnet that confronts the sonnet itself as a poetic form and thereby confronts also the impossibility of that form's embodying successfully the authentic emotional matrix arising out of the historical reality that it addresses. The poem raises the question of its own cultural legitimacy, one could say, by bringing an established European poetic tradition into direct and uneasy juxtaposition with the status of the African American writer and the black American citizen.[41] Through the discipline of the sonnet's organization the author seeks to establish, as if carving an intractable but long-lasting material, an appropriate poetic memorial for Shaw and the 54th Massachusetts and to confront the impossibility of achieving that purpose by selecting a poetic form that satirizes its own perfection with a subtle drawing of attention to both its formal contingency and its epistemological insecurity. In many respects, Dunbar's text (and indeed the broad mass of his work, both "dialect" and "lyric") supports the reigning and largely justifiable critical view that the core sensibility of American poetry at the end of the nineteenth century is oriented far more to the subjectivity of the poet's expressive act than to any formal experimentation. The only problem with that evaluation is that it fails to see, as German Romantic critics such as Schlegel and modern critics such as Benjamin saw clearly, the necessity of the poetic confrontation between the contingent and the absolute, and the "helplessness" (to use Benjamin's word) of the former's recognition of the unreachability of the latter. The turn that Paul Laurence Dunbar gives to the theory of the restrictions the form itself places on the poet, and of the consequent celebration of the indestructibility of the work in the moment of its ironic dismantling, is the conscious choice of a form that, in its overdetermined stylistic constraints and the impossibility of its relationship to the political and cultural realities facing an African American writer in 1900, mirrors both the impossibility and the historical reality of the attack and the sacrifice at Fort Wagner.

The discursive context within which the *Atlantic* published "Robert Gould Shaw" in 1900 was national. The ceremony at Boston Common on Memorial Day three years earlier had not been, however, part of the seemingly irresistible advance of sectional reconciliation that had as its goal the reuniting of the veterans of "the Blue and the Gray" for the price of an ideological rewriting of the meaning of the Civil War. Rather, it had been a local elegiac gesture to a complex of ideas and individuals that embodied, in their motives and in their persons, a tradition that was essentially regional (Boston and New England) in its historical and emotional resonance. Nevertheless, the event went beyond local boundaries. The evocative power of the unveiled memorial opposite the State House, with its majestic bronze figures of Shaw, the platoon of black soldiers following him, and the strange angel that seems to hover protectively over them; the addresses made on the day by influential figures such as William James and Booker T. Washington, and the appearance of William Carney, the first African American to win the Medal of Honor, carrying the regiment's original battle colors: all these elements combined to lend the ceremony its significance for the broader and more uncertain question of the nature and direction of American culture, a question also at the heart of Dunbar's poem. As David Blight remarks, "Saint-Gaudens' relief forced the thoughtful citizen to consider how a struggle in the 1860s . . . became a struggle for blacks over whether they had any future in America at all."[42] This entangling of a sense of national identity and a recognition – on both intuitive and intellectual levels – of the implacable forces facing African Americans gives Dunbar's poetry its curious and sometimes overlooked atmosphere of what one might call "lyric strain." By that I mean that Dunbar is trying to carry out multiple and sometimes contradictory tasks in his poetry, and the forms reveal the pressures that are the inevitable accompaniment to such a poetic process. These tasks have, primarily, to do with the institution of the nation and the dynamics of communicating cultural memory.

Both institution and communication require investment in language. The sensitive and, for some, politically dangerous linkage between language, cultural memory, and political self-assertion is intimately bound up with the role of the creative writer, the political theorist, and the pedagogue in the struggle for national self-realization. Although such professions or job descriptions may sound slightly off-key or even foreign in the American context, the tasks they carried, and carry, out were clearly on the agenda for the United States at the end of the nineteenth century. The waves of immigration that changed America between the 1880s and the 1920s provoked a wide range of responses from all parts of the society, including from immigrant communities themselves. In this shifting configuration, African Americans were in a special and unenviable position as the one ethnic group in the United States that had not come to the New World voluntarily. The cross-thread of intercommunity tension and individual interaction was thus not composed uniquely of exchanges between immigrants and "native-born" white Americans.[43] As an African American poet and fiction writer, Paul Laurence Dunbar stood at a peculiar angle to the changes in American society, a posture in which language, nation, and racialized identity were held in a fragile balance. Dunbar's poetry can in some way be seen as an African American staking of claims in a new and diverse United States where a more complex map of vernaculars and accents (and of people who, furthermore, had no collective memory of the war) had supplanted an older, simpler demographic reality, particularly in the urban and industrial centers.[44]

As Ross Poole has argued in his study of the identity structures underpinning modern nationalism, "the nation has appropriated to itself the linguistic and cultural means necessary for the articulation of the sense of self of its members."[45] If this position can be maintained as viable in terms of historical scholarship and conceptual coherence, then it proposes a very fraught and difficult problem for African American literature and its relationship to the national entity in which its work has been done, the United States of America. To put it simply, how were black writers to articulate a "sense of self" in a social context in which their assertion of linguistic citizenship and their access to cultural legitimacy

were constitutionally uncertain and subject to inner doubts from their
various communities as well as to outer pressures from the reigning ideology of white America at large? Indeed, Poole's comments go as far as
suggesting that a sense of self, rather than constitutional rights or various types of economic or legal status, is the most important thing that
the nation can disburse to its citizens. In a complex and dispiriting political environment, Dunbar attempted to deal with the problem of stabilizing the self and asserting African American cultural citizenship by
mounting a two-pronged intervention: appropriating the energies of the
English lyric to express an individuality that both celebrates and questions the assumptions of that particular literary ideology, and using the
double-edged humor and covert judgments of "dialect" poetry to explore the potential of black folklore to shift the issue of race from a site of
social resentment and psychological cowardice to one of cultural process
and an open-ended discourse on national identity. In these poetic texts,
however, an ideal of reconciliation through cultural exploration is undermined by the ironies emerging from Dunbar's ultimate intuition that
that ideal was an impossible equation to solve.[46]

Dunbar takes the cultural memory of the English lyric tradition as his
own, indicating that it is open to him as much as to any other poet, but
does not fall into the trap of believing that the mere display of his facility
with the form will amount to his acceptance as an original poet within
the Anglo-American language community, or his race's acceptance as
full citizens of the American nation. Nonetheless, for Dunbar, as important as not falling into that trap is the uncompromising assertion that, as
an English-speaking American writer of the late nineteenth century, he
has a right to the cultural energies of the language that is nonnegotiable.
In appropriating and deploying these lyric forms – essentially, the "dialect" of English poetic expression – Dunbar appropriates a cultural
legacy and deploys it to sketch a future in which he will be accepted as an
original poet and his people will achieve their right of equal citizenship.
As Poole expresses it:

> Every identity carries a conception of its past and its future. The
> self which acts is always a temporarily extended self. It exists, not
> merely at the moment of action, but through time. . . . [M]emory
> and anticipation are not merely modes of cognitive access to what

we did in the past and will do in the future, but are the very forms through which our identity is constructed. As in memory and anticipation we identify with past and future selves and appropriate their action as ours, so we make ourselves one with those past and future selves.[47]

In a move that links psychology and polity, Dunbar makes his pitch for the reconfiguring of an American national culture, knowing that culture is, as Gregory Jusdanis puts it, "simultaneously the mode of representation and the represented object . . . [and] a territory of codes, symbols, norms, and the signifying practices like texts, tropes, rhetoric, discourse."[48] That Dunbar's leap of faith toward a new sense of nation and belonging fell, ultimately, at the fence of American racism does not render his project illegitimate or the texts produced thereby unworthy of critical attention. That racist assumptions and the claims of citizenship can meet in an unequal battle for ideological and cultural power is no surprise; nor is the phenomenon uniquely American. Dunbar's irony is, at its core, the knowledge that the strength of the individual poetic act will fail to match that of the forces that come between reality and vision.

Dominick LaCapra in *History in Transit*, his study of the relationship between historical writing, modes of experience, and the status of contemporary cultural theory, argues for a nuanced understanding of the relationship between the audience and cultural texts of various kinds:

> One always has some tendency to project or to identify (whether positively, negatively, or ambivalently), and one may also be tempted to repress or deny any involvement in the other. Objectivity in a desirable sense should be seen as a process of attempting to counteract identificatory and other phantasmatic tendencies without denying, or believing one can fully transcend, them. Rather, limited but significant objectification should be cogently related to other discursive and signifying possibilities depending on the nature of the object of study and how one is able to negotiate one's own subject positions. Objectification is bound up with reality-testing that . . . may check unmediated identification and related modes of phantasmatic investment, including the sense of being haunted or possessed by the other (something I indicated may be

inevitable for victims of trauma and perhaps for those empatheti-
cally unsettled by their experience).[49]

One of the great problems of the literature of race and politics in the
United States is that the shape of emotional and intellectual response to
literary and other texts does not remain static across different communities of readers. In LaCapra's sense of it, the map of identification alters
according to different reading contexts. Exceptionally rigid "identifica-
tory" processes can, however, lead not only to an essentializing of experience, in which writing becomes subordinated to the requirements of an
already established identity, but also to an equivalent disciplining of
reading and response, in which, for example, membership in a racially or
ethnically constituted group is implied to be a prerequisite for true understanding of a particular work. In respect of African American writers
and readers, this posture has often been a response to a tradition (stretching from, say, *Uncle Tom's Cabin* and *Huckleberry Finn* to *Porgy and
Bess*) in which white American artists have rendered blacks according to
their own needs and desires. An assertion of black identity, as something
that exists quite apart from its representation in American literary culture, is a predictable and legitimate countering force in this process.
Nevertheless, the danger is always present that a new set of assumptions
can take root, in which any imaginative leap into the perspective and
meanings of the racial Other is declared a priori to be an outdated, illegitimate, or at the very least embarrassing procedure. The "phantasm"
of Dunbar's rendering of the state of mind of Robert Gould Shaw forty
years earlier could be described, from that perspective, as an attempt to
validate a historical event in a way that gives a white Boston-Brahmin
Abolitionist a cultural status denied to the hundreds of black men who
followed him to their deaths.

One could take LaCapra's commentary a little further and note that
the issue of trauma is also relevant here. The poem "Robert Gould Shaw"
is haunted, as discussed earlier, by the failure of the project of racial
emancipation and, at another remove, by the attempt to construct an
authentic memorial to the unredeemed sacrifice at Fort Wagner. The pressure to objectify is, for Dunbar, complicated, because he wants to remember a sacrifice and condemn the historical irony that tends to degrade its
meaning, while simultaneously enacting a poetic form that matches the

utopian architecture – the biracial self-sacrifice – of the earlier historical event. To that extent, Dunbar is trying to counter the trauma or traumas (of slavery, of the doomed assault by the 54th Massachusetts, of the new white supremacy) with a vision of cross-racial loyalties and sacrifices under extreme circumstances. If this is a phantasmatic procedure, then it would seem to be one that asserts Dunbar's own rights, as a black American poet, to take on the task of "projecting" himself into Robert Gould Shaw, a white Abolitionist and martyr in the antislavery struggle, who in turn, and in his own right, had sought enough of an identification with his African American troops that they can, historically, never be completely separated from him. Dunbar's delicate balance between race community and spiritual community, between the anonymity of the unnamed black soldiers and the individuality of their commanding officer, is not in my reading an unresolved division but a determined setting of limits to trauma, a declaration that being "haunted and possessed" cannot be the final story. Memory is not only injury, Dunbar seems to say, but potentially also a repository of alternatives that cannot be judged absolutely on narrow criteria of success or failure.

Nevertheless, there is a powerful strand of hopelessness to Dunbar's act of remembering and reminding. The lack of superficial optimism, indeed the assimilation of a deep pessimism into the argument of the poem, as I have laid it out, enables a willingness to challenge the assumptions of the Shaw memorial by bringing up the reality of the social amnesia that corrodes any commemorative act. Poetically, it is a self-reflexive move, embodying the fact that the formal elegance of the sonnet, like that of the memorial design itself, offers no guarantee of its political or cultural influence. That does not hide the ambition to wield such influence, since "Robert Gould Shaw" is clearly a poem that desires to, at the very least, set the tone for the reading of a particular item of history and memory. To that extent, there is in Dunbar's wider body of work a poetic speculation around what a national cultural formation might look like: the voices of English poetry, mainstream American eclecticism, and African American folk culture woven together into a new design. But that was a quixotic ideal to struggle for, because the politics of cultural memory were against such a project at the turn of the twentieth century. It might have been possible in some alternative future in which Dunbar lived on (and it is interesting to speculate what his contribution might have been to modern poetry and modern fiction during World War I or in the 1920s).[50] Dunbar's nation, the inclusive nation of poetic culture, may not be merely a kind of nostalgic fantasy, however. Although the call of the nation continued to have a cynical and bitter echo for black Americans well into the twentieth century, there is a less-theorized (and perhaps less well-researched) paradigm of African American patriotism that is often obscured by the kind of assumption mentioned earlier: that of an invariably oppositional posture on the part of black writers, for example. Paul Laurence Dunbar stood, at 1900, in a vanishing cultural context that nevertheless still had enough vitality to enable him to invoke the sheltering trope of national service and sacrifice for the memory of the United States Colored Troops of the Union Army, even as the real social composition of the American armed forces – deploying in a quasi-colonial war in the Philippines at the same time as his poem appeared in the *Atlantic* – reflected increasingly the humiliation of black servicemen and the ideological reintegration of Northerners and Southerners into a white national military.

As the contribution of black soldiers to the Union victory receded into forgetfulness, and as the ideological implications of that contribution were obscured and ignored, so went the poetry of Dunbar after his death in 1906. The subversive irony at work in "Robert Gould Shaw," "A Corn-Song," "Accountability," and many other poems faded into the standard black-and-white photographs of Dunbar, reflecting the ambiguous fate of their author in American literary history. Broadly speaking, Dunbar's work persisted on the fringes of the American poetic canon, although he was not by any means the only poet of his generation to suffer the consequences of being too late for one poetic century and too early for another. He did survive, however, in a more substantial form as the popular poet of black American households – a fate that in a curious way echoes that of Robert Frost. Although Frost clearly held a place of prestige in the cultural record of the American twentieth century that Dunbar never achieved, there are nonetheless certain parallels between Dunbar's popular reputation and Frost's. Both were interested, in their early careers, in controlled experiments in the lyric mode that combined unexpected tones and perspectives within traditional structures. Both, also, wrote poems that passed into the fabric of American popular culture, such as

"When Malindy Sings" for Dunbar and "Stopping by the Woods on a Snowy Evening" for Frost.

The major difference is that Dunbar's work remained for many decades a kind of shadowy absence in American poetic history, while Frost's long creative life built an ever-increasing presence. Whereas Robert Frost survived to write "The Gift Outright" and attach it to his inaugural poem of January 1961, making possibly the last New England--centered gambit for management of the national cultural imaginary in the twentieth century, Dunbar's early death meant the disappearance of both his sense of a convergent (not unified) American poetic culture and his understanding that the loss of the emancipatory narrative of the Civil War was both a destruction of memory and an irony of memorialization. As Michael S. Roth has suggested, the knowledge of the dynamics of historical development have led to the "ironist's cage," a paralysis of political vision on the part of the intellectuals who have assembled and theorized such knowledge.[51] Dunbar's "Robert Gould Shaw" can be regarded as a brief poetic manifestation of that same perception. The poem is a vision of how the cage looks from the inside. Dunbar is not, I think, denying all possibility of an emancipatory politics reemerging in the future. But if even the most courageous and insouciant actions, the most self-sacrificing and morally elegant commitments, cannot bring about the desired and natural change (from slavery to human rights and racial equality, for example), then the death and commemoration of Shaw and the men of the 54th Massachusetts regiment are, to repeat, suffused with an irony that it is very difficult to escape from, and especially difficult to escape from in aesthetic terms.

Nevertheless, Dunbar's poems can be also, in many respects, regarded as tentative answers to such difficult questions. For example: How can one reconcile social form with experience ("We Wear the Mask")? How can one balance saying and not-saying ("The Secret")? How can one reconcile nostalgia and history ("A Corn-Song")? How can one balance political frustration and poetic possibility ("Robert Gould Shaw")? The more profound question, and one even less easy to answer, has to do with how well, or how at all, the human capacity for memory and the desire to memorialize an act can be reconciled with a configuration of power in the real world that denies the truth of particular memories and moves one act of commemoration to the margins while granting another pride of place in the schedule of collective national ritual.

I have arrived at the argument that the issue of reconciliation is – with all its attendant utopian impossibility – a trope that cannot be avoided in the landscape of post-Civil War literature. Much more than for Lowell, Melville, James, or Bierce, however, reconciliation is a defining moment for the imaginative structure of Dunbar's poetry. It is furthermore simultaneously an attractive political objective and, in terms of the literary text, a site of formal ambivalence. In Dunbar's vision, the reconciliation that could be the embodiment of a new national culture is freighted with the realization that the gap between the gesture and the reality mirrors the gap between the contingent poetic work and ideal manifestation it cannot reach. In this way, the force of poetic irony meets the social reality of the black writer in fin-de-siècle America. The question of irony signals the problem of reconciliation as a literary trope. As the critic and psychoanalytic theorist Julia Kristeva has argued, reconciliation demands "a partial, temporary identification with the subject of the act and with the act itself." This process is essentially private and interpersonal, because "the social sphere . . . is that of judgment, and . . . a community cannot maintain itself unless it gives itself laws that are impossible to transgress."[52] Kristeva draws a clear distinction between the private act of forgiveness and the social process of law and justice, suggesting that the liberating potential of an individual's surrender of his retributive anger cannot be translated into collective, political action, or at least not without considerable danger (creating the impression, for example, that major war crimes could be expiated by an anonymous, collective apology). What is interesting here is that literature seems to occupy a position somewhere between the individual and the collective sites of experience. The interpretive act of writing and the interpretive act of reading demand some opening to, or empathy with, the object in and of the text, and poetry – perhaps more than other genres – carries both the timbre of individual expression and the aura of a public declaration.

Some of the various respondents who engage with Kristeva's arguments locate the crucial problem in the slippage from the personal to the public, and the implications of the work of the Republic of South Africa's famous Truth and Reconciliation Commission are taken up by more

than one commentator.[53] The five years of the commission's proceedings between 1995 and 2000, offering individuals who had committed
acts of violence within the political context of apartheid the prospect of
immunity from prosecution in return for full disclosure of their involvement, were more about narrative, emotion, and the individual leap of
faith than they were about documented evidence, rational choice, or impersonal judgment. Without drawing oversimplified parallels between
slavery and apartheid, it could be argued that literature in the post-
Emancipation United States was the only arena, the only "commission,"
in which anything remotely like an authentic public discourse on slavery
took place, in which the implications for both whites and blacks, individuals and communities, men and women, ethics and philosophy, or love
and politics could be explored. Literary texts, among them Dunbar's poetry, are neither solely the private voice in the public arena alone nor the
public voice heard, or consumed, in a private retreat. To offer an act of
writing is to signal a configuration in which each of these voices is sometimes amplified and (depending on the writer's interests and the critic's
agenda) at other times muffled. In the poem "Robert Gould Shaw," to
take a relevant example, the two registers are in a delicate but almost
perfect balance.

In my discussion of that poem, I suggest that its form is both a display
of the aesthetic balance achieved and an ironic reversal of that very accomplishment to concede the difficulty of reconciling the memory of the
act of sacrifice at Fort Wagner with the act of commemoration manifested on Boston Common. Nevertheless, the poem also argues that the
sacrifice of the 54th Massachusetts was a moment of aesthetic and emotional rupture – a productive disturbance in the American national
imaginary. For Dunbar, the defeat of slavery has generated a new dynamic of national identity and cultural practice, at least in its imaginative potential. The possibility of white, Anglo-American culture meeting
black culture from the South in a creative fusion that would transcend
the history of racism and violence becomes, in Dunbar's writing, a political vision for which his poetry is a metonymic exercise. When the black
vernacular of Dunbar's rural characters meshes with the metrical legacy
of the English lyric, and when the English lyric is reshaped by the pressure of African American experience, the kind of cultural product that
emerges has the potential for reconciliation. While reconciliation cannot

escape from the pressure of history, the metaphor embodied in work such as Dunbar's can, at certain moments, invoke "an ethos of generosity whose lyrical strength becomes its main justification," as Wole Soyinka describes it in an essay on the legacy of colonialism and slavery for the literatures of the African diaspora.[54] The significance of that lyrical strength and formal accomplishment in Dunbar, as I point out, is not answered by taking these aspects of his work as a given. Rather, our response as readers must be to look carefully at how his poetic syntax is as subtly constructed in his dialect poems as in his lyrics (they are, in fact, two varieties of "dialect"), and how the architecture of the poetry is a model for a national cultural diversity that does not demand the subordination of one cultural sensibility to another. In contemporary terms, Dunbar's poetry of fusion is not a set of static forms, but rather, as one critic has put it in an essay on racial versus national philosophies of American art at the turn of the twentieth century, an attempt, "to transform cultural heterogeneity into U.S. nationality . . . to establish a national people in the United States."[55]

How feasible is, or was, such an attempt? As Terry Eagleton has expressed it, there is a danger of neurosis in the kind of utopianism that persuades us to "desire uselessly rather than feasibly."[56] Confronted with the unchanged reality of our situation, we suffer the reality as well as the sharper edge of ambitious but unfulfilled ideals. Although this and other confrontations may well have affected Dunbar negatively in his own life, his work somehow avoids that fate.[57] Dunbar's poetic experiment manages to be both feasible and utopian, in that the poetry is often the wishful projection of a society that, while failing in many things, has passed significant tests of historical responsibility (for example, it has ended slavery), social diversity (it is made up of individuals and communities of many different backgrounds who can get along as citizens and groups), and national cultural maturity (there is an American literature that is not merely a copy of models from elsewhere). The fact that the nation has not passed other tests, however, such as facing the fact of racism and the hypocrisies that mar its political discourse, is only to state that it has yet to become the embodiment of the spirit of its governing documents.[58] Either way, Dunbar is prepared to let stand the poetic resolution of that which cannot be resolved in the world of 1890s America and take the consequences of the ironic dismantling of his achievement by the social and political context that overshadows it. Beyond that, however, my argument is that he is prepared to take the consequences because he has already admitted the contingency of the poetic act as an epistemological countermovement that subverts from within the text. As "Robert Gould Shaw" does its commemorative duty while knowing that no commemorative words can ever achieve their full and desired purpose, so does Dunbar live the unachieved national reconciliation "passionately, ironically, in all of its elusive impossibility."[59]

The tale of the Northern writer and American memory does not offer easy access to the dream of historical justification that Southern literature made its own, and the tale of the black Northern writer even less so. Paul Laurence Dunbar, for his part, partakes of both the world of modernity and the shackles of an unresolved past. In his Dayton, Ohio, upbringing, his high-school friendship with the aviation pioneer Orville Wright, and his easy facility with the dialects of a diverse population, he commands a view of the world made electric by change and progress; in contrast, his color, his family history, and the stony callousness of much of American society all go to make him part of a tradition of black poetic meditation against white racial culture. Neither of these modes of being secured his complete allegiance. If there were ashes left by 1900, then Dunbar certainly tasted some of them as he reflected on the ironies of American historical amnesia and the desire for an easygoing folk-memory of an unproblematic national past. In many ways he was the Northern writer par excellence, certain that there had once been a victory in a civil war but finding only the re-engineered cultural memory imposed by the ostensibly defeated party. Like Lowell, Melville, James, and Bierce in their different ways, Dunbar recognized that, at particular historical moments, culture may need to be resisted as well as embraced.

Coda

LONG ROAD

> no scar,
> But internal difference,
> Where the Meanings, are –
>
> *Emily Dickinson*

WHY MEMORY? The question is worth raising. As I argue throughout this book, literary texts are a form of memory that walks a thin line between the subjectivities of individual experience (and their imaginative reinterpretation) and the public dynamics of collective memory and commemorative politics. Some of that argument is explicit, but much of it is woven into the readings of the individual texts. One particular objection to my basic approach, however, might be expressed as follows: despite its usefulness as a way of describing certain cultural phenomena, collective memory is nothing more than a metaphor, a conceit, and evidence of its autonomous existence as an object of study is impossible to locate in any scholarly framework, whether that of psychology, history, sociology, or literary and cultural studies. After all, it is hovering on the borders of mysticism to conceive that there is a kind of community brain, a place where memories that were not just individual memories would have to reside. There is no commonly held psyche, so to speak, and indeed contemporary literary texts that foreground the trope of collective memory can find themselves burdened with difficulties emerging from the increasingly fraught interactions between American recollection and American history.[1] The same critic might point out that while it is an attractive rhetorical turn to suggest that geographical locations, institutions, and texts are "realms of memory" (as in Pierre Nora's *Lieux de memoire*), there are other terms and formulations that would serve as well, and with greater scholarly accuracy.

I would concede the argument, to a certain extent. A considerable number of institutions such as history museums and historical associations devoted to specialized topics are involved with the task of preservation and presentation for the Civil War as much as for any other historical event or period in America, or indeed elsewhere. All have something to do with "memory" in a casually associative way, but to designate, say, the Smithsonian's National Museum of American History as a component of American collective memory is perhaps to apply a whimsical description to a place of rational procedures, educational standards, and scholarly reputation. Nevertheless, contemporary cultural studies as well as older, more established disciplines, such as anthropology and sociology, would be open to the idea that cognition and communication are distributed across people, their social interaction, and the natural and the built environment. To that extent, the institution of the Smithsonian has, beyond the verifiability and the scholarly legitimacy of its procedures and presentations, a role as a setting for metaphor, symbol, and the subjective perceptions of the visiting audience (or audiences) within the framework of a project of national historical understanding. Indeed, like the Smithsonian, many less permanent and less high-profile entities also have that dual role as rational and symbolic doorways into American memory.

Looking at the matter from a different perspective, an argument could be made for decoupling the concept of institution from a rather inflexible relation to the realms of higher social organization and bringing it home to the immediate context of human experience, perhaps even experience beneath the level of individual conscious recollection. One might look at the question as Philip Kuberski does in *The Persistence of Memory*:

> The originative memory is organism itself, the persistence of organized patterns and cycles passing from stars to rivers to bodies. We tend to think of memory as the possession of an individual ego, but it is perhaps more accurate to see that the individual ego is

remembered – or lives – because of the patterned forces of organic memory. The cardio-vascular system is autonomic (or self-ruling) only because of the millions of years of accumulated memory implicit in each breath and heartbeat. Cybernetic theorists recognize this fact, but they refer to an organism in this general sense as a feedback system. Such phrasing cannot conceal its mythological basis: a system is very like an abstracted river, the originative image of cyclicity. And our body, [the German Romantic author] Novalis wrote, is a moulded river.[2]

As the memory of the Civil War was rendered present in everything from the injuries and missing limbs of veterans and the absence of deceased family and friends, through the subtle and obvious social and economic changes in life over the succeeding decades, to the stream of fictional and nonfictional writings that appeared with no end in sight, so the ideology of commemoration changed according to both the distance from the original loss and demands for what Robert Pogue Harrison has called the "creative retrieval" and "reprojection" of the memories of the dead.[3] This is not a particularly American phenomenon, but it took on an American stamp in those years: in particular, the dead were not merely inoperative functions within a new principle of mechanized warfare but rather retained a republican status: "citzens were selves – bodies and names that lived beyond their own deaths, individuals who were the literal lifeblood of the nation," however differently the term nation was interpreted.[4] For their part, Southerners lost little time in fabricating (in the technical sense of the word) a culture of commemoration and justification that tapped, retrieved, and – where it could – reprojected memory to create a pattern that linked the experience of the war to the consensus narrative of Southern identity, that of struggle, unearned defeat, and honor. The political discourse of the South at the end of the nineteenth century brought the sacrifice of the body and the body of cultural thought into urgent and active juxtaposition.

The North, in contrast, had lost its grip on the memory of the war by the beginning of the twentieth century, in which memory would become a crucial nexus of politics and psyche, of power, injury, and identity. To use Kuberski's terminology, the South succeeded where the North did not in transforming the memory of the war into organic memory, and not just the mental recollection of the past. The social topography of memory had shifted between the end of the war and the end of the century, and with primarily negative consequences for the meanings of what one might call the liberations of 1865: the liberation of African Americans into an uncertain future; the rescue of the Union from the potentially greatest threat to its existence; the freeing of the South in general from the psychic prison-house of slavery. Whether personal or community recollection was what was at stake, it was clear that by 1900 both had circulated through a filter of ideological cleansing and restoration. The once-victorious North had finally arrived at a stage where it reflected, rather than challenged, the contours, if not the precise content, of the collective memory of the former Confederacy on its journey to national cultural hegemony. The South's new position of cultural dominance had been secured by writing and rhetoric, by popular cultural forms and elite modes of discourse, and by appeals to racial fears and to common values alike. Whether sentimentally progressive, querulously conservative, or sardonically detached, the literature of Civil War memory at home in the North had discovered, perhaps somewhat to its discomfiture, that it had failed the test of resilience. In Harrison's terms, the North failed to creatively retrieve and reproject its own loss.

The selection of texts and authors in *Ashes of the Mind* is meant, however, not to constitute a precise map of collective or community memory – that would require a larger base of textual evidence – but to examine how particular Northern writers perceived and understood the changes in politics and conviction that had infused the commemorative culture at the time of the Union victory. Lowell's elegiac celebration, Melville's recalcitrance, James's complex sympathies, Bierce's nihilism, and Dunbar's irony are way stations on that path from 1865 to the end of the century. Despite the authority of these exemplary texts, however, one achieves only a narrow focus on the broader issue of collective memory – coming back to Maurice Halbwachs's statement that "it is language, and the whole system of social conventions attached to it, that allows us at every moment to reconstruct our past"[5] – if the objects of analysis are restricted to those validated, to a greater or lesser degree, by their presence in the literary canon or within a consensus of culturally approved production. The justification I would advance to counter that implied charge is essentially disciplinary: the fact is that literary studies still maintain a bias, even after many decades of challenge and reconsideration, toward a study of the kind of text that can repay the investment of time and intellectual energy. Complexity has certain advantages. There is also, however, a more personal argument: the selection of what should be studied is rooted inevitably, to some degree, in unpredictable and subjective preference.

I want to glance briefly, therefore, at three works that cast light from a very different angle on the theme of conflict and subjectivity, and on the paths that memory takes. These are the novel *Like unto Like* by the expatriate Southerner Sherwood Bonner, the long career in advocacy and charitable organizations of Josephine Shaw Lowell, and a study by one of the most influential social activists and thinkers of the period, Jane Addams. An important aspect of this final section is also that the meaning of "work" can be expanded to include the performative, the political, and the anthropological.

The assertion that women remember differently from men can be deployed for different ends, including the slightly suspect construction of an exclusive relationship between women and "sentiment," one of the popular foci for literary scholarship in recent years. Although one can certainly recover previously dismissed texts on the very legitimate grounds that *sentiment* has been conflated with *sentimentality* and that fiction that was rooted in the former has become the target of a general indictment for the latter, critics can also fall into the trap of merely celebrating a subgenre for the same characteristics for which it has been previously condemned. One can inadvertently cement a link between writer, gender, form, and readership that has simply changed from being an object of patronizing dismissal in the past to one of current academic approbation. The problems with the critical vocabulary of sentiment become obvious when we look at a notably unsentimental work within the sentimental tradition, Sherwood Bonner's *Like unto Like* (1878). This novel tells the story of a doomed relationship between Blythe Herndon, a young Southern woman, and Roger Ellis, an older Union army officer stationed in her home town in Alabama during the Reconstruction era. *Like unto Like* is one of the few works of fiction (if not indeed the only one) produced by a female author during the postwar decades that takes a decidedly ironic, and at times almost comic, perspective when dealing with the questions of defeat, remembrance, and the potential for North–South reconciliation up to and including marriage between partners from the previously warring sides.

It is important to note that, although its author was a Southerner, *Like unto Like* was written and published in Boston, the city of smug Yankee self-regard to which Sherwood Bonner (the pen name of Katherine Sherwood Bonner MacDowell) had exiled herself in 1872. One of the many interesting things about Bonner's novel is that it addresses how unexpectedly and unhappily an attempt to manage the memory of the war by intimate sectional reconciliation (love and marriage) can founder on the one thing that nobody wants to talk about: race. The social status of a black youth called Bill (whose nickname is, somewhat improbably, Civil Rights Bill) becomes the metaphorical mine that blows up in the face of the newly married couple, Blythe and Roger. To that extent, *Like unto Like* is the lost radical classic of Southern Reconstruction literature whose heroine, a loquacious maverick, rejects the dull, sententious culture of her rural Alabama upbringing to fall in love with, and eventually marry, an intellectual and political reformer from the abolitionist North. And yet, although Blythe dismisses the reverential circling around the memory of the war and the Confederacy that her family and community engage in, she discovers ultimately that she has taken a step too far in her project of self-liberation and falls prey to prejudices she had previously regarded herself as having left behind. She does not believe, however, that those prejudices are what caused her marriage to collapse.

Sherwood Bonner's own move to Boston (and far away from her husband and children), and her entry into the city's literary and intellectual circles, together embody an act of defiance in the face of the deeply rooted expectations placed on women in the South. Women enjoying a certain social status were meant to, above all, use their skills to influence the cultural politics of education and to nurture a local historical sensibility that had the purity of the Confederate cause as its core belief. Ironically, however, her major literary achievement, *Like unto Like*, can be seen as an account of how difficult it may be to simply declare the victory of individual destiny over community feeling, or of a liberated future over neurotic re-enactments of the past. At the conclusion of the novel, Blythe knows that her memory of her marriage, and of why it failed, will not be accepted at home, and the collective memory of the family and community will assert its dominance, irrespective of factual truth. The peculiar position taken on by Bonner, as an assertive Southern woman in the (by then somewhat fading) national cultural metropolis of Boston becomes a metaphor for the complex two-directional negotiation that women can find themselves engaging in, as both repositories of family memory and potential vehicles for future relationships – and indeed she is perhaps the only female author whose writing really captures the irony endemic to that role in post-Civil War America.

Representing a very different style and posture, Josephine Shaw Lowell stood at the angle-point of memory and change for four decades after the end of the Civil War. Lowell was the sister of Robert Gould Shaw, commander of the 54th Massachusetts, and the widow of James Russell Lowell's nephew Charles, also killed on active duty. Lowell's forty-year career as a social worker, organizer, and activist is a testimony to her husband's short life and his death in a cause that was almost a family inheritance. It is also a method of transforming her memory of him (and her brother), and of the war, into a commemorative act that is ongoing and convivial, that attempts to escape the morbidity of a ritualistic invocation of loss. Josephine Shaw Lowell, a soldier's widow and the sister of a dead hero, constructed a very individual life of social and moral engagement and high-minded reformism, although one distinctly scripted by the traditions and expectations of the milieu she grew up in.

Joan Waugh in her biography of Josephine Lowell emphasizes the emotional cost of Lowell's early bereavement (she had only a few months of married life, much of it spent apart, before Charles Lowell was killed in late 1864) but argues that her youthful widowhood directed Lowell to a path that would offer her a way of being a "useful citizen," a popular term in her circle, and embody the ideals for which she believed her husband and brother had died.[6] Social historians have not been kind, however, to the theory and practice with which she is identified. The intrusive and mechanical charity procedures of the Gilded Age, often seen as pressuring the poor into accepting respectable middle-class behavior and values as a quid pro quo for urgently needed help, have come to be regarded as a conservative force in American culture. Waugh opposes this interpretation of Lowell's work and writings and argues that her career reveals in fact strong threads of feminist thought, a radical moral politics, and a broad concept of political liberation traceable to the abolitionist milieu of her youth and the experience of the war years.[7]

The influence of that long tradition emerges, in particular, in the way in which Josephine Shaw Lowell created, in the Charity Organization Society, an active and institutional equivalent to the bronze monument to her brother's regiment on Boston Common. This step brought Lowell into the senior management of New York social work and philanthropic activity, and in many ways she and other like-minded reformers embodied the era's combination of business efficiency and humanitarian impulse.[8] One can speculate that Lowell believed that a focused practice of social amelioration, embedded in an understanding of the swiftly changing structure of the American economy, would be one method of signifying a link with a lost past and a long-dead but psychologically present loved one. Her life path and career between 1864 and 1905 reveal the presence of not only a sense of personal history and inherited values but also an organic memory (to use Kuberski's phrase again) that flows from the days of youth, marriage, and an idealists' war, through the decades of functional memorialization, to the unexpected reshaping of Civil War memory as a new political trope that was no longer about the meanings of distinct Union and Confederate histories.

As Waugh notes in *Unsentimental Reformer*, the sudden emergence of an assertive American imperialist philosophy at the turn of the century, and the opposing campaign to end the war against the nationalist insurgents in the Philippines, altered the easy relationship with the image of the military that Josephine Lowell had embraced in her younger years. Her perspective had changed into something we would now recognize as an early form of the civil protest that marked, for example, the antiwar movement of the Vietnam era.[9] Lowell also found herself at a distinct disadvantage here. The assumption on the part of Lowell and many of her fellow activists that the Civil War had been – in contrast to the contemporary operations in the Philippines – a noble undertaking to save the Union and eradicate slavery was countered very effectively by those who invoked the memory of the conflict as a site of generalized American military prowess and fighting spirit, with the particular aims of each side dismissed as irrelevant. Most Americans took the latter view, and the sudden projection of a weak-willed femininity onto the dissenting camp underlined the nature of that particular culture war.

As Lowell's younger fellow activist and reformer Jane Addams declares in her original and often overlooked study *The Long Road of Woman's Memory* (1916): "In this moment of almost universal warfare there is evinced a widespread moral abhorrence against war, as if its very existence were more than human nature could endure."[10] Written against the background of World War I, Addams's evaluation of the women she spoke with at Hull-House and elsewhere over several years focuses on the capacity of women to keep in balance a self-deprecating obedience to authority and an implicit challenge to the dynamics of organized patriotism and nationalist ideology. Her account in the chapter entitled "Women's Memories – Challenging War" of mothers with sons fighting in the "great European War," as Addams calls it, details the confused attitudes women have to the social norms that suddenly demand the mass recruitment and sacrifice of males of military service age. Seeing the men in their families disappear, but unused to openly criticizing the state of affairs in public, most women go along with war until such time as its depredations appear to put all civilization in danger, including the basic humane structures for which they, as women, feel themselves responsible. Indeed, the very persistence of the nation as a touchstone for stability and social meaning can suddenly appear threatening rather than reassuring. As Josephine Shaw Lowell, widow of a soldier and sister of a hero with his own memorial opposite the Massachusetts State House, suddenly found herself on the "unpatriotic" and "anti-American" side of the public debate on America's first Pacific war, so the tribal nationalism of the women in Addams's book gives way to what she calls a "humble internationalism," a sense of an alternative world based on real human connections and progressive interactions across national borders, including the delicate webs of communication between immigrants in the United States and families left behind in Europe.[11]

The movement from the mother's memory of her child to the realization that the basic dynamics of existence are placed in question by the continuation of war is long. In anthropological as much as individual terms such a movement will inevitably arrive at the site of "an ever-recurring struggle, often tragic and bitter, between two conceptions of duty, one of which is antagonistic to the other."[12] The duty to the beliefs of the society in which you live and to its duly constituted authorities grinds against the duty to humanity, the duty to not engage in violence and killing that destroys not only lives and property but also the capacity for moral outrage. In *The Long Road*, it is the sharpest edge of all to be caught on – to send out one's sons and brothers and lovers to kill other women's sons and brothers and lovers, but to come to disbelieve in the warrant for that action. And no relief from memory is granted. To recall the child in precise detail as he was before he was lost is both an achievement and a terrible burden, and the women in Addams's accounts are tempted to retreat from an unbearable reality into the reassurance of memory.

War, memory, and commemoration do not exist, therefore, in some obscure conceptual or cultural realm. rather, they are there within and alongside the organic response and the domestic routine. Human beings are bereaved by war, because war transforms the context in which human beings live, for good or ill. The realization of injury may well be a gendered experience, as Bonner, Lowell, and Addams suggest; women's memories may be assigned longer and less prestigious roads to travel and may confront greater pressure to adjust the incommunicable meaning of loss to locally authorized political and institutional forms, including within the family. And the human organism may stimulate or enact things that are below the level of moral or rational awareness and therefore take no account of where the political weight comes down. Blythe Herndon's sudden racial paranoia that, against the force of her open mind and generous spirit, fixates on the unacceptable bodily otherness of the young African American boy in *Like unto Like*; Josephine Lowell's dedication of her life to practical social objectives as a kind of active or virtual memorial to the values for which, she believed, her soldier men had died; Jane Addams's attentive and persistent drawing out of the real meanings of female traumatic loss: all the foregoing, despite their differing ideological content, testify to the physicality of memory, an organically lived dimension predating the verbal, the social, or the institutional.

Gender may draw some crucial and unavoidable distinctions, but the human capacities for recollection and forgetting, loss and commemoration, are all equally at stake, and make the knowing of the past both an institutional and a personal matter. Often, if not all the time, people in their role as readers, as members of communities, as citizens of nation-states, as makers and consumers of cultural production (including academic scholarship), and perhaps even at certain times and places as victims will accept that there are conflicts and, subsequently and inevitably, in time, will work through the memory of those conflicts. They are not surprised by such phenomena, on either the collective or the individual level, as the burial of unpleasant recollections, the increasing self-doubt of the ostensibly victorious entity, or the unexpected resurfacing, in politics and poetics, of historical forces that one believed long since put to sleep.

Neither are many people taken aback by the discovery that the political and the aesthetic moments are not safely removed from each other's influence. With World War II, the Holocaust, Stalin's mass purges, Vietnam, the first Gulf War, and Rwanda behind us, we also have no problem grasping that war and liberation, trauma and commemoration have been all part of the global grammar of the twentieth century and look as though they are going to abide – as both text and context – well into the twenty-first. To that extent, the series of writings by Lowell, Melville, James, Bierce, and Dunbar explored in this book point to something beyond the achievement of complex representations of the American Civil War and its long historical aftermath, beyond merely the metaphor of individual or collective injury or recovery. These texts gesture, in fact, toward the reality that the literary culture is not protected from the fires of history, and that even their ashes can hide still-burning embers – something that James Russell Lowell no doubt understood very well, as he sketched out his poem the night before the ceremony on July 21, 1865.

Notes

Introduction

1. Maurice Halbwachs, *On Collective Memory*, ed. and trans. Lewis A. Coser (Chicago: University of Chicago Press, 1992), 173.

2. Military campaigns against Native American resistance had always aimed at (at least) intimidating the nonwarring part of the population too, but that strategy comes from a branch of military thinking that is different from that of large-scale engagements of equivalent regular forces. To a certain extent, the "cabinet wars" of the eighteenth century, in which strategic aims were modest and the impact on civilian life reduced, still wielded some influence over staff officers on both sides of the Civil War, and the economic and psychological warfare conducted by Sherman in Georgia in 1864, for example, was a relatively late development.

3. Ralph Ellison, "Stephen Crane and the Mainstream of American Fiction," in *Collected Essays of Ralph Ellison*, ed. John F. Callahan (New York: Modern Library, 2003), 119.

4. Vernon Louis Parrington, *Main Currents in American Thought: An Interpretation of American Literature from the Beginnings until 1920*, vol. 2, *1800–1860: The Romantic Revolution in America* (New York: Harcourt, Brace, and World, 1927), 474.

5. See Wolfgang Schivelbusch, *The Culture of Defeat: On National Trauma, Mourning, and Recovery*, trans. Jefferson Chase (New York: Henry Holt, 2005), esp. 91–101, for a broader discussion of the success of the cultural work done by the defeated South.

6. Robert Lowell, *Selected Poems*, expanded ed. (New York: Farrar, Straus and Giroux, 2006), 178–80.

7. In his ambitious study *The Material Unconscious: American Amusement, Stephen Crane, and the Economies of Play* (Cambridge, MA: Harvard University Press, 1996), Bill Brown suggests that the photographic record of the Civil War, through, for example, battlefield images of corpses, offered the first "countermemory" (147), a piece of evidence to challenge the calculated and sanitized narratives of war. He also calls the culture of documentary war photography a way of making "a technology of the psyche apprehensible as a technology of the

visual" (145). A question arises whether the achievement of the technology of the literary is not only a similar but much older one. I would argue that literary texts offer, in contrast to photography, not so much a choice between memory and countermemory as the setting for a type of guerilla warfare between the two.

8. I am more interested in the role of memory in cultural life than in the individual functions of memory as either a psychological or a neurological issue. However, although the neuro-scientific aspects of memory are beyond the scope of this book (and the expertise of the author), I should emphasize nonetheless that this is an area that is becoming difficult for literary and cultural scholars to ignore. For a brief but persuasive summary of some recent developments, see Suzanne Nalbantian, *Memory in Literature: From Rousseau to Neuroscience* (New York: Palgrave Macmillan, 2003), esp. chap. 8.

9. Barry Schwartz, *Abraham Lincoln and the Forge of National Memory* (Chicago: University of Chicago Press, 2000), 17.

10. Coincidentally, as I worked on this introduction one day I heard a radio report about the emotional case of a baby's being born to a woman who already had been brain-dead for several weeks (and who was taken off life-support just after the delivery). A family member stated that she had given "the last, full measure of devotion" to the life of her child. Whatever the medical and ethical issues in this case, the quotation from the Gettysburg Address was clearly meant to be widely understood and to place the mother's situation on a high moral plateau validated by national collective memory.

11. Randall Jarrell, "The Death of the Ball Turret Gunner," in *Anthology of Modern American Poetry*, ed. Cary Nelson (New York: Oxford University Press, 2000), 713.

12. R. Clifton Spargo, *The Ethics of Mourning: Grief and Responsibility in Elegiac Literature* (Baltimore: Johns Hopkins University Press, 2004), 222. Chap. 6 of Spargo's book is, broadly speaking, an impressive and highly critical analysis of Jarrell's use of the elegy.

13. For example, when visitors arrived in Charleston, SC, in April 1961 for the official commemoration of the Fort Sumter attack, the city's hotels refused to put up the African American guests. Eventually, on instructions from the Kennedy administration, the U.S. Navy offered them accommodation on a military installation. See John Wiener, "Civil War, Cold War, Civil Rights: The Civil War Centennial in Context, 1960-1965," in *The Memory of the Civil War in American Culture*, ed. Alice Fahs and Joan Waugh (Chapel Hill: University of North Carolina Press, 2004), 238-41.

14. Stuart McConnell, *Glorious Contentment: The Grand Army of the Republic, 1865-1900* (Chapel Hill: University of North Carolina Press, 1992), 215-18.

15. David W. Blight, *Race and Reunion: The Civil War in American Memory* (Cambridge, MA: Harvard University Press, Belknap Press, 2001), 266.

16. Nell Irwin Painter, "Honest Abe and Uncle Tom," *Canadian Review of American Studies/Revue canadienne d'études américaines* 30 (2000): 246-72. Painter's exploration of the cultural meanings of visual images (those of Lincoln and

of Stowe's character Uncle Tom) and her analysis of the capacity of a dominant social group to (partly) unconsciously mold and reconfigure its collective memory – in other words, to determine the history that it wants to remember and that which it desires to forget – is a good example of the "history and memory" studies that became popular during the 1990s. These were in turn influenced to a significant extent by the French historian Pierre Nora and his *Lieux de mémoire* project, which appeared in English in three volumes as *Realms of Memory*, trans. Arthur Goldhammer (New York: Columbia University Press, 1996).

17. Lowell, *Selected Poems*, 179.

18. Murray Shane, "The Psychology of Monuments," in *"Remove Not the Ancient Landmark": Public Monuments and Moral Values*, ed. Donald Martin Reynolds (Amsterdam: Gordon and Breach, 1996), 49.

19. Sometimes I feel that Margaret Mitchell has a claim to be in that line-up, too, but I have already mentioned *Gone with the Wind* once in this introduction, and I am not certain it really embodies the kind of searching return to origins I am discussing.

20. Thomas Nelson Page, *In Ole Virginia; or, Marse Chan and Other Stories* (Nashville, TN: J. S. Sanders, 1991), 171.

21. See Daniel Aaron, *The Unwritten War: American Writers and the Civil War* (New York: Oxford University Press, 1973), 275-76, 288.

22. See Kathleen Diffley, *Where My Heart Is Turning Ever: Civil War Stories and Constitutional Reform, 1861-1876* (Athens: University of Georgia Press, 1992), esp. xix-xlii for a survey of the regional publishing landscapes. I should note that Diffley has compiled much useful detail and delivers a more nuanced assessment of the situation in the South than does my brief comment.

23. Edward Tabor Linenthal, *Sacred Ground: Americans and Their Battlefields*, 2nd ed. (Urbana and Chicago: University of Illinois Press, 1993), 118. See also Painter, "Honest Abe and Uncle Tom," 267-68, for a comment on Gettysburg as a place of highly charged and nonreconciled memorial politics, and thus of implicit struggles over meaning, rather than the site of an uncomplicated and static remembrance of a Union victory.

24. Bob Newhart, "Abe Lincoln vs. Madison Avenue," in *The Button-Down Mind of Bob Newhart*, 1960, Warner Bros. Records Inc. (Transcription by the author.)

25. Some readers may be familiar with Peter Norvig's parody of the Gettysburg Address, for example, developed to show the limitations of some current audiovisual presentation tools whose capacities are often overrated. The Gettysburg Powerpoint Presentation can be viewed at http://norvig.com/Gettysburg/, accessed May 18, 2008.

26. Michael Kammen, *Mystic Chords of Memory: The Transformation of Tradition in American Culture* (New York: Vintage Books, 1993), 101.

27. Alfred Kazin, *On Native Grounds: An Interpretation of Modern American Prose Literature* (1942; San Diego: Harcourt Brace, 1995), 69.

28. See Painter, "Honest Abe and Uncle Tom," 267, on the absence of any memorial specifically dedicated to black soldiers in the Union army until the late 1990s.

29. Dunbar's reading tour of Britain in 1897, the first such tour in which a black American writer enjoyed the goodwill of the U.S. minister (ambassador) to the Court of St. James's, could be seen as a move on the transatlantic cultural and racial chessboard.

1. Cambridge Interiors: Lowell's Commemoration Ode

1. Lowell's nephews killed in battle were Charles Russell Lowell, his brother James Jackson Lowell, and their cousin William Lowell Putnam. These were not James Russell Lowell's only losses: Charles Lowell's widow was the sister of Robert Gould Shaw of the 54th Massachusetts regiment, killed in 1863 leading his African American troops in the famous assault on Fort Wagner. See also Steven Axelrod, "Colonel Shaw in American Poetry: 'For the Union Dead' and Its Precursors," *American Quarterly* 24 (1972): 523-37, for an account of the resonance of these casualties within American poetry over the succeeding century.

2. Betsy Erkkila, *Whitman the Political Poet* (New York: Oxford University Press, 1989), 309.

3. Ibid., 308-9. Erkkila points out that, although there had been much press hostility over the years, the first public legal challenge to Whitman's work was the opening of obscenity proceedings against *Leaves of Grass* by the Boston district attorney in 1882.

4. F. DeWolfe Miller, introduction to *Walt Whitman's Drum-Taps (1865) and Sequel to Drum-Taps (1865-6)* (Gainesville, FL: Scholars' Facsimiles and Reprints, 1959), li.

5. One should note that repeated efforts have been made to recover the work of the so-called Schoolroom Poets and give them appropriate space in the history of poetry in the United States. Apart from John Hollander's notable achievement with the Library of America's *American Poetry: The Nineteenth Century* (New York: Literary Classics of the United States, 1996), Longfellow and Whittier are undergoing a revival of sorts, clearly a result of the Library of America's bringing out substantial anthologies of their work in 2000 and 2004, respectively. In particular, Angela Sorby, *Schoolroom Poets: Childhood, Performance, and the Place of American Poetry, 1865-1917* (Durham: University of New Hampshire Press, 2005) is a welcome addition to the scholarship. Earlier interventions include George Arms, *The Fields Were Green: A New View of Bryant, Whittier, Holmes, Lowell, and Longfellow, with a Selection of Their Poems* (Stanford, CA: Stanford University Press, 1953); Robert Penn Warren's powerful essay on Whittier from 1971 entitled "John Greenleaf Whittier: Poetry as Experience," in *New and Selected Essays* (New York: Random House, 1989), 235-83; and Thomas Wortham's introduction to *James Russell Lowell's "The*

Biglow Papers [First Series]": A Critical Edition (DeKalb: Northern Illinois University Press, 1977), ix–xxxiv, among others. There are some interesting remarks on the international reputation and following that Longfellow enjoyed in an undated essay by Randell Jarrell ("Is American Poetry American?"), published in *Yale Review* 87.3 (1999): 5-7.

6. *Four American Poems, Metrically Translated into German by Charles Theodore Eben* (Philadelphia: F. Leypoldt, 1864).

7. Arms, *Fields Were Green*, 5. The concept of "urbanity and wit" needs some qualification also: in Lowell's *Biglow Papers: First Series*, for example, the truculent "Debate in the Sennit" verses with their sarcastic and hypnotic refrain, "Sez John C. Calhoun, sez he," are aggressive political satire, less urbane than angry. On the issue of literary-historical nomenclature, because the descriptors "Schoolroom" and "Fireside" are negatively loaded for critical discussion, I would like to re-introduce the older term "the New England Poets" into this chapter as the most appropriate rubric for Lowell and his colleagues.

8. And even the dogged interiority of Whitman's "Lilacs" is a statement made within the parameters of civil interaction in the United States in the months following the surrender of the Confederacy and the Lincoln assassination.

9. For a succinct discussion of the topic of party loyalties, see Joel H. Silbey, *The American Political Nation, 1838–1893* (Stanford, CA: Stanford University Press, 1991), 215-24.

10. Vernon L. Parrington, *Main Currents in American Thought: An Interpretation of American Literature from the Beginnings to 1920*, vol. 2, *1800–1860: The Romantic Revolution in America* (New York: Harcourt, Brace and World, 1927, 1930), 474.

11. Lowell to R. W. Gilder, January 16, 1886, *Letters of James Russell Lowell*, ed. Charles Eliot Norton, 3 vols. (Boston and New York: Houghton, Mifflin, 1904), 3:149. The original title of the poem, on the assumption that it was retained for the privately printed version, was "Ode Recited at the Commemoration of the Living and Dead Soldiers of Harvard University, July 21, 1865." For an extensive account of the progress of the ode from composition through performance to publication, as well as a useful appendix with a tabular listing of the various emendations to the text, see Hamilton Vaughan Bail, "James Russell Lowell's Ode Recited at the Commemoration of the Living and Dead Soldiers of Harvard University, July 21, 1865," *Papers of the Bibliographical Society of America* 37 (1943): 169-202.

12. In his path-breaking study of the elegy in English poetry, Peter Sacks argues that American poetry has always had problems with the elegiac form. As a result of the "severe repression and rationalization of grief" involved in Puritan culture, he asserts, "American culture seems to have had a particular difficulty in accommodating genuine mourning" (Peter M. Sacks, *The English Elegy: Studies in the Genre from Spenser to Yeats* [Baltimore: Johns Hopkins University Press, 1985], 313). Sacks suggests that American poets have concentrated on the suffering of the isolated consciousness rather than the emotion of the

community for their elegiac projects. This may well be true for Whitman, but Lowell's Commemoration Ode does not, I would argue, fit Sacks's paradigm.

13. The edition of the poem used in this chapter is from *The Poetical Works of James Russell Lowell*, Cambridge ed., rev. Marjorie R. Kaufmann (Boston: Houghton Mifflin, 1978), 340–47; text references are to stanza number.

14. Elaine Scarry, *The Body in Pain* (New York: Oxford University Press, 1985), 114. Scarry is engaging in a critical but diplomatic reading of the Prussian general and scholar Carl von Clausewitz in this section of her book; she draws attention (98-105) to his discussion of the elements of war in *Vom Kriege*, in particular the problem he has in establishing the "power of enforcement" as an indispensable component of, and indeed a logical justification for, war. To put it simply, a war that purported to be against institution X that ended in victory for the anti-X forces, but after which for whatever reason X continued to exist, would be not only psychologically confusing but also contrary to any rational logic of war. As historians and other scholars have shown in different contexts, the interpretation of the Civil War in the North within abolitionist and related ideologies was often couched in terms of a national trial to expiate sin, a moral testing of an extreme kind. Thus, in the Harvard Commemoration Ode Lowell is intensely focused on the justification for the experience of the war, for violence given and violence suffered, a process in which the moral thought – the self-definition – flows effortlessly into the political belief. Clausewitz also has something to say about that other dimension of the Civil War – which he did not live to see – the issue of physical endurance and battle-field trauma. This further point emerges in book 1, chapter 5 of *Vom Kriege*, where he comments on the unknown limits to which the body can be pushed in military engagements, defining the atmosphere of war by four elements: danger, physical effort, uncertainty, accident (Carl von Clausewitz, Helmuth von Moltke, *Kriegstheorie und Kriegsgeschichte* [Frankfurt am Main: Deutscher Klassiker Verlag, 1993], 62-67). In the context of 1865 the war has subjected the American body to more pressure that it can be expected to endure – a theme that dominates Whitman's "Lilacs" and provides a more submerged note in Lowell's Commemoration Ode.

15. James Russell Lowell, "Abraham Lincoln (1864)," in *My Study Windows* (Boston: James R. Osgood and Company, 1871), 176; Thomas Gustafson, *Representative Words: Politics, Literature, and the American Language, 1776–1865* (New York: Cambridge University Press, 1992), 386.

16. The quatrain is perhaps particularly memorable when put up against some of Whitman's strained and least convincing passages. As a counterpoint, however, it is worth remembering the final stanza from Melville's "The College Colonel" ("But all through the Seven Days' Fight, / And deep in the Wilderness grim, / And in the field-hospital tent, / And Petersburg crater, and dim / Lean brooding in Libby, there came – / Ah heaven! – what *truth* to him") as a more ambivalent poetic statement on – this time uncapitalized but italicized – truth (Herman Melville, *Battle-Pieces and Aspects of the War* [New York:

Harper and Brothers, 1866; reprinted with a new introduction by Lee Rust Brown, New York: Da Capo Press, 1995], 121).

17. Wolfgang Schivelbusch, *The Culture of Defeat: On National Trauma, Mourning, and Recovery*, trans. Jefferson Chase (New York: Henry Holt, 2003), 5.

18. Henry James, *Autobiography*, ed. Frederick W. Dupee (Princeton, NJ: Princeton University Press, 1983), 463.

19. Harold Bloom, "Freud: Frontier Concepts, Jewishness, and Interpretation," in *Trauma: Explorations in Memory*, ed. Cathy Caruth (Baltimore: Johns Hopkins University Press, 1995), 113-27.

20. Ibid., 117.

21. Bloom suggests that literary criticism and psychoanalysis are the two contemporary "belated versions" of this tradition of speculative prophecy. And "speculative" is a good adjective for the writing that Emerson and his contemporaries were producing in the 1840s and 1850s, work that had the energy of creative experimentation without taking the form of conventional literary genres. In his analysis of the Transcendentalists and their writing, Lawrence Buell suggests that the peculiarity of their approach was that it combined the metaphoric energy and imaginative leaps of poetry with ostensibly inappropriate genres, such as the natural history essay, the autobiographical account, and the sermon, none of which permits entry to the traditional kinds of critical readings as readily as the "normal" literary modes do. This mingling of genres has led, in the past, to the marginalization of writing that just will not align itself with the reigning academic categories (Lawrence Buell, *Literary Transcendentalism: Style and Vision in the American Renaissance* [Ithaca, NY: Cornell University Press, 1973], 13-17). Echoes of this speculative mingling are to be heard at moments during Lowell's "Ode."

22. *Selected Essays of John Crowe Ransom*, ed. Thomas Daniel Young and John Hindle (Baton Rouge: Louisiana State University Press, 1984), 28. Ransom's assertion appeared originally in a brief essay for *The Fugitive* in 1925.

23. An even more contemporary variant (that I take up briefly at the conclusion of the chapter) would be the influence of deconstructionist approaches to the lyric by critics such as Paul de Man. From a deconstructionist point of view, Lowell's Commemoration Ode is as useful a poetic object on which to expose the figural sleight of hand trying to disguise its grammatical/syntactic system (literal reading as the return of the repressed, perhaps) as a passage from *The Waste Land* would be. The overdetermination of some of the elegiac motifs in the Commemoration Ode might even operate, in that critical context, as a kind of protection for the poem.

24. Cleanth Brooks, *The Well Wrought Urn: Studies in the Structure of Poetry*, rev. ed. (London: Dennis Dobson, 1968), 136.

25. Ibid., 142.

26. Sacks, *English Elegy*, 19.

27. Lowell, *Poetical Works*, xxx.

28. Hamilton Vaughan Bail, "Harvard's Commemoration Day, July 21, 1865," *New England Quarterly* 15.2 (1942): 268. Bail's account of the sequence of events at

Harvard on July 21 and his related essay "James Russell Lowell's Ode" (see n. 11) are still the two most helpful and informative articles on, respectively, the ceremonies on the day in question and the gestation of Lowell's poem.

29. Jörn Rüsen, "The Development of Narrative Competence in Historical Learning: An Ontogenetic Hypothesis Concerning Moral Consciousness," *History and Memory* 1.2 (1989): 44-45. Rüsen's conceptually intriguing article provides four examples of "narrative competence" for the mediation of history. His example is based on a story told by Samuel Johnson in his *Journey to the Western Isles of Scotland* about a centuries-old and unqualified duty accepted by one Scottish clan to help members of another clan, arising out of a significant act of assistance in the past. The question would be, if a clan member (on the run from the authorities, for example) appealed for help today, what is the appropriate response? Rüsen divides the possible solution into four variants: the traditional (help given without question), the exemplary (help given to discharge abstract principle of upholding historical values), the critical (help refused because anachronistic debt has no value or meaning today), and the genetic (help offered, but within the context of transforming historical debt into contemporary values). Rüsen's argument is that "narrative competence" increases as one goes through the different stages of response. It might be difficult to isolate which variant is most intensely present in the Commemoration Ode, since it invokes both the values of uncritical loyalty to one's nation and those of the inherited commitment to the intellectual (and by implication critical and transformative) values embodied in Harvard University.

30. Lowell to R.W. Gilder, *Letters*, 3:149.

31. See Allen Grossman's 1983 essay "My *Caedmon*: Thinking about Poetic Vocation" on Caedmon's hymn for some comments on the meaning of political pressure for a poet and the appropriation of a poetic text – the real existing product of the creative impossibility made possible, as Grossman expresses it – by the reigning politico-cultural authorities. The essay is reprinted in his collection *The Long Schoolroom: Essays in the Bitter Logic of the Poetic Principle* (Ann Arbor: University of Michigan Press, 1997), 1-17. Applying this paradigm, Lowell would be a Caedmon who is, confusingly, simultaneously a member of the cultural establishment and an outsider, both the voice of an elite community and the lone singer of a risky poetic project.

32. Two letters, one from an individual named "Mr. W." (Bail identifies him as Charles P. Ware in "James Russell Lowell's Ode") and one from Lowell, can be found in *Proceedings of the American Society for Psychical Research* 1.4 (1889): 372-74. "Mr. W." writes to William James and testifies to waking up on the morning of July 21, 1865, and hearing in his mind the line "and what they dare to dream of dare to die for." Later on that day he is in the audience for Lowell's performance of the Commemoration Ode, and when he hears "Those love her best" he feels he knows what is coming, although the line Lowell actually spoke was slightly different ("And what they dare to dream of, dare to do"). "Mr. W." agreed to have his letter sent to Lowell for comment. Lowell replied

in a somewhat jocular tone, hoping that he had not stolen the ode in any way but also taking the opportunity once again to repeat his own account of having nothing ready as late as the night before the event, and finally showing F. J. Child a section of the poem in the morning of July 21 (presumably what he had written during the night). The letters, accompanied by William James's linking comments, are reproduced in full in the *Proceedings*.

33. Bail, "Harvard's Commemoration Day," 261.

34. Martin Duberman, *James Russell Lowell* (Boston: Houghton Mifflin, 1966), 224.

35. Bail's survey of memoirs, diary entries, and letters reveals that, for many present, the most remarkable experience of the day was an extemporized prayer or invocation by Phillips Brooks, a Harvard graduate and a young Episcopalian minister in Philadelphia, delivered during the morning. Members of the audience described it variously as "a man talking straight into . . . the heart of God," "a spontaneous and ultimate expression," and "a fiery stream of thanksgiving and supplication the like of which I never knew." Neither Brooks himself nor, as far as we know, any of his listeners kept notes on or wrote down phrases from the prayer, but the trace of this "lost" but memorable text in the recollection of many participants does suggest that Lowell made a duller impression with his textually robust and unashamedly "written" poem later on in the day (Bail, "Harvard's Commemoration Day," 265-67).

36. For a negative, even hostile, assessment of the female/maternal influence on the New England values (collective and individual) that led to the sacrifice celebrated by Lowell, see Lewis P. Simpson, *Mind and the American Civil War: A Meditation on Lost Causes* (Baton Rouge: Louisiana State University Press, 1989), 69.

37. See *Harvard Memorial Biographies*, 2 vols. (Cambridge, MA: Sever and Francis, 1867). The two "Supplementary Biographies" that conclude the second volume, however, fall outside the established parameters. The entries on Ebenezer Pierce Hinds and Charles Edward Hickling strike a different note from the others. Hickling, a sergeant in the 45th Massachusetts Volunteer Infantry, caught a fever in 1861 that attacked his spinal cord, with the result that he had to use a wheelchair for much of his succeeding life (2:491). He died in 1867. Hinds was much older than the average Harvard college man in the military, having graduated in the 1840s. "Eccentric and reticent to excess," he appears to have been somewhat of a dropout (2:485). He joined the Union army as a private and died with that rank, after being taken ill on a troopship. He was buried in an unmarked mass grave. The unglamourous suffering and death of the two men lend the conclusion of the *Biographies* an astringent note of stoicism in the face of the ironies of war, as well as revealing a genuinely egalitarian editorial policy.

38. Thomas Wentworth Higginson, preface to *Biographies*, 1:iii. It should be noted that this attitude was not peculiar to Harvard and Cambridge: Frederick Douglass also welcomed the war as a clearing of the political and social decks,

a chance to roll back the frustrations and unresolved tensions of the 1850s, and the 54th Massachusetts Volunteer Infantry regiment, in which his sons served, was regarded by very many blacks – and some whites – as the ideal vehicle to restore the manhood of African Americans once and for all.

39. *The Journals and Miscellaneous Notebooks of Ralph Waldo Emerson*, vol. 15, *1860–1866*, ed. Linda Allardt, David W. Hill, and Ruth H. Bennett (Cambridge, MA.: Harvard University Press, Belknap Press, 1982), 300.

40. Anne Mellor, *English Romantic Irony* (Cambridge, MA: Harvard University Press, 1980), 24-25.

41. Lowell, *Poetical Works*, 339.

42. The broader question of the relationship between national identity, intellectual activity, and the Transcendentalist inheritance has been raised by Charles Capper in " 'A Little Beyond': The Problem of the Transcendentalist Movement in American History," *Journal of American History* 85.2 (1998): 502-39. In particular, Capper suggests that the assumptions made along the way by American Studies about the relationship between Transcendentalism and various ideologies of the nation require some revisiting of the evidence. His exhaustive inventory of earlier and current scholarship on a wide range of connected issues largely leaves out the Civil War, however, with the exception of a brief mention of George Frederickson's *The Inner Civil War*. Although Lowell's relationship to the movement is vaguer than that of other New England literary intellectuals, his essays on Emerson and Thoreau are anything but the writings of a complete outsider, and the Commemoration Ode, in my view, contains a substantial presence of the poetic and social languages that the Transcendentalists had brought to the national cultural discourse. The concept of the poet-priest (for a brief discussion, see Buell, *Transcendentalism*, 50-53), for example, is useful for understanding Lowell's role and that of the poem itself at the Harvard memorial ceremonies.

43. Walt Whitman, *The Complete Poems*, ed. Francis Murphy (Harmondsworth, UK: Penguin Classics, 1996), 573-74.

44. Whitman, *Sequel to Drum-Taps*, 14.

45. Although war wounds and injuries were a common aspect of life, there was some controversy over a romanticized image of the Union veteran that emphasized (or overemphasized) his social and medical problems and led to demands for special privileges as a legitimate recompense for military service. See Eric T. Dean Jr., *Shook Over Hell: Post-Traumatic Stress, Vietnam, and the Civil War* (Cambridge, MA: Harvard University Press, 1997) for a discussion of the origins of the "disturbed veteran" syndrome and the provision of health care denied to other American citizens.

46. John Carlos Rowe, *At Emerson's Tomb: The Politics of Classic American Literature* (New York: Columbia University Press, 1997), 150-51.

47. Sacks, *English Elegy*, 37.

48. Or, to put it another way, the general absence of recent and current work on the New England Poets may be at least prima facie evidence of their inability to

attract and hold scholarly interest – but it also reveals the critical consensus of inactivity. Nevertheless, as I mention elsewhere, what is curious about the attitudes to Lowell, Longfellow, and others is that the kind of rejection of nineteenth-century poetry formulated by New Critics such as Yvor Winters and John Crowe Ransom has largely survived until today, even among academics for whom the New Criticism is *the* prime example of an elitist formalism that projected an ideological map of Anglo-American culture while simultaneously denying an interest in any agenda outside the borders of the text. It may be that the New Critical paradigm for teaching poetry in particular is just too useful to jettison, even decades after the New Critics' intellectual influence peaked and declined. A transatlantic comparison can be illuminating: for an account of recent developments in scholarship on British Victorian Poetry, inviting some suggestive contrasts with the Americanist tradition, see Joseph Bristow, ed., *The Cambridge Companion to Victorian Poetry* (Cambridge: Cambridge University Press, 2000).

49. Cleanth Brooks, "Irony as a Principle of Structure," in *Literary Opinion in America,* ed. Morton Dauwen Zabel, rev. ed. (New York: Harper & Brothers, 1951), 737.

50. Irwin Silber, ed., *Songs of the Civil War* (New York: Columbia University Press, 1960; repr., New York: Dover, 1995), 119, 137-39.

51. The song title was appropriated by Reid Mitchell for his study of the effect of the Civil War on family relations and the domestic sphere entitled *The Vacant Chair: The Northern Soldier Leaves Home* (New York: Oxford University Press, 1993).

52. George M. Frederickson, *The Inner Civil War: Northern Intellectuals and the Crisis of the Union* (New York: Harper & Row, 1968), 80-81.

53. Silber, *Songs of the Civil War*, 137.

54. Mitchell's work also involves a commitment to the value of ordinary life, something about which the Commemoration Ode, with its more demanding criteria, is rather dismissive.

55. Paul de Man, *Allegories of Reading: Figural Language in Rousseau, Nietzsche, Rilke, and Proust* (New Haven, CT: Yale University Press, 1979), 11-12.

2. A Strange Remorse: Melville and the Measure of Victory

1. Herschel Parker, *Herman Melville: A Biography*, vol. 2, *1851–1891* (Baltimore: Johns Hopkins University Press, 2002), 615-23.

2. Stanton Garner, *The Civil War World of Herman Melville* (Lawrence: University Press of Kansas, 1993); see also Parker, *Herman Melville*, esp. chaps. 19-30.

3. See John Limon, *Writing after War: American War Fiction from Realism to Postmodernism* (New York: Oxford University Press, 1994), 36-55, for an intriguing discussion of the counterintuitive significance of noncombatant status (that is, missing the war) for authors such as William Dean Howells and Mark Twain. Limon is dealing exclusively with fiction, but a good argument could be made for reading *Battle-Pieces* from this theoretical approach also.

4. Guert Gansevoort's name has remained in historical memory mostly in connection with his role, as a ship's officer, in the execution of three sailors on the U.S. brig *Somers* in 1842; it was a case that achieved considerable notoriety at the time and later supplied Melville with material for *Billy Budd*.

5. Parker, *Melville*, 567-72; Garner, *Civil War World*, 308-21.

6. See Timothy Sweet, *Traces of War: Poetry, Photography, and the Crisis of the Union* (Baltimore: Johns Hopkins University Press, 1990), 168; see also 166-68 for Sweet's reading of Melville's slightly contradictory declaration in the preface to *Battle-Pieces* that he took the details of the poems from news reports but also, as he put it, "placed a harp in a window" to catch the breezes as it might – that is, to allow a spontaneous unfolding of poetic inspiration unconstrained by the authority of fact.

7. Shira Wolosky, "Poetry and Public Discourse, 1820-1910," in Cambridge *History of American Literature*, vol. 4, *Nineteenth Century Poetry, 1800–1910* (New York: Cambridge University Press, 2004), 240.

8. Lawrence Buell, "Melville the Poet," in *Cambridge Companion to Herman Melville*, ed. Robert S. Levine (New York: Cambridge University Press, 1998), 135.

9. Herman Melville, *Battle-Pieces and Aspects of the War* (New York: Harper and Brothers, 1866; reprinted with a new introduction by Lee Rust Brown, New York: Da Capo Press, 1995), 63. Cited hereafter in text as *B-P*.

10. Franny Nudelman, *John Brown's Body: Slavery, Violence, and the Culture of War* (Chapel Hill: University of North Carolina Press, 2004), 102.

11. Joshua Scodel, *The English Poetic Epitaph: Commemoration and Conflict from Jonson to Wordsworth* (Ithaca, NY: Cornell University Press, 1991), 385.

12. Ann Douglas, "Heaven Our Home: Consolation Literature in the Northern United States, 1830-1880," in *Death in America*, ed. David E. Stannard (Philadelphia: University of Pennsylvania Press, 1975), 57.

13. If Melville had not become the canonical "Melville," then we would not care so much what his poetry says: but he did, so we do. The resurrection of Melville by both the academy and freestanding intellectuals in the 1920s is a crucial moment in modern American culture – the assertive reinstatement of a writer whom both the genteel and the popular cultures had forgotten – and also an act of selective remembrance, particularly with regard to the low prestige of Melville's poetic output. That work remained, in many ways, "forgotten" until much more recently; even the epic *Clarel* (1876) has been avoided by scholars as a somewhat troublesome anomaly in the arc of Melville's literary career: see Buell, "Melville the Poet," 141.

14. Wayne R. Dynes, "Monument: The Word," in *Remove Not the Ancient Landmark: Public Monuments and Moral Values*, ed. Donald Martin Reynolds (Amsterdam: Gordon and Breach, 1996), 30.

15. See Faith Barrett, introduction to *"Words for the Hour": A New Anthology of American Civil War Poetry*, ed. Faith Barrett and Cristanne Miller (Amherst and Boston: University of Massachusetts Press, 2006), 5-6. Barrett and Miller's

selection of poems for this book also emphasizes the crucial interplay of domestic and political arenas during the war years, as both men and women struggled with various demands on their principles and sensibilities.

16. Martin Heidegger, *Poetry, Language, Thought*, trans. Albert Hofstadter (New York: Harper & Row, 1971), 224.

17. Helen Vendler, "Melville and the Lyric of History," in *Battle-Pieces and Aspects of the War: Civil War Poems* (Amherst, NY: Prometheus Books, 2001), 255. This edition includes four "interpretive essays," by Vendler, Rosanna Warren, Richard H. Cox, and Paul M. Dowling.

18. Robert Milder, "The Rhetoric of Melville's *Battle-Pieces*," *Nineteenth Century Literature* 44.2 (1989): 188–89; see also a revised version of this article in Robert Milder, *Exiled Royalties: Melville and the Life We Imagine* (New York: Oxford University Press, 2006), chap. 8.

19. Lee was deposed on February 17, 1866; the transcript is contained in the *Report of the Joint Committee on Reconstruction of the First Session Thirty-Ninth Congress* (Washington: Government Printing Office, 1866), 2:129–36.

20. See Parker, *Herman Melville*, 612–13, for related comments on the Lee-Melville parallel.

21. Allen Grossman, *The Long Schoolroom: Lessons in the Bitter Logic of the Poetic Principle* (Ann Arbor: University of Michigan Press, 1997), 61.

22. Ibid., 72.

23. Nudelman, *John Brown's Body*, 131. Nudelman's chapter on Civil War photography contains a persuasive argument about audience reaction to images of battlefield corpses, and she notes that the "staged" dimension of some of the more famous photos would not have been especially disturbing to contemporary viewers, who would not yet have imbibed the naturalistic claims of documentary photography. Likewise, I see Melville as "staging" some of the poems in *Battle-Pieces* as traditional notions in a new technical posture, or as novel notions inside a traditional rhetoric.

24. Garner, *Civil War World*, 33.

25. Ibid., 368.

26. To paraphrase Clint Eastwood in *Dirty Harry*, perhaps poetry must know its limits too. One wonders what Melville would have thought of modern poetry such as that which came from World War I or out of the European Holocaust, in which new forms and languages had to deal with the historical reality of some of Melville's own bleaker premonitions.

27. Carolyn L. Karcher, "The Moderate and the Radical: Melville and Child on the Civil War and Reconstruction," *ESQ: A Journal of the American Renaissance* 45.3-4 (1999): 229.

28. It might also be that the best parallel to the imaginative relationship between Whitman's poetry and Lincoln's policy, as set out by Allen Grossman, is a mapping of Melville's poetry onto the policy of President Andrew Johnson.

29. For a recent account of key aspects of this larger story, see James M. McPherson, "Long-Legged Yankee Lies: The Southern Textbook Crusade," in *The*

Memory of the Civil War in American Culture, ed. Alice Fahs and Joan Waugh (Chapel Hill: University of North Carolina Press, 2004), 64-78.

30. The journey from *Moby-Dick* to the final poems in *Battle-Pieces* has often been studied as a movement from ambitious art to disciplined craft, or from the visionary Melville of the late 1840s and early 1850s to the Melville of silence and existential caution. One might also see that passage as being Melville's movement from Romantic democracy to a grudging embrace of the political and cultural status quo. As Betsy Erkkila has argued recently, the book by the marxist C. L. R. James, written while the author was in detention in the United States on immigration charges in the early 1950s (*Mariners, Renegades, and Castaways: The Story of Herman Melville and the World We Live In* [Hanover, NH: University Press of New England, 2001]), places the political dimension of Melville's work center-stage and reads *Moby-Dick* as an epic rendering of a coming multiracial democracy (see Erkkila, *Mixed Bloods and Other Crosses: Rethinking American Literature from the Revolution to the Culture Wars* [Philadelphia: University of Pennsylvania Press, 2005], 189-97). The failure of *Battle-Pieces* to understand the terminus of its own political vision points to Melville's implied admission that he no longer thinks a multiracial democracy is possible. "A Meditation" would be his closing effort at universalizing that local, and resigned, posture.

3. The Road from Memorial Hall:
Memory and Culture in *The Bostonians*

1. Of the three short stories of the late 1860s that dealt with the war experience, "The Story of a Year," "Poor Richard," and "A Most Extraordinary Case," only the last is of any great interest.

2. Henry James, *Notes of a Son and Brother* (1914); reprinted in Henry James, *Autobiography* (Princeton, NJ: Princeton University Press, 1983), 463-64; Leon Edel, *Henry James*, vol. 1, *The Untried Years: 1843-1870* (Philadelphia: J. B. Lippincott, 1953; repr., Avon Books, 1978), 230.

3. [Henry James], "Mr. Walt Whitman," *The Nation* 1.20 (November 16, 1865): 626.

4. Gary J. Handwerk, *Irony and Ethics in Narrative: From Schlegel to Lacan* (New Haven, CT: Yale University Press, 1985), 44.

5. Henry James, *The Bostonians* (New York: Penguin Putnam, 1986), 243-44. Cited hereafter in text. The Penguin Classics edition follows, with two minor emendations, the text published by Macmillan in their 1921-23 series of James's complete fictional works that, in turn, was a reprint of the original 1886 Macmillan edition. The novel first appeared in several installments, between February 1885 and February 1886, in *The Century Magazine*, New York.

6. See C. Vann Woodward, *Origins of the New South, 1877-1913* (1951; rev. ed., Baton Rouge: Louisiana State University Press, 1971), particularly chapter 16 for a commentary on the state of Southern higher education in the postwar pe-

riod. Although Ransom's education would have been earlier, Woodward's classic account of poverty-stricken, dysfunctional colleges allows one to read back
the realities of the postwar decades into the prewar era. Whatever qualities may
have been found in certain schools in the South, the Civil War had worn them
down to a barely functional minimum (437).

7. This brand of stoicism was the "Anglo-Saxonism" for which Southern intellectuals in particular developed a taste in the postwar decades. For an interesting
account of the ways Anglo-Saxon poetry and its motifs of dour heroism flowed
into Southern thinking, see Gregory A. VanHoosier-Carey, "Byrhtnoth in
Dixie: The Emergence of Anglo-Saxon Studies in the Post-Bellum South," in
Anglo-Saxonism and the Construction of Social Identity, ed. Allen J. Frantzen
and John D. Niles (Gainesville: University Press of Florida, 1997).

8. The inclusion of Göttingen in this list suggests that either Verena Tarrant or
Henry James was unaware of the fact that the Georg-August-Universität Göttingen was, in comparison with Harvard as well as Oxford and Padua, a relatively
new institution (founded in the 1730s, Göttingen is younger than Harvard by a
century) with a reputation for modern scholarship and scientific research. In
fact, once again in contrast to both Oxford and Padua, Göttingen had been
home to a regular stream of (male) American students ever since a modest beginning with four individuals in 1816 (see Carl Diehl, *Americans and German
Scholarship, 1770–1870* [New Haven, CT: Yale University Press, 1978]). Göttingen's admissions policy regarding women was presumably as discriminatory as
those of all institutions of higher education anywhere else in Europe or the
United States at the time.

9. Two views of the Memorial Hall transept section can be seen at http://www.fas
.harvard.edu/~memhall/transept.html. There is also a link to the full list of
names, now numbering 136, on the marble tablets. Accessed May 19, 2008.

10. Although the majority of Harvard students who joined up served in the Union
forces as officers, a small number did in fact experience the war as enlisted men.

11. Verena Tarrant's comment that Memorial Hall is "very peaceful too" echoes
Whitman's stanza 15 in "Lilacs." Both suggest that the war dead are at peace,
but those that survived them are not. Verena Tarrant, belonging to a generation
that did not experience the war as an adult, reflects in the balance of her own
personality the peaceful atmosphere of the commemorative complex, and in a
curious reversal embodies a challenge to Lowell's nationalism and also to the
tragic isolation of Whitman's vision.

12. Elizabeth Young, *Disarming the Nation: Women's Writing and the American
Civil War* (Chicago: University of Chicago Press, 1999), 11–14.

13. Ibid., 16–17.

14. In Millicent Bell's chapter on *The Bostonians* in her book *Meaning in Henry
James* (Cambridge, MA: Harvard University Press, 1991), 123–51, for example,
her exploration of the mind of Olive Chancellor moves in very close to the fabric of motivation as it reveals the shifting sympathies of the character, the narrator, and the author but fails to take up that one strand that seems to be almost

dangling there, waiting to be seen. Bell discusses "the crucial scene between Ransom and Verena in Harvard's Memorial Hall" but misses the connection between Olive and Memorial Hall (that her brothers are, at least indirectly, commemorated there also).

15. We can assume, however, that James would have addressed problem passages and refined, modified, or otherwise dealt with problematic narrative elements if he had included *The Bostonians* in his final selection of works for the New York edition. There is an important discussion of this issue in Martha Banta, "The Excluded Seven: Practice of Omission, Aesthetic of Refusal," in *Henry James's New York Edition: The Construction of Authorship*, ed. David McWhirter (Stanford, CA: Stanford University Press, 1995), 240–60. My argument in this chapter is predicated on the assumption that the dead brothers represent a traumatic loss in Olive's past and consequently an absence that shapes her negotiations with her social environment and, by implication, the narrative as a whole. Whether James would have agreed with this reading of his novel is an open question, of course.

16. Although to a degree a class issue, Olive's distaste for the Tarrants appears to go beyond her unpredictable snobbery: their liminal, almost parasitic social status threatens her in some way, as if it were contagious, while clearly offering her the opportunity to purchase Verena's move to Charles Street with a generous check.

17. Freud recounts the anecdote, in his 1915 essay "Thoughts for the Times on War and Death" (in *The Standard Edition of the Complete Works of Sigmund Freud*, vol. 14, trans. James Strachey [London: Hogarth Press, 1957], 286) of an English colleague who was giving a presentation in the United States on dream analysis and put forward a thesis on the egoistic impulses behind all dreams. The presenter was then challenged by a woman in the audience who insisted that, whatever might be true in Europe, she and her friends "were altruistic even in their dreams." On that model, Olive Chancellor is the daughter of an American Puritan tradition in which the constraints of the superego are so deeply internalized that it is impossible to concede the presence of any selfish or otherwise dubious impulse – there is no such thing as an unbidden thought, so to speak – or to transform the discharge of duty openly into the enjoyment of pleasure. The conscience may no longer be God's presence in the psyche, but the rigor with which it will seek out and arraign weakness has not lessened.

18. Janet A. Gabler offers an elegant discussion of Olive Chancellor's "tragic flaw," her inability to reflect self-critically on her own attitudes and desires, in "James's Rhetorical Arena: The Metaphor of Battle in *The Bostonians*," *Texas Studies in Literature and Language* 27.3 (1985): 270–83. I would extend that assessment to include her unwillingness (or inability) to see that she might have invited Ransom to Boston as an emotional re-investment in the memory of her deceased brothers.

19. Richard Terdiman, *Present Past: Modernity and the Memory Crisis* (Ithaca, NY: Cornell University Press, 1993), 3–32.

20. Ibid., 244.

21. See Kristin Boudreau, "Narrative Sympathy in *The Bostonians*," *Henry James Review* 14.1 (1993): 17–33, for a discussion of James's response to negative criticism (during the serialization of the novel) from various sources, including William James, about the portrayal of Miss Birdseye.

22. Olive Chancellor tends to idealize all social constituencies as functions of her ideological preferences of the moment, sometimes in unexpected ways: in her argument with her sister, for example, Olive becomes a class warrior of the more aggressive type with a note of socialist pathos. When discussing the most appropriate pedagogical environment for her spoiled and troublesome nephew Newton, Mrs. Luna's son, she comments that the "place for him . . . was one of the public schools, where the children of the people would teach him his small importance, teach it, if necessary, by the aid of an occasional drubbing" (172). This invocation of the healthy ideological benefits of school bullying seems a little out of character, or at least an oddly enthusiastic version of conservative theories of boys' education for someone so committed to root-and-branch reform, but the more shadowy implication is the idea that an irreducible core of virtue can be found in "the people." Olive ascribes essential qualities to an abstract Boston working-class population, creating a mythical image of "the people" as she has created a similar one of her sex.

23. Olive's feeling that Verena is too weak to resist Ransom's advances is reflected in the comments of some critics. To take three examples appearing decades apart: Leon Edel's patronizing description of Verena in his discussion of the novel in *Henry James*, vol. 3, *The Middle Years: 1882–1895* (Philadelphia: J. B. Lippincott, 1962; Avon Books, 1978), 139, is of a girl "who does not have an idea in her rather pretty little head"; "pretty," "sweet" and "vapid" are Martha Banta's adjectives in *Henry James and the Occult: The Great Extension* (Bloomington: Indiana University Press, 1972), 180; these judgments are echoed more recently by "a pretty redhead of no particular substance" in Joyce A. Rowe, "'Murder, what a lovely voice!': Sex, Speech, and the Public/Private Problem in *The Bostonians*," *Texas Studies in Literature and Language* 40.2 (1998): 158–83. In contrast, Michael Kearns makes a rare attempt to take Verena Tarrant seriously, but in a different critical context from this chapter, in his "Narrative Discourse and the Imperative of Sympathy in *The Bostonians*," *Henry James Review* 17.2 (1996): 162–81.

24. The continual humiliation by Southern spokesmen of Northern politicians (not only open Abolitionists) and the nonslave states in general is an important element in the cultural history of the antebellum years: the most dramatic enactment of this paradigm was the brutal physical attack on Charles Sumner by South Carolina congressman Preston Brooks on the floor of the Senate after a controversial debate in May 1856, to which Sumner had contributed much polemic, on admitting slave-owning into the Kansas territory. The cultural significance of the act for the South was that Sumner was a "Yankee blackguard" who "deserved a horsewhipping," rather than a gentleman who could be challenged to a duel, for

example. See James M. McPherson, *Battle Cry of Freedom: The Civil War Era* (New York: Ballantine Books, 1989), 149–51. A further consideration for the reading of *The Bostonians* is that, although the slave states were represented by legendary, powerful public speakers, such as South Carolina's John C. Calhoun, the most attractive motif for the Southerners was one of a hysterical, expostulating North being silenced by a short, sharp masculine response on the part of the South – something the Brooks incident seemed to embody perfectly.

25. Ulysses S. Grant, *Memoirs and Selected Letters* (New York: Literary Classics of the United States, 1990), 207–10. Grant included facsimiles of the original letters in his 1884 *Personal Memoirs of U.S. Grant*. Interestingly, the facsimile shows that the key sentence was itself the concluding paragraph in the original, something that is not typographically reproduced in the letter printed in the main text of the *Memoirs*.

26. For various accounts of the Donelson message and its reverberations, historical and folkloric, see, for example: Helen Todd, *A Man Named Grant* (Boston: Houghton Mifflin, 1940), 44–45; Harry J. Maihafer, *The General and the Journalists: Ulysses S. Grant, Horace Greeley, and Charles Dana* (Washington, DC: Brassey's, 1998), 97–99; Jean Edward Smith, *Grant* (New York: Simon & Schuster, 2001), 162–66.

27. See Nina Silber, "Intemperate Men, Spiteful Women, and Jefferson Davis," in *Divided Houses: Gender and the Civil War*, ed. Catherine Clinton and Nina Silber (New York: Oxford University Press, 1992), esp. 285–91.

28. For one of the best explanations of the significance of the capitulation of Radical Reconstruction, see C. Vann Woodward, *Reunion and Reaction: The Compromise of 1877 and the End of Reconstruction* (Boston: Little, Brown, 1966); esp. 204–15.

29. For a number of sometimes contradictory reasons, the artisans and working classes of the Northern cities, including New York, had often revealed a certain sympathy for the culture of the slaveholding aristocracy and the race rhetoric of Southern political leaders. Ransom may have found himself quite welcome, even popular, among the regular clientele of his local bar.

30. Alan Trachtenberg, *The Incorporation of America: Culture and Society in the Gilded Age* (New York: Hill and Wang / Farrar, Straus and Giroux, 1982), 163–64.

31. Ransom is also the man who spends "a long, empty, deadly summer on the plantation" learning German (46). This challenging pursuit, which parallels Olive's desire for Verena to learn German, is an odd echo of the struggles of the earlier generation of American Transcendentalist intellectuals to connect with the cultural discourse of a distant Europe. One of the more heroic achievements in the history of the acquisition of German under unpropitious circumstances was that made by the writer and journalist Margaret Fuller in the 1830s in Boston. Fuller's family duties (looking after her younger siblings) and work schedule (teaching junior school) left her little time to learn a foreign language to a such a high level of fluency that she was in a position to

translate Eckermann's *Conversations with Goethe* after only two years. Ransom's long, empty summer must have offered a more relaxed opportunity for study.

32. I am not suggesting that American political discourse before the Civil War consisted of neutral debate on the technical merits of various positions with no ideological agendas (which would be ludicrous) but rather that the tensions and animosities became more active around identity and culture in the last third of the nineteenth century as the industrial age put both identity and culture under heretofore unknown pressures.

33. Trachenberg, *Incorporation of America*, 173.

34. Carl E. Schorske, *Fin-de-Siècle Vienna: Politics and Culture* (New York: Alfred A. Knopf, 1980); see esp. 3-23, 116-80.

35. Michael S. Roth, *The Ironist's Cage: Memory, Trauma, and the Construction of History* (New York: Columbia University Press, 1995), 50. The links between the European experience of the politics of the irrational and American sociopolitical fantasies at the end of the nineteenth century invite more focused study in a transatlantic context. See also Schorske, *Fin-de-Siècle Vienna*, 128-29, for an interesting example of transatlantic influence: the Chinese Exclusion Act of 1882, one of the principal successes of the race-specific anti-immigration movement, was taken up as a model by the populist anti-Semitic politician Georg von Schönerer in his polemical attacks on Jews and Slavs.

36. Schorske, *Fin-de-Siècle Vienna*, 134.

37. For two significantly different approaches to this issue, see Richard Salmon, *Henry James and the Culture of Publicity* (Cambridge: Cambridge University Press, 1997), esp. 39-45; and Brook Thomas, "The Construction of Privacy in and around *The Bostonians*," *American Literature* 64.4 (1992): 719-47.

38. Trachtenberg, *Incorporation of America*, 140-41.

39. As Elsa Nettels writes in *Language and Gender in American Fiction: Howells, James, Wharton and Cather* (Charlottesville: University Press of Virginia, 1997), 82: "[James's] hostility to feminist causes . . . is part of a greater mistrust of all political causes and the oratory that promotes them. *The Bostonians* indicates one source of his mistrust – his recognition of the power of speakers to mesmerize audiences by their charismatic personalities, sexual magnetism and seductive voices." See also Susan Wolstenholme, "Possession and Personality: Spiritualism in *The Bostonians*," *American Literature* 49.4 (1978): 580-91, for some comments on James's use of the social phenomena of spiritualism, inspirational feminism, and the like as a metaphor for the moral chaos of Boston society.

40. Scholars have tended to assume, without further examination, the Booth/Lincoln parallel when looking at Ransom's meditation in the Music Hall: for example, Susan L. Mizruchi, "The Politics of Temporality in *The Bostonians*," *Nineteenth Century Fiction* 40.2 (1985): 187-215; and Lynn Wardley, "Women's Voice, Democracy's Body and *The Bostonians*," *ELH* 56.3 (1989): 639-65. As my discussion shows, the language of the relevant passage can be seen as pointing in

a different direction. John Wilkes Booth did not assassinate President Lincoln out of obscure, nihilistic motives aimed at the concept of political authority itself; rather, his action embodied, in an extreme form, the shock and resentment of the defeated Confederacy.

41. An entertaining and sophisticated analysis of the meaning of Verena's performances and Olive's fate of having to go before the audience to deny them their expected satisfaction can be found in Thomas F. Bertonneau, "Like Hypatia before the Mob: Desire, Resentment, and Sacrifice in *The Bostonians* (An Anthropoetics)," *Nineteenth Century Literature* 53.1 (1998): 56–90. Bertonneau takes the narrator's allusion to Hypatia, a fifth-century Alexandrian woman murdered by a Christian mob, as a starting point for his investigation of the complex relationship between sacrifice – the willingness to sacrifice oneself in a cause and the readiness to sacrifice others in one's own interests – and individual autonomy in the novel. In particular, he sees Verena's position at the end as having recovered some control over her own "value" even if her future with Ransom is not going to be happy: you have to be allowed to make a bad choice yourself rather than a good one under someone else's direction is the sense of Bartonneau's argument.

42. Barbara L. Packer, "The Transcendentalists," in *The Cambridge History of American Literature*, vol. 2, *1820–1865* (New York: Cambridge University Press, 1995), esp. 331–49.

43. Robert C. Jeffrey, "Southern Political Thought and the Southern Political Tradition," in *Confederate Symbols in the Contemporary South*, ed. J. Michael Martinez, William D. Richardson, and Ron McNinch-Su (Gainesville: University Press of Florida, 2000), 29.

44. With Verena standing in for the North in general, the analogy is almost overdetermined. Ransom will not try to beat Verena into intellectual submission with detailed arguments but rather by way of a passive-aggressive assertion of masculine virtue. Again, the deployment of stoicism in the postbellum construction of Southern cultural identity (see n. 7 on the new interest in Anglo-Saxon literature) involved the conviction that there was a specific kind of victory in defeat, particularly if that defeat could be rewritten to detach effect (contingent, compromised) from motive (pure, justified). This conviction won the hearts and minds, as David Blight comments, and toward the end of the century "by the sheer virtue of losing heroically, the Confederate soldier provided a model of masculine devotion and courage in an age of gender anxieties and ruthless material striving" (David W. Blight, *Race and Reunion: The Civil War in American Memory* [Cambridge, MA: Harvard University Press, Belknap Press, 2001], 266).

45. Thomas L. Connelly and Barbara L. Bellows, *God and General Longstreet: The Lost Cause and the Southern Mind* (Baton Rouge: Louisiana State University Press, 1982), 22.

46. Ibid., 86.

47. Ernest Gellner, *Language and Solitude: Wittgenstein, Malinowski and the Habsburg Dilemma* (Cambridge: Cambridge University Press, 1998), 19.

48. Paul H. Buck, *The Road to Reunion, 1865-1900* (Boston: Little, Brown, 1939), 209. See also Michael Davitt Bell, *The Problem of American Realism: Studies in the Cultural History of a Literary Idea* (Chicago: University of Chicago Press, 1993), 89-91, for some more nuanced discussion on whether the form of *The Bostonians* embodies a struggle between realism and romance, between Olive Chancellor's struggle to demystify "aesthetic and erotic susceptibility," on one hand, and Basil Ransom's successful attempt to rescue Verena Tarrant and make her "a character in his romance-narrative" on the other. As Bell observes, however, the equation is complicated: Olive is open, on occasion, to aesthetic pleasure herself, and she feels an intense desire to prove herself capable of heroism and martyrdom; I would add that Ransom, for his part, is open to a friendly acquaintanceship with the angular and professional Doctor Prance, the most thoroughly unromance-like figure in the novel.

49. *The Century Magazine* led the way with its extensive and influential series of Civil War articles and autobiographical accounts with a strong reconciliationist orientation that appeared between 1884 and 1887 (*The Bostonians* ran from February 1885 to February 1886). This series had to, and did in fact, appeal to the magazine's large Southern readership; see Blight, *Race and Reunion*, 173-81. *The Century*'s editorial practice was more nuanced, however, as dissenting Southern voices also made themselves heard: for example, George Washington Cable's essay "The Silent South," his analysis of the racial paranoia at large in Southern thinking, appeared in the magazine in issue for September 1885 (Blight, *Race and Reunion*, 294-95). Curiously, Cable's article ends on page 691 of that issue (vol. 30, no. 5) and that month's installment of *The Bostonians* begins on page 692. Readers would have moved from Cable's severe, unwavering analysis of the South directly into the more ambivalent tones of Ransom's and Verena Tarrant's journey to Memorial Hall.

50. Handwerk, *Irony and Ethics*, 16.

51. To suggest some of the difficulties that surface in this regard, Mary Doyle Springer, "Closure in James: A Formalist Feminist View," in *A Companion to Henry James Studies*, ed. Daniel Mark Fogel (Westport, CT: Greenwood Press, 1993), 270-75, argues for the feminist implications of James's refusal of energetic closure and, at the same time, for the unambiguous, rather one-dimensional meaning of the narrator's final comment – Verena's gloomy fate as Basil's wife. The more subtle analysis by Millicent Bell in *Meaning in Henry James* (e.g., 139), suggests that James is giving in to the formal demands of the marriage plot while struggling with its moral and political inadequacies.

52. Leland S. Person Jr. offers an intriguing discussion of gendered rewriting of historical motifs in "In the Closet with Frederick Douglass: Reconstructing Masculinity in *The Bostonians*," *Henry James Review* 16.3 (1995): 292-98. Person suggests that Ransom's pulling of Verena's cloak over her face is a satirical replay – this time with a Southerner in charge and enacting the defeat of Radical Reconstruction – of the incident in 1865 when Jefferson Davis's wife tried to disguise him as a woman, with her shawl over his head, to help him evade capture by

Federal troops. As with Grant's letter at Fort Donelson, this was another incident that articulated the distribution of gendered authority to the disadvantage
of the South's masculine self-image.

53. Homi K. Bhabha, "DissemiNation," in *Nation and Narration*, ed. Bhabha
(New York: Routledge, 1990), 292. Bhabha argues in this essay, among other
things, that the question of narrative temporality is crucial for understanding
the way in which an imperial narrative is imposed on a subordinate, colonized
people. Resistance to the denigration of one's own community's memory and
historical legitimacy must be organized in the field of culture also (as Franz
Fanon has asserted in *On National Culture*), but a danger lurks in the narrative
strategies of renascent nationalism: to create a national alternative to the cultural dominance exercised by the ruling political authority that nevertheless
continues to accept that authority's vision of history as a progressive teleology
is to accept the dynamic of the imperial world view, thus compromising the potential for real liberation. In *The Bostonians*, however, and the sentimental literature of the post–Civil War decades that James's novel is, to an extent,
satirizing, the resistance to the temporal rhythms and cultural energies of the
dominant power is coming from the forces of conservative and regional reaction, rather than from, say, African Americans as the nearest obvious victims of
racism and imperialism.

4. Bierce and Transformation

1. For example, *The Heath Anthology of American Literature*, 2nd ed., vol. 2 (Lex-
ington, MA: D.C. Heath, 1994), provides space for one representative item
each by Bierce, George Washington Cable, John Milton Oskison, Alice Dunbar-
Nelson, Hamlin Garland, Frank Norris, and Jack London. William Dean Howells, in contrast, gets over thirty pages of excerpts and complete short texts, and
Stephen Crane almost forty.

2. Robert von Hallberg, ed., Kenneth J. Northcott, trans., *Literary Intellectuals
and the Dissolution of the State: Professionalism and Conformity in the DDR*
(Chicago: University of Chicago Press, 1996), 239. The conversations took
place between 1990 and 1992, in the immediate aftermath of the collapse of the
Soviet Bloc and the reunification of Germany.

3. Roy Morris Jr., *Ambrose Bierce: Alone in Bad Company* (New York: Oxford University Press, 1995), 223-27.

4. For example, Poe's short story "The Purloined Letter" was once the stimulus
for a dispute between Jacques Lacan and Jacques Derrida, two of the most influential figures in late twentieth-century intellectual life; see Claude Richard,
American Letters, trans. Carol Mastrangelo Bové (Philadelphia: University of
Pennsylvania Press, 1998), 35-37, 165-66.

5. Lawrence I. Berkove, *A Prescription for Adversity: The Moral Art of Ambrose
Bierce* (Columbus: Ohio State University Press, 2002), and Cathy N. Davidson,
The Experimental Fictions of Ambrose Bierce: Structuring the Ineffable (Lincoln:

University of Nebraska Press, 1984), are distinctly scholarly book-length engagements with Bierce's writing, as opposed to the various biographies that include discussion of it as an extra dimension of varying quality and depth. The two definitive surveys of the Civil War in American writing, Edmund Wilson, *Patriotic Gore: Studies in the Literature of the American Civil War* (New York: Oxford University Press, 1966), and Daniel Aaron, *The Unwritten War: American Writers and the Civil War* (New York: Oxford University Press, 1975), also contain brief chapters on Bierce, again with rather more psychologizing than criticism. Wilson's comment that Bierce suffered "an impasse, a numbness, a void, as if some psychological short-circuit had blown out an emotional fuse" (632) is memorable, however. Davidson's phenomenological approach highlights, in contrast, the relationship between Bierce and modernist and postmodernist fiction, emphasizing the presence in his work of the interpretive nature of experience, the indeterminacy of language and communication, and the fictionality of fiction. In her concluding chapter, for example, Davidson shows clearly the substantial echoes of Bierce's "Occurrence at Owl Creek Bridge" in Jorge Luis Borges's "The Secret Miracle." It should also be noted that Berkove's reading of "Owl Creek Bridge" in *Prescription for Adversity* (113–35) is a magisterial performance.

6. The status of Bierce or, indeed, any other American author among East German scholars and intellectuals is not the subject of this chapter, but it might be relevant to point out that the context for Lange-Müller's remarks is one in which the study of American literature and culture was subject to an ideological and institutional pressure that valorized a highly restricted concept of "realism" and sought to identify politically progressive streams in American culture even at the price of a ludicrous degree of oversimplification. For some recent, and partly autobiographical, work on this theme, see the various essays in Rainer Schnoor, ed., *Amerikanistik in der DDR: Geschichte - Analyzen - Zeitzeugenberichte* (Berlin: trafo Verlag, 1999). In Eberhard Brüning's contribution to that volume ("Die Amerikanistik an der Universität Leipzig"), for example, there is a brief account of the way in which the East German Americanists, who managed to avoid the savage battles over the supposed "decadence and formalism" of modernist art and literature by a pragmatic commitment to textual reading and a strategic invocation of the socially progressive dynamic of American writing, were then accused by others in the GDR academy of being "theoriefeindlich" (73). Though the word meant "unwilling to subject their discipline to the dull and exacting criteria of Marxist-Leninist philosophy," rather than a hostility to contemporary literary theory, it is an amusing echo nonetheless.

7. Michel Foucault, "Nietzsche, Genealogy, History," in *Language, Counter-Memory, Practice: Selected Essays and Interviews*, trans. Donald F. Bouchard and Sherry Simon (Ithaca: Cornell University Press, 1977), 144. One imagines *The Devil's Dictionary* as a suitable home for a similar, Biercean definition of "Truth."

8. *The Complete Short Stories of Ambrose Bierce*, comp. Ernest Jerome Hopkins (Lincoln: University of Nebraska Press, 1984), 335. Cited hereafter in text as *CSS*. Hopkins comments that "not more than fifteen of his Civil War stories are familiar to most readers; they actually number twenty-five, an additional ten not having been included in 'In the Midst of Life,' but left scattered and half-concealed in Volumes III, VIII, and XI of *The Collected Works*" (261).

9. At certain times and places, however, the notoriously bad marksmanship of soldiers in execution details led to many grotesque and brutal incidents (see, for example, Gerald F. Linderman, *Embattled Courage: The Experience of Combat in the American Civil War* [New York: Free Press, 1987], 58-59). Counterintuitively, hanging may have offered Adderson the quickest and most reliable death.

10. Frank Kermode, *The Sense of an Ending: Studies in the Theory of Fiction, with a New Epilogue* (1966; New York: Oxford University Press, 2000), 44-45.

11. Ibid., 45. In the "New Epilogue," Kermode comments that there has been much disagreement over, among other things, his *tick-tock* paradigm since *Sense of an Ending* first appeared over thirty years ago. He defends his having "started these hares," however, because they have opened the way, for other critics as well as for Kermode himself, to new ideas about fiction.

12. See Berkove, *Prescription for Adversity*, 54-56, for some comments on the connections between this narrative and Bierce's interest in classical Stoicism.

13. See Morris, *Alone in Bad Company*, 9-10. Morris points out that Bierce's parents were members of the First Congregational Church of Christ in a part of northern Ohio branded with the most fervent varieties of frontier evangelism. The family had originally emigrated from Massachusetts.

14. One aspect of the ending is a little opaque. It is not completely certain whether the officer who says "Dead a week" is Lieutenant Searing or some other character. In a recently published guide to Bierce's work, the assumption is made that it is his brother (see Robert L. Gale, *An Ambrose Bierce Companion* [Westport, CT: Greenwood Press, 2001], 214), but there could be some justification for identifying that officer as "the officer" who gives Adrian Searing the order to have his unit advance. Also, the death by fright of Private Searing is implied clearly but not described in so many words. Finally, the penultimate paragraph of "One of the Missing" (and that paragraph only) is written in the present tense, suggesting a slightly different relationship between time and narrative at this one point. Some questions remain about time in this story.

15. Robert Coles, *Irony in the Mind's Life: Essays on Novels by James Agee, Elizabeth Bowen, and George Eliot* (New York: New Directions, 1978), 11. Coles discusses Adam's desire, or even compulsion, to name the creatures of his world (Genesis 2) in the light of the suggestion of loneliness in his lack of a "help meet." The creation of Eve seems to give Adam's existence a more concrete sense of reality and the slight intimation that the two are now in time (there is the prospect of a future that was not there in the past) as well as in the Garden: the first hairline crack, perhaps, in the timeless prelapserian structure. The

naming is a way of exerting a narrative control over one's world, dealing with a sense of "aloneness" and mediating the unknown (including time). Coles also observes at a later point that literature can be, among other things, writers engaging with "habits, practices, or states of mind" that arise from childhood experience and have remained compelling "beyond daily comprehension" (55). The mental struggles of Bierce's youth, against a background of family oppression and strict religious imperatives, yet confused both by a father who was something of an eccentric cultural autodidact and by his own tendency to morbid speculation, have clearly many echoes in his war fiction and his stories of the uncanny.

16. Saint Augustine, *Confessions*, trans. R. S. Pine-Coffin (Harmondsworth, UK: Penguin Books, 1961), 276. See also Kermode's comments on chapter 11 of *Confessions*, in which Augustine develops his theory of time and memory (*Sense of an Ending*, 53, 71-72).

17. Augustine, *Confessions*, 278. Augustine sees memory as being only words, representations of the impressions left by events in the mind. To that extent, our memory of a psalm, which consists of words (and music, perhaps) both in reality and in memory, would have a closer relationship to the fact of its real existence than, for example, our memory of an action in which we took part, because that action would exist only in memory as "words based on memory-pictures" (267).

18. Ibid., 274.

19. Julius Caesar Scaliger, "Poetics," in *Dramatic Theory and Criticism: Greeks to Grotowski*, ed. Bernard F. Dukore (Orlando, FL: Harcourt Brace Jovanovich, 1974), 142.

20. Davidson, *Experimental Fictions*, 3.

21. See Alfred Kazin, *On Native Grounds: An Interpretation of Modern American Prose Literature* (1942; New York and San Diego: Harcourt Brace, Harvest, 1995), 193-94, for his account of the way the "rebels" – writers who had hidden from or refused the literary mainstream of fin-de-siècle America – had clearly carried the day by 1920; apart from contemporary figures such as Sherwood Anderson and H. L. Mencken, their ranks included deceased writers in an unlikely proximity: Bierce, Henry Adams, and Emily Dickinson, for example. Kazin sees the Melville revival as also belonging to this cultural phenomenon.

22. Possibly Wayne Booth's "implied author" would be the appropriate designation, but my sense of this story is that there is something placed between that entity and the narrator. I use *authorial voice* and *editor* more or less interchangeably, however, as I am not searching for the precise term so much as emphasizing this important level of structuring authority in the text.

23. With respect to the military justice regime touched on by this narrative, the prevailing legal parameters in the Union forces during the Civil War were much more fluid than they became in the future. It is clear, nevertheless, that Ransome as battery commander should have determined that they were shelling their own forces and instructed the battery (or ordered Lieutenant Price to

instruct the battery) to cease firing. As the junior executive officer, Price would not have had the authority to make this decision himself. Ransome's defense, from the military legal point of view, would be unlikely (even if Cameron were still alive to confirm his original order) to impress a court-martial. For this information I am indebted to Steve Sanders of Fort Worth, Texas, former U.S. Army JAG officer, and Civil War re-enactor.

24. Edith Wharton, *The House of Mirth* (New York: Oxford University Press, 1999), 131–33.

25. "One Kind of Officer" provides an interesting illustration of the problem of narrative reliability discussed exhaustively by Ricoeur in his long study *Time and Narrative*. Ricoeur writes: "The question of reliability is to the fictional narrative what documentary proof is to historiography. It is precisely because novelists have no material proof that they ask readers to grant them not only the right to know what they are recounting or showing but to allow them to suggest . . . an evaluation of the main characters" (Paul Ricoeur, *Time and Narrative*, trans. Kathleen McLaughlin and David Pellauer, 3 vols. [Chicago: University of Chicago Press, 1984], 3:162). At the beginning of that particular chapter, "The World of the Text and the World of the Reader," Ricoeur comments that the "enigma of pastness" cannot be solved, in historiography, by appeal to testimony, as this merely shifts the central problem from event to witness (Ricoeur, *Time and Narrative*, 3:157). Bierce provides a malicious turn on this entire problematic, in fact, as the story pretends that a kind of historical truth might be, at least potentially, available if the question of authorial reliability were to be solved on the fictional level. But it cannot be solved: "One Kind of Officer" enacts the fatal sequence of testimony and conclusion that an actual military justice investigation would face.

26. Søren Kierkegaard, *The Concept of Irony with Continual Reference to Socrates*, ed. and trans. Howard V. Hong and Edna H. Hong (Princeton, NJ: Princeton University Press, 1989), 258.

27. Kierkegaard, *Concept of Irony*, 542 n. 39.

28. As Cathy Davidson points out, Bierce was writing "at the same time that many veterans of the Civil War were foisting upon a public being primed for another armed conflict their self-justifying accounts of glory won in the battles of the recent past" (*Experimental Fictions*, 18).

29. Ambrose Bierce, *The Devil's Dictionary*, with an introduction by Roy Morris Jr. (New York: Oxford University Press, 1999), 200.

30. Walter Benjamin, "The Storyteller: Reflections on the Works of Nikolai Leskov," in *Illuminations*, trans. Harry Zohn (New York: Schocken Books, 1969), 109.

31. Kierkegaard, *Concept of Irony*, 259.

32. Ibid., 261. Kierkegaard's position was largely a more complex and less paranoid iteration of Hegel's earlier attack on German Romanticism's theories and practice of ironic discourse. Intriguingly, the passage contains an odd foreshadowing of Walter Benjamin's image of the angel of history, being pushed

continually backward into the future while the rubble of the past mounts at his feet.

33. One way of understanding this kind of irony-into-alienation is as if a trauma or wounding were reversed and directed back into the outside world. Some critics have, consciously or not, merged the language of wounding with the limits, the maximum possible extension, of Bierce's fiction: "Bierce not only choked on the blood of the Civil War, he practically drowned in it" (Aaron, *Unwritten War*, 181). See also the chapter on Maupassant and Bierce in Richard Fusco, *Maupassant and the American Short Story: The Influence of Form at the Turn of the Century* (University Park: Pennsylvania State University Press, 1994), 103-18, for a brief discussion of possible influences on Bierce through the translations of Maupassant's work by Lafcadio Hearn and Jonathan Sturges. Fusco suggests that Bierce could well have seen some atmospheric similarities between the French writer's imagination and his own and deals with some specific compositional influences, including in "One of the Missing." The "objectionable" aspects of Maupassant's fiction for many mainstream readers, reviewers, and authors (such as O. Henry) might well have been a spur for Bierce to sound his own dark and cynical notes more unapologetically. Although they avoid the kind of sexual motifs that Maupassant uses, Bierce's narratives achieve their own shock effects, emphasizing that "tumultuous insight cannot enrich an individual's life – it becomes merely the last ironic twist of fate's knife" (Fusco, *Maupassant*, 118).

34. Wolfgang Iser, "Indeterminacy and the Reader's Response in Prose Fiction," in *Aspects of Narrative: Selected Papers from the English Institute*, ed. J. Hillis Miller (New York: Columbia University Press, 1971), 40. Iser is discussing *Ulysses* at this point, but his comments have wider application.

35. Davidson, *Experimental Fictions*, 125-34.

36. Ross Chambers, *Story and Situation: Narrative Seduction and the Power of Fiction* (Minneapolis, University of Minnesota Press, 1984), 217. Chambers's comments could be regarded as a line of argument, coming from a different critical standpoint, parallel to that of Paul Ricoeur when he writes that the self-effacement of the author "is one rhetorical technique among others; it belongs to the panoply of disguises and masks the real author uses to transform him or herself into the implied author" (Ricoeur, *Time and Narrative*, 3:161).

37. Walt Whitman, *The Complete Poems*, ed. Francis Murphy (Harmondsworth, UK: Penguin Classics, 1996), 358. The question of the physical absence of the war dead and whether their souls have bodily manifestation of some kind is an undercurrent in certain Bierce stories as well as in the passage from Whitman. It is also the theme of Elizabeth Stuart Phelps's *The Gates Ajar*, an exceptionally popular postwar novel from 1868. See Lisa A. Long, " 'The Corporeity of Heaven': Rehabilitating the Civil War Body in *The Gates Ajar*," *American Literature* 69.4 (1997): 781-811, for a discussion of the way in which the spiritualist movement provided consolation for those family members of soldiers who could not accept the idea that their deceased loved one had be-

come a kind of floating, neutral spirit. It is as if the scope of bodily destruction that the war brought triggered a deep but unorthodox commitment to
Christian redemption as promising the physical restoration of the body, and
thus of individuality.

38. Stephen Crane, *Prose and Poetry* (New York: Literary Classics of the United
States, 1984), 212.

39. Ibid.

40. This debate is a modern moment in the reception of *Red Badge*, since the presence of an all-pervading irony was a nonissue for most contemporary readers in
the 1890s. Even in more recent times, there has been some ambivalence in the
air. See, for example, various approaches to the issue such as John Berryman,
"The Freedom of the Poet," in *Stephen Crane's "The Red Badge of Courage,"*
ed. Harold Bloom (New York: Chelsea House, 1987), 10, 14; Ralph Ellison's introduction to the 1960 Modern Library edition, reprinted as "Stephen Crane
and the Mainstream of American Fiction" in *The Collected Essays of Ralph Ellison*, ed. John F. Callahan (New York: Modern Library, 2003), 113–27; Chris-
tine Brooke-Rose, "Ill Logics of Irony," in *New Essays on "The Red Badge of
Courage,"* ed. Lee Clark Mitchell (New York: Cambridge University Press,
1986), 129–46. Brooke-Rose's is an unusual study, however, in that she foregrounds a structural-linguistic, rather than a discursive, perspective on the
irony in Crane's narrative.

41. Robert H. Davis, introduction to *Tales of Two Wars: The Work of Stephen
Crane*, vol. 2 (New York: Alfred A. Knopf, 1925), x.

42. [Ambrose Bierce], The Prattle, *San Francisco Examiner*, July 26, 1896, 6.

43. This is a somewhat murky affair, to this day. There is, for example, the question
of the demands made on Crane by Ripley Hitchcock, his editor at Appleton &
Co., which clearly pressured the author into toning down a too-sharp portrayal
of Henry as a self-deluding adolescent, hence reducing the ironic charge of the
published text. See Hershel Parker, "Getting Used to the 'Original Form' of
Red Badge of Courage," in Mitchell, *New Essays*, 36–41.

44. Chris Hedges, *War Is a Force That Gives Us Meaning* (New York: Random
House /Anchor Books, 2003), 10.

45. Ibid., 11.

46. Michael Herr, *Dispatches* (1977; repr., New York: Vintage Books, 1991), 6.

47. John F. Lynen, *The Design of the Present: Essays on Time and Form in American
Literature* (New Haven, CT: Yale University Press, 1969), 36.

48. Bierce, *Devil's Dictionary*, 158.

5. Paul Laurence Dunbar: Memory and Memorial

1. William Dean Howells, "Paul Laurence Dunbar," in *Selected Literary Criticism*, vol. 2, *1886–1897* (Bloomington: Indiana University Press, 1993), 279–81;
Langston Hughes, "Two Hundred Years of American Negro Poetry," *Transi-
tion: An International Review* 7:3-4 (1997–78): 92; Henry Louis Gates Jr., *The*

Signifying Monkey: A Theory of African-American Literary Criticism (New York: Oxford University Press, 1988), 113-15, 176-77.

2. Henry Louis Gates provides a good example of this curious phenomenon. At one point in *Signifying Monkey* he uses a quotation from a letter from Dunbar when he was visiting London in 1897 ("I am entirely white") as an admission that clearly supports his (Gates's) theory that Dunbar felt himself forced to "write white" (115). The problem is that the complete text – a letter to his mother in Ohio – can be read easily as a witty account of the lack of an American-style color bar in London (see Jay Martin and Gossie H. Hudson, eds., *The Paul Laurence Dunbar Reader* [New York: Dodd, Mead, 1975], 439). Indeed, Dunbar writes elsewhere that the color line in England does exist but that the black American is on the "right" side of it, in contrast to people from the Indian subcontinent, for example (21). Gates's larger point about the poetry might be correct, but the letter from London is not the most convincing evidence.

3. See, for example, James A. Emanuel, "Racial Fire in the Poetry of Paul Laurence Dunbar," in *A Singer in the Dawn: Reinterpretations of Paul Laurence Dunbar*, ed. Jay Martin (New York: Dodd, Mead, 1975), 75-93, for an argumentative but balanced assessment of Dunbar's work informed by the race politics of the 1970s. The period in which this essay was published manifests itself, however, in Emanuel's dismissal of a comment by Dunbar to the effect that black writers and white writers are now living the same lives (79). He reads Dunbar's remark as self-deluding political fantasy rather than as, for example, a recognition of the way in which modernity is proceeding remorselessly to remake all Americans in its image, regardless of racial identity. For a somewhat different approach, see Houston A. Baker Jr., *Modernism and the Harlem Renaissance* (Chicago: University of Chicago Press, 1987), 37-41, 49. Baker argues that the problem with Dunbar was that his aesthetic ambitions were disengaged from the potential resources of black culture. Thus his sense of individual frustration is mediated through, for example, "wearing the mask" as a self-inflicted impediment, rather than the trope of adopting the mask tactically – and indeed drawing attention to it – to enable communication on a more subversive level to happen (something that Baker suggests Booker T. Washington managed to do).

4. Regarding Dunbar's feel for the musical dimension of poetic composition, Arna Bontemps relates that James Weldon Johnson once had told him that Dunbar's voice "was a perfect musical instrument and he knew how use it with extreme effect." See "The Relevance of Paul Laurence Dunbar," in Martin, *Singer in the Dawn*, 50. In the same volume, Myron Simon's essay "Dunbar and Dialect Poetry" (114-34) is a focused and balanced account of the qualities of Dunbar's work as a dialect poet. Simon discusses the ambivalence in James Weldon Johnson's attitude to Dunbar's work (Johnson was a crucial link between the black writers of Dunbar's generation and the Harlem Renaissance) and also highlights the fact that Dunbar wrote a significant amount of dialect verse that was trying to render not a black vernacular but white ethnic speech.

My point is that English lyric poetry is also a type of "dialect." Simon also, incidentally, makes a brief comparison between Dunbar and James Russell Lowell as dialect poets.

5. *The Collected Poetry of Paul Laurence Dunbar*, ed. Joanne M. Braxton (1913; repr., Charlottesville: University Press of Virginia, 1993), 5. All subsequent quotations from the poem are from this source.

6. The word *accountability* itself, taking public responsibility for one's actions, connects the poem to the distinctive culture formed by the reformist politics and muckraking journalism of the time, a culture that included experiments with various artistic forms with the objective of achieving social honesty. Examples of such work would include Jacob Riis's photography, Lincoln Steffens's *Shame of the Cities*, Thomas Eakins's painting The Agnew Clinic and Frank Lloyd Wright's houses. Dunbar's poem does, however, suggest an ironic evasiveness about the concept, as if the poet concedes the value of accountability as a virtue but sympathizes with the speaker of the poem, who cannot afford it.

7. See Darwin T. Turner, "Paul Laurence Dunbar: The Poet and the Myths," for a brief discussion of Dunbar's prosody (in Martin, *Singer in the Dawn*, 62–64). A fact worth mentioning is that there is no consistency among different editions of Dunbar's poetry as far as line breaks are concerned. In the Braxton reprint edition of *Collected Poetry*, a two-column page layout demands that the poems' lines be split rather than continuous, creating in "Accountability" an eight-line stanza; in contrast, John Hollander's Library of America College Edition of *American Poetry: The Nineteenth Century* (New York: Literary Classics of the United States, 1996) prints "Accountability" with four long lines in each stanza. The texts are otherwise identical, but I believe that the long line with the caesura gives the poem a more dynamic presence than the Braxton edition division into two lines, as I hope my quotation from the poem reflects.

8. Houston A. Baker Jr. in his *Blues, Ideology, and Afro-American Literature* (Chicago: University of Chicago Press, 1984) comments that Dunbar's work, like that of other black writers, has been undervalued because of the critical assumption that "Afro-American expressive works of any given historical moment [are] a report on the state of the race at that moment in time" (118). Dunbar's poetry is perhaps such a report, but not in a way that the phrase might usually be understood.

9. Graham Hough, "The Modernist Lyric," in *Modernism: A Guide to European Literature 1890–1930*, ed. Malcolm Bradbury and James McFarlane (Harmondsworth, UK: Penguin Books, 1991), 316–17.

10. Quoted in ibid., 317. I have made minimal alterations to Hough's translation of the lines from the poem.

11. Ibid., 314.

12. *The Poetry of Robert Frost: The Collected Poems, Complete and Unabridged*, ed. Edward Connery Latham (New York: Henry Holt, 1979), 68–69.

13. Dunbar, *Collected Poetry*, 59. All subsequent quotations from the poem are from this source.

14. Frederick Douglass, *Autobiographies*, Library of America College Edition (New York: Literary Classics of the United States, 1994), 184.

15. See Timothy Sweet, *Traces of War: Poetry, Photography, and the Crisis of the Union* (Baltimore: Johns Hopkins University Press, 1990), 101–2, for some comments on how the pastoral vision in America had already combined an "organicist aesthetic" with a conservative political vision long before the Civil War, which in turn had a powerful influence on the images through which the war might be remembered and interpreted. Taking Sweet's model as a measure, "A Corn-Song" would be a poetic enactment of the failure of pastoralism to provide a valid tool of representation for plantation slavery.

16. Roger D. Abrahams, *Singing the Master: The Emergence of African American Culture in the Plantation South* (New York: Pantheon Books, 1992), xxii–xxiv.

17. Ibid., 85.

18. "Appendix I" to Abraham's book contains a large number of accounts of corn-shucking ceremonies, both contemporary and after the fact. These accounts often involve the songs and rhymes written down at the time or remembered by participants. Abrahams calls these "multiple-voice, complex metrical practices" (xviii). Several of the accounts were published in the 1880s and early 1890s (for example, William Wells Brown, *My Southern Home; or, the South and Its People* [1880]), and Dunbar would have had opportunity to consult them, in addition to whatever he learned of his mother's experiences in her youth.

19. "Lyric and Modernity," the final chapter in Paul de Man, *Blindness and Insight: Essays in the Rhetoric of Contemporary Criticism* (New York: Oxford University Press, 1971), is among other things a defense of the relevance of lyric poetry for the theoretical exploration of modernism's relationship to its vehicles of artistic expression. De Man quotes Yeats's comment that modern poetry is "the conscious expression of a conflict within the function of language as representation and within the conception of language as the act of an autonomous self" (171). Early warnings of these conflicts can be found, I suggest, in Dunbar's poetry also, as – like Yeats's struggle with the Irish political imagination – it explores a division not only within social reality but also within the American cultural consciousness.

20. David Simpson, *Irony and Authority in Romantic Poetry* (London: Macmillan, 1979), 27.

21. See, for example, Michael North on the experience of the Jamaican poet Claude McKay in *The Dialect of Modernism: Race, Language, and Twentieth-Century Literature* (New York: Oxford University Press, 1994), 103. On a more general note, Eric J. Sundquist writes in *To Wake the Nations: Race in the Making of American Literature* (Cambridge, MA: Harvard University Press, Belknap Press, 1993), 304: "For . . . Dunbar, the use of dialect was fraught with the tension between capitulation to stereotypes and the desire to find an audience for African American literature, whether one took that desire to be rank minstrelsy or a literary act of cultural consciousness akin to the publication of dialect verse

by nationalist poets such as Robert Burns and John Synge." His remarks could be supplemented by mentioning the problem of some white critics' inherited or adopted "mimetic prejudice," that black writers' creative productions did not represent original work but rather were copies of European literary forms. This mirror-image of this prejudice appeared later in the criticism by black writers and intellectuals who saw an overenthusiastic investment in Eurocentric models. The joke is perhaps that Dunbar foresaw the liberation of the fragmentary procedures of modernism ("A Corn-Song" begs for a more radical poetic treatment) but could attempt to capture those intuitions only within the "given" of conventional verse forms.

22. Paul de Man, "The Concept of Irony," in *Aesthetic Ideology*, ed. Andrzej Warminsky (Minneapolis: University of Minnesota Press, 1996), 182. There is a complex critical genealogy at work at this point in de Man's essay, involving de Man's interpretation of Benjamin, as well as an earlier treatment of his work by Peter Szondi. De Man's footnotes 24 and 25 (182) provide extensive citations. Friedrich Schlegel's essay "Über die Unverständlichkeit" appears in *Kritische Schriften* (Munich: Carl Hanser Verlag, 1956), 340-51; an English translation, entitled "On Incomprehensibility," appears in *Dialogue on Poetry and Literary Aphorisms*, trans. Peter Firchow (Minneapolis: University of Minnesota Press, 1971). Warminsky comments that de Man often provides his own translations of Schlegel in "The Concept of Irony."

23. Walter Benjamin, "Der Begriff der Kunstkritik in der deutschen Romantik," in *Gesammelte Schriften* I:1 (Frankfurt am Main: Suhrkamp Verlag, 1974), 85. The translation is de Man's. The quotation in the original German runs as follows: "Es ist also bei dieser Art der Ironie, welche aus der Beziehung auf das Unbedingte entspringt, nicht die Rede von Subjektivismus und Spiel, sondern von der Angleichung des begrenzten Werkes an das Absolute, von seiner völligen Objektivierung um den Preis seines Untergangs." Benjamin's next sentence reads: "Diese Form der Ironie stammt aus dem Geiste der Kunst, nicht aus der Willen des Künstlers" (This form of irony emerges from the spirit of art, and not from the will of the artist) (my translation). I return to the question of the ironization of form as something born out of the work and unconnected to any intentionality on the part of the artist later in the chapter, when I deal with the implications of Dunbar's struggle with the conflicting forces in his poetry.

24. De Man, "Concept of Irony," 183.

25. Alan Trachtenberg, *The Incorporation of America: Culture and Society in the Gilded Age* (New York: Hill and Wang, 1982), 194-98. See also Richard Hofstadter, *The Age of Reform: From Bryan to F.D.R.* (New York: Vintage Books, 1955), 192-98. Although more than fifty years old, Hofstadter's study survives to impress with its implacable analytic focus and the authority of its style. It is also worth mentioning in this context that Alfred Kazin, *On Native Grounds: An Interpretation of Modern American Prose Literature* (1942; repr., New York: Harcourt Brace, 1995), still offers, in its first two chapters in particular, one of the most readable and intellectually convincing accounts of how American

writing came to be what it was at the turn of the twentieth century. The development of poetry is different from that of prose fiction, but there are more common factors than might be assumed.

26. Frank Lentricchia, "On the Ideologies of Poetic Modernism, 1890-1913: The Example of William James," in *Reconstructing American Literary History*, ed. Sacvan Bercovitch (Cambridge, MA: Harvard University Press, 1986), 245.

27. Examples of this phenomenon include, besides many of Dunbar's poems, Lazarus's "Long Island Sound," passages from Vaughan Moody's "Ode in Time of Hesitation," and Robinson's "Eros Tyrannos." Crane's brief, enigmatic verses in his collection *The Black Riders and Other Lines* (Boston: Copeland and Day, 1895) are already somewhat more experimental, but the atmosphere of the whole work is characterized by an awkward lyric diction that seems at odds with the imagery and thought. These poems are all, in general, looking for a new relationship between form and emotion, between form and idea, and part of their attraction might well be the sense of a struggle with an overcontrolling poetic legacy.

28. The issue presented itself more urgently, in some senses, during and after the Harlem Renaissance. The African American intellectual and cultural milieu that existed in Washington, DC (where Dunbar lived) at the turn of the century, however, experienced similar energies, successes, and doubts connected with black cultural expression, although the memory of the Washington milieu has been marginalized to the advantage of the later history in New York City. One reason is possibly that the Harlem Renaissance was more interesting to white readers and audiences, in the sense that it provided a thrill connected with exotic/sexual images and a primitivist aesthetic. See Wilson J. Moses, "The Lost World of the Negro, 1895-1919: Black Literary and Intellectual Life before the 'Renaissance,'" *Black American Literature Forum* 21.1-2 (1987): 61-84.

29. David W. Blight, *Race and Reunion: The Civil War in American Memory* (Cambridge, MA.: Harvard University Press, Belknap Press, 2001), 319.

30. Lentricchia, "Ideologies of Poetic Modernism," 221.

31. Dunbar, *Collected Poetry*, 221. All subsequent quotations from the poem are from this source.

32. The *Atlantic* version of the poem has "bold" instead of "cold," which appears to be a typographical error corrected at a later point.

33. Richard Kearney, *Modern Movements in European Philosophy*, 2nd ed. (New York: Manchester University Press, 1994), 13.

34. The opposing transatlantic journeys and expatriate lives of writers and intellectuals such as Hannah Arendt and Richard Wright could be seen as later developments in this complex cultural process.

35. Martin Heidegger, *Being and Time: A Translation of "Sein und Zeit,"* trans. Joan Stambaugh (Albany: State University of New York Press, 1996), 251-66 (cited hereafter in text). The translation problems involved in Heidegger texts begin with his key term "Da-sein," a different concept from the normal German word "Dasein," which means existence. "Da-sein" could be regarded as a process of

ontological becoming, or self-exploration: the Be-ing (or the being-there) that seeks to understand its being. It is difficult, as Stambaugh remarks in her introduction, to use any English term (such as capitalized Being) that does not either mislead or bring unwanted psychological baggage with it, leading to too-quick assumptions by the reader that he or she has grasped the central concepts. As she says, "It was Heidegger's insight that human being is *uncanny*: we do not know who, or what, that is, although, or perhaps precisely because, we *are* it" (xiv).

36. It would be a reasonable assumption that Heidegger, in these passages, is in some way seeking to appropriate and redefine the traditional Christian concept of the "vocation." I think it is important also that Dunbar, in "Robert Gould Shaw," is conscious of the Puritan sense of an inner calling but chooses to desacralize the meaning of Shaw's choice – while elevating its existential character.

37. An early intimation of W. B. Yeats's "An Irish Airman Foresees His Death" ("A weary impulse of delight / Drove me to this tumult in the skies above") can perhaps be heard in "Robert Gould Shaw." The mixture of revolutionary, self-sacrificial, and elitist tendencies in Yeats's artist-aviator, Major Robert Gregory, makes such a comparison inviting. The implication that Colonel Shaw was also driven by some other than purely altruistic motives remains a stubborn if minor note in the poem. On the issue of social class and the cultural reverberations of Shaw's death, see George M. Frederickson, *The Inner Civil War: Northern Intellectuals and the Crisis of the Union* (New York: Harper & Row, 1965), 152-55, for a discussion of the class sensitivities surrounding the events at Fort Wagner and how they played out among the higher Boston social circles. For a brief but iconoclastic reading of Shaw psychology and motivation (and by implication those of the New England reformist tradition), see Lewis P. Simpson, *Mind and the American Civil War: A Meditation on Lost Causes* (Baton Rouge: Louisiana State University Press, 1989), 65-66, 69. For a more balanced but largely sympathetic reading of Shaw and his milieu, see Joan Waugh, *Unsentimental Reformer: A Life of Josephine Shaw Lowell* (Cambridge, MA: Harvard University Press, 1997), chaps. 2 and 3 in particular.

38. David Blight comments that William James's address at Boston Common involved a complex view of the meaning of the war for the nation, perhaps too subtle a presentation for the occasion (*Race and Reunion*, 342).

39. Benjamin, "Der Begriff der Kunstkritik," 83-87. It is also useful to keep in mind that, for Benjamin, Romantic criticism (and his implication is that the effect has been deeply felt in Western culture) operates on the principle that it must, as a quasi-creative act, engage and assimilate the work under discussion into itself, for not to do so would be to already make a final judgment and reject the work as below criticism. This raises some issues for Dunbar's writings and how they have been valued.

40. Ibid., 86-87.

41. The broad thrust of Benjamin's theory of the ironization of form could be seen as remarkably similar to Gates's investigation of the procedures of signifyin(g), although Gates does not discuss Benjamin's work in *Signifying Monkey* The

major difference would be, again, that Benjamin sees the moment of formal disruption as coming from a force within the dynamic of the work, rather than a conscious act on the part of the artist. Nevertheless, the matter of whether creative artists in disadvantaged social and historical situations (black writers in Jim Crow America, for example) have the duty to raise one final and possibly fateful question about the status of the literary artifact they have produced remains open, for Dunbar as for others.

42. Blight, *Race and Reunion*, 339.

43. The question of immigration could provoke some angry reactions. Charles W. Chesnutt, for example, expressed himself as follows in a letter (to Booker T. Washington) of October 31, 1903: "To my mind it is nothing less than an outrage that the very off-scourings of Europe, and even of Western Asia may pour into this Union, almost by the millions annually, and be endued with full citizenship after a year or two of residence, while native-born Americans, who have no interest elsewhere and probably never will have, must be led around by the nose as members of a 'child race,' and be told that they must meekly and patiently await the result of an evolution which may last through several thousand years, before they can stand upon the same level of citizenship which any Sicilian, or Syrian or Turk or Greek or any other sort of European proletarian may enjoy in the State of Alabama." The passage is quoted in Joseph R. McElrath Jr., "W. D. Howells and Race: Charles W. Chesnutt's Disappointment of the Dean," *Nineteenth Century Literature* 51.4 (1997): 479.

44. According to Trachtenberg, foreign immigration alone "represented a third of the total population increase between 1860 and 1900" (*Incorporation of America*, 87). The connections between the perceived breakup of a monocultural American society, the politics of literacy, and the popularity of dialect writing during this period are dealt with in Gavin Jones, *Strange Talk: The Politics of Dialect Literature in Gilded Age America* (Berkeley and Los Angeles: University of California Press, 1999). See also North, *Dialect of Modernism*, chap. 1, for an assessment of the situation in relation to early modernism, about ten to twenty years after Dunbar was publishing. North is more interested, however, in the kind of Harlem Renaissance writers and their white colleagues who would have regarded Dunbar's "dialect" and "standard" poetry as compromised and derivative, respectively.

45. Ross Poole, *Nation and Identity* (New York: Routledge, 1999), 69.

46. Dunbar's double-edged statement in his essay "Recession Never" (in Martin, *Singer in the Dawn*, 39) that "so long a time has the black man believed that he is an American citizen that he will not be easily convinced to the contrary" transfers the confirmation of citizenship from constitutional and legal regulation onto psychological conviction. The belief outweighs any contingent state of affairs, and in the area of conviction art carries more truth content than positivist social science, for example. The persistence of a justified belief, however, may not be enough to translate that belief into political reality: it may indeed be continually confronted with the impossibility of its realization.

47. Poole, *Nation and Identity*, 64.

48. Gregory Jusdanis, *The Necessary Nation* (Princeton, NJ: Princeton University Press, 2001), 67.

49. Dominick LaCapra, *History in Transit: Experience, Identity, Critical Theory* (Ithaca, NY: Cornell University Press, 2004), 71.

50. It is even possible to imagine Dunbar as a middle-aged antifascist poet in the 1930s, since his ability to straddle different popular forms and literary legacies would have been attractive to the cultural Left in the Depression era.

51. Michael S. Roth, *The Ironist's Cage: Memory, Trauma, and the Construction of History* (New York: Columbia University Press, 1995), 148.

52. Julia Kristeva, "Forgiveness: An Interview," *PMLA* 117.2 (2002): 281–82.

53. Among the respondents who reply to Kristeva in the same issue of *PMLA* are Peter Brooks, Ruth Kluger, and Cary Nelson. Rather surprisingly, the question of literature as an autonomous or even subordinate site of political and individual expression is not discussed by anyone, although Cary Nelson suggests that "inculcating a refusal to forgive can be an integral part of our scholarly commitments" (ibid., 318), which certainly raises some interesting pedagogical and intellectual issues.

54. Wole Soyinka, *The Burden of Memory, the Muse of Forgiveness* (New York: Oxford University Press, 1999), 105. Soyinka's remark is slightly double-edged. Soyinka's essay "L. S. Senghor and Negritude" discusses the work of Léopold Sédar Senghor within the context of an exploration of memory and forgiveness, the memory of the destruction of the African life-world by colonialism, and the conflicting cultural pressures that brought some writers to reject European cultures and structures, and others to embrace them. In a connected essay in this book, Soyinka suggests that the gap between "truth" and "reconciliation" needs to be occupied by something like "restitution," to avoid the possibility that crimes will be excused on the basis of mere confession (including crimes committed by, for example, black African leaders against their populations). Soyinka's assessment of Senghor's drive to dispense forgiveness and to merge a West African cultural identity with the assumptions of French national history is that it attempts to achieve an impossible synthesis, or at least one that "is possible only for a poet and priest" (139), in the sense of having to be both, which mirrors my argument for Dunbar's "impossible" achievement, and perhaps some criticisms of it also.

55. Jack Kerkering, " 'Of Me and of Mine': The Music of Racial Identity in Whitman and Lanier, Dvořák, and DuBois," *American Literature* 73.1 (2001): 168.

56. Terry Eagleton, "Nationalism: Irony and Commitment," in *Nationalism, Colonialism, and Literature*, by Eagleton, Frederic Jameson, and Edward W. Said (Minneapolis: University of Minnesota Press, 1990), 25.

57. See Martin, *Singer in the Dawn*, 42, for a comment on Dunbar's widow's saying after his death, "There was much bitterness in Paul that he had to suppress."

58. The nationalism of African American patriots has been fraught with contradiction and subject historically to an array of critical pressures from black intellectuals who reject the assumptions of American republicanism, and it continues
to be a loaded topic. For comparison, see one recent book and two recent articles that approach the issue with radically different assumptions: Roger
Wilkins, *Jefferson's Pillow: The Founding Fathers and the Dilemma of Black
Patriotism* (Boston: Beacon Press, 2001); Roumiana Velikova, "W. E. B. Du
Bois vs. 'The Sons of the Fathers': A Reading of *The Souls of Black Folk* in the
Context of American Nationalism," *African American Review* 34.3 (2000):
431–42; Krista Walter, "Trappings of Nationalism in Frederick Douglass's *The
Heroic Slave*," *African American Review* 34:2 (2000), 233–48.
59. Eagleton, "Nationalism," 38.

Coda: Long Road

1. For a relatively recent discussion of how non-collective collective memory can
seem if you're in a different collective, see Walter Benn Michaels's reading of
Toni Morrison's *Beloved* in his *The Shape of the Signifier: From 1967 to the End
of History* (Princeton, NJ: Princeton University Press, 2004), 135–39; the upshot of Michaels's analysis is that Morrison's novel (like other contemporary
texts) is part of a cultural shift that has made racial, ethnic, or national particu-
larity a requirement for bringing memory into history – to bring it from literary
metaphor into political reality, as it were. Whereas I argue in the case of Paul
Laurence Dunbar, for example, that the politics of "Robert Gould Shaw" tend
toward a transcendence of race within a new national or even international culture (without, however, denying the existential reality of racism), Michaels appears to be suggesting that the modern politics of African American memory,
as fictionalized in *Beloved*, now demand race as a basic and absolute category of
understanding. Identity becomes co-extensive with memory, in fact. Without
opening up a debate on whether Michaels's reading of Morrison is a reasonable
one, it is worth noting that there was already a more "organicist" view of racial
identity held by some African American writers and intellectuals at the turn of
the twentieth century. In *The Souls of Black Folk* (1903), for example, W. E. B.
DuBois walks a thin line between the indelible and identity-creating trauma of
slavery and the potential for cross-cultural understanding and communication.
2. Philip Kuberski, *The Persistence of Memory: Organism, Myth, Text* (Berkeley
and Los Angeles: University of California Press 1992), 132.
3. Robert Pogue Harrison, *The Dominion of the Dead* (Chicago: University of
Chicago Press, 2003), 124.
4. Drew Gilpin Faust, *This Republic of Suffering: Death and the American Civil
War* (New York: Knopf, 2008), 269.
5. Maurice Halbwachs, *On Collective Memory*, ed. and trans. Lewis A. Coser
(Chicago: University of Chicago Press, 1992), 173.

6. Joan Waugh, *Unsentimental Reformer: The Life of Josephine Shaw Lowell* (Cambridge, MA: Harvard University Press, 1997), 85-87, 91-93.

7. Ibid., 9-11.

8. Ibid., 153-54.

9. Ibid., 235-41.

10. Jane Addams, *The Long Road of Woman's Memory* (New York: Macmillan, 1916), 139.

11. Ibid. 132; indeed, Addams notes that the idea of the United States involved in war at all (for example, by selling munitions to belligerent powers) was often bewildering for people abroad who had nurtured idealistic notions of America as a community run on principles of mutual fairness and interethnic fellowship.

12. Ibid., 115.

INDEX

MARTIN GRIFFIN was born and grew up in Dublin and earned his BA and MA from the National University of Ireland. He lived in Germany for several years, working as a journalist and translator and as a civilian paralegal for the U.S. Army JAG Corps; he also served as European coordinator for a Berlin-based NGO advocating for community economic empowerment. Picking up the threads of his academic career once more, he completed his doctorate in American literature at UCLA, and subsequently taught at Pomona College and Claremont Graduate University. He has been at the University of Tennessee since 2007. He currently lives in Knoxville.